EXPLORING NEW ZEALAND'S COAST & ITS PEOPLE

Coasters

WITH AL BROWN

RANDOM HOUSE
NEW ZEALAND

Dedicated to my children, William, Nina, Matai and Harper —
may the coast be your playground for years to come.

A RANDOM HOUSE BOOK published by Random House New Zealand
18 Poland Road, Glenfield, Auckland, New Zealand

For more information about our titles go to www.randomhouse.co.nz

A catalogue record for this book is available from the National Library
of New Zealand

Random House New Zealand is part of the Random House Group
New York   London   Sydney   Auckland   Delhi   Johannesburg

First published 2010

© 2010 text Fisheye Films, images Fisheye Films unless otherwise credited
on page 288

The moral rights of the author have been asserted

ISBN 978 1 86979 443 9

This book is copyright. Except for the purposes of fair reviewing no part
of this publication may be reproduced or transmitted in any form or by
any means, electronic or mechanical, including photocopying, recording
or any information storage and retrieval system, without permission in
writing from the publisher.

Maps: Stephen Fuller
Cover photographs: main image, Kieran Scott; small images, Fisheye Films;
front flap, Colin Monteath/Hedgehog House/www.photonewzealand.co.nz;
back flap, Daisy Day
Design: Gary Stewart, Gas Project
Printed in New Zealand by Printlink

Foreword

What a pleasure it has been to present this series, *Coasters*. I've always had a strong affinity with our coastline, so to travel and discover different sections has been a truly special experience.

The wonderful thing about the coastline is that as each tide draws back, it takes away any indication of what happened between tides. So, if you're lucky enough to be making the first footprints as you walk down the beach in the morning, it may be easy to imagine what it might have been like when Maori or early European settlers first stepped onto the shores of Aotearoa.

Most New Zealanders have a special part of the coastline that they consider theirs and have a strong connection with — and for everyone that's different.

Like me, a lot of people spent time at a campground, or returned to a certain beach for holidays as children and, as a result, they feel it's part of who they are. There's a sense of arrival when they get there, and they protect it like it's theirs.

For others, the coast is where they live, and for many it sustains their livelihoods.

In this show, I have been fortunate enough, through the seven journeys, to experience other people's special piece of coast. And after finishing the series, what was really reinforced for me was the importance of protecting our coastline and the need to guard it for future generations. We must treasure it as one of the most precious things that we as Kiwis can call our own.

So to all the coasters that I've connected with through this series, I feel honoured to have met you and shared your harbours, your beaches, your rocky outcrops and to have listened to your stories.

Finally, it's been fantastic to share the experience with producer Peter Young and the terrific 'Fisheye' team that make all the magic happen behind the scenes. We are now bonded by our 'coasters' experience.

Thank you everyone.
Al Brown

Contents

Foreword	3
Introduction	6
Wellington	8
The West Coast	48
The Bay of Islands	94
Doubtful Sound	134
The Coromandel	170
Banks Peninsula	206
Taranaki	250
Image credits	288

Introduction

There is something very special about the edge of this country — the narrow strip of land where *terra firma* meets the ocean. New Zealand's long convoluted coastline is dynamic, dramatic, wild and stunningly beautiful.

It was the coast that greeted our forebears and after navigating its sandbars, river mouths and harbours, it went on to become an integral part of their lives — a wonderful food source, an essential means of transport, a place of great tragedy and triumph.

Generations later I find myself strongly connected to the coast and have been ever since I first learnt how to surf at Fitzroy Beach in New Plymouth. In my early working years, the surf determined where I lived and worked — my life revolved around the swell and the tides and I always kept an eye on the sea, waiting for that next wave. I found something calming in its constant movement, something refreshing with each tide and each storm. Without ever really thinking about it, I was a *coaster*. And I think that's the case for many New Zealanders.

The seed for *Coasters* was sown a few years ago when, as a freelance cameraman, I had the privilege of flying over long stretches of the New Zealand coastline, filming aerials for a TVNZ documentary series called *Explorers*. From the air, the coastline was absolutely gob-smacking and I knew then, somewhere, somehow there was a great television series to be made.

When we finally put the proposal on paper, it comprised a series of separate journeys along the coast of New Zealand. After getting the green light and doing further research, the first thing we did was reduce the length of our journeys — such was the richness of stories and characters we found. Every stretch of coast — even the most remote and isolated coasts, have a wealth of fascinating tales that collectively speak volumes about where we come from and who we are.

Making this series with Al Brown has been thoroughly enjoyable — for the places we have been, the people we met and the stories we have told. I would like to thank the many coasters who opened their doors and shared their lives with us and hope that we have done justice to you and your section of coast. Thanks to NZ On Air and TVNZ for their support of the series.

The book has been a real collaboration. A BIG thanks goes to Janet Hunt and John McCrystal who have contributed enormously to its writing. Jenny Hellen from Random House was instrumental right from the start and provided wonderful support throughout. Gary Stewart for his brilliant design and Sue Lewis for bringing it all together. Elizabeth Koroivulaono at Fisheye has been awesome and our researchers Katherine Bonner, Ange Davidson and Sally Airey. To my film crew Nigel Gordon-Crosby and Matt Tuffin thanks for the long days and photos. Finally to my partner Tracy Roe who has also been involved with research, writing, editing as well as raising the family while I was away, for crossing the T's and dotting the I's — I appreciate your support so much.

I hope the television series and the book resonate with you, our audience, and turn your eyes towards that wonderful part of our country — the coast and the people who live there.

Peter Young
Producer
Coasters

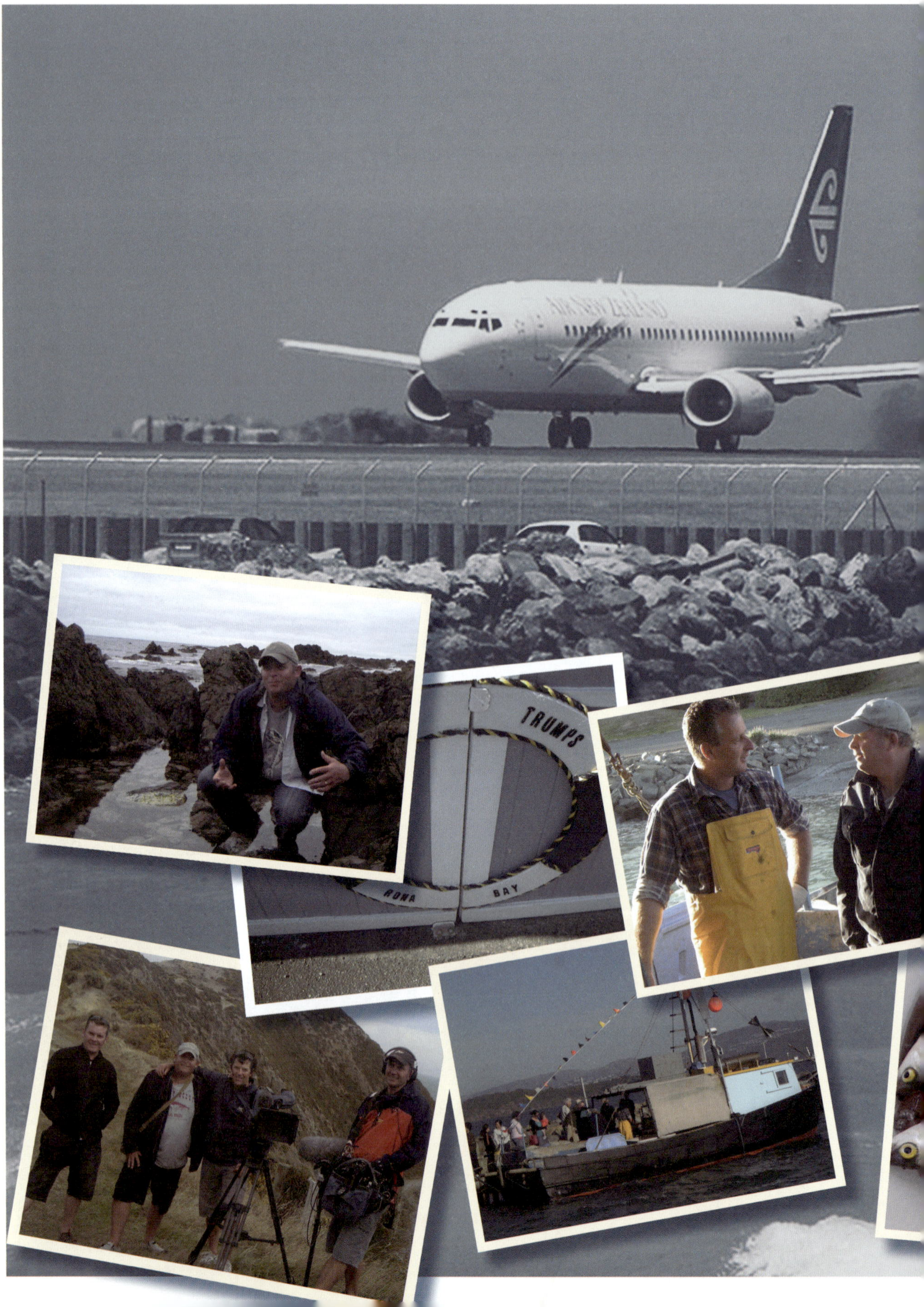
AIR NEW ZEALAND
TRUMPS
RONA BAY

Welcome to... Wellington

The Capital Coast

New Zealand has an exceptionally long coastline relative to its land mass — something in the region of 15,000 kilometres, almost as long as that of the United States.

Previous page: Touching down and taking off at Lyall Bay, Wellington.

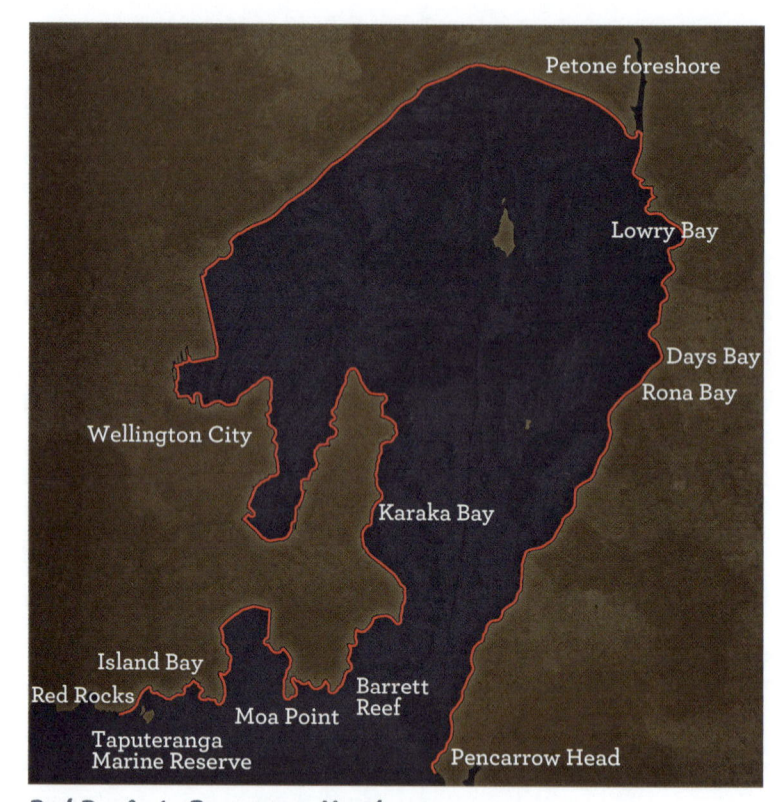

Red Rocks to Pencarrow Head

It's got a lot to do with the convoluted outlines of our three main islands and the frequency of long inlets, large harbours and intricate fiords, and if length is anything to go by, its influence on us has been huge.

For Maori and early European settlers, that coastline was everything: it was a point of arrival and departure both for ocean-going expeditions and for inshore activities such as fishing; it was a means of transport — a route more easily travelled than the bush-clad hills and mountains of the interior; it was a trading point and a meeting point; its reefs and seas provided food; it was where we put down our roots. It's natural that much of our lives, our histories and our cultures revolve around it and evolve from it. The coast is not only the edge of our world, it is a place in itself: a rich, wide swathe that connects land to sea, and Kiwis to the world.

The journey from Red Rocks to Pencarrow Head is a great entrée to the New Zealand coastline and the place it has in our lives. Al travels from the wilds of Wellington's southern shores east along the edge of Cook Strait to the harbour entrance. Passing baches that cling to the seaside, he continues through increasingly built-up suburbs and on to the city's heart and the seat of government, before making his way around the harbour to Pencarrow Lighthouse. Along the way, he meets some great coasters, people whose lives are interwoven with the sea and its rhythms, who live and breathe the coastal life and wouldn't have it any other way.

Red Rocks Reserve on Wellington's south coast, the start of Al's journey.

Wild winds and waters

Al's coastal odyssey begins at Pariwhero or Red Rocks, a jagged point on Wellington's southern shore on the outskirts of the city. His feet sink deep into a fine-shingle beach as he gets his bearings, looking south-east across the swell in Cook Strait to the Kaikoura mountains and east towards Wellington harbour, while towering behind and above him are the massive hills and scarps of the lower edge of the North Island. It's an isolated, harsh section of coastline, a good spot to stretch the legs and exercise the dog on a weekend. Today, however, there's no one else around. A stiff wind through the strait raises large waves that hurl themselves landward in a froth of foam. A squall is coming through, the first drops sharp on the skin. It's all very familiar — this is Al's home coast and one that he's grown to love. 'I get as much pleasure out of the turbulent ocean as I do a soft sunrise over a flat sea. I simply love the coast.'

Jandals in hand, Al heads towards the city, looking forward to encountering some of the capital's coasters along the way.

BLOOD ON THE ROCKS

The Polynesian explorer Kupe Raiatea was New Zealand's first coaster, arriving in his waka *Matahourua* sometime over 1000 years ago, whereupon he gave the country its first name, 'Ao-tea-roa' after the long drift of white cloud he and his party saw from far out at sea. The cloud told them that an unknown but substantial land mass lay ahead. It must have been an exciting yet daunting moment — who knew what wonders and what terrors this new world might hold?

Sailing around the edges of the new land, they would have found a great variety of coastlines — plains, wetlands, high cliffs and hills, covered in forest with clefts made by ravines and river mouths, and occasional stretches of long sandy foreshore.

As they neared the lower North Island, legend has it that a giant octopus rose from the sea and fled before them, leading them into what is now known as Cook Strait. After battling and defeating the creature, they rested in Wellington harbour, where Kupe named the islands Matiu (Somes) and Makaro (Ward) after his daughters. He then set off alone to explore the area to the south, but when he did not return as expected, one of his daughters believed him to be lost at sea and in her grief threw herself onto the rocks, staining them with her blood.

In fact, the red rocks are pillow lava, from undersea volcanic eruptions 200 million years ago. Their russet colour comes from iron oxides in the rock. You will sometimes see the large, sleek, sleepy forms of New Zealand fur seals sunning themselves on the rocks. They have come from the larger colony a little further around the coast at Sinclair Head and are bachelor males who are mainly too young yet to breed.

This remote little reserve of national importance gives little indication of the city that begins just around the next point, and that's where Al is heading, east towards the nation's capital.

A DIP A DAY KEEPS YOU SPRIGHTLY

After he leaves the Red Rocks, Al follows a narrow track around the base of the cliffs, past a disused quarry that, since its purchase by Wellington City Council in 2000, is being progressively replanted with native species. It's all part of a new way of looking at the coast: no longer seeing it purely in terms of a place to blast for rock or dump rubbish or sewage, but something to care for, to be proud of.

A little further on, where the baches and houses leave the shoreline and sprawl up the valley behind Owhiro Bay, Al meets Sheila Natusch, a bright-eyed woman in her senior years who enjoys what is perhaps one of the most basic and intimate relationships we can have with the coast, an invigorating dip in the sea. Sheila, who was born in Invercargill in 1926, comes from a long line of artists and naturalists. She is not only a passionate and lifelong coaster, but an

Sheila Natusch starts most days with a refreshing dip in the chilly waters at Owhiro Bay. 'I usually have the pool to myself.'

Sheila and Al under the mural at Owhiro Bay.

Wellington 13

author with at least 21 books of non-fiction to her name. In the 2007 New Year Honours she was made a Member of the New Zealand Order of Merit (MNZM) for services as a writer and illustrator. Sheila and her husband Gilbert moved to their house on the windswept hillside overlooking Owhiro Bay in 1951.

It's cold and Al can't believe she's about to get in, but Sheila assures him that it's a regular if not always daily occurrence. Temperatures in the strait range from an icy 14 to an only slightly better 19°C. 'You brave, brave soul,' he says admiringly as she walks into the sea. Then he thinks about it. He may be minding her towel, but how can he remain on the beach while a woman of 80+ years goes in? 'If she does it, I've got to do it,' he says. He's down to undies and bare skin in a flash and joins her, gasping at the chill. 'It feels like the middle of winter — but you feel brilliant when you get out!'

Where the city meets the sea — Taputeranga Marine Reserve near Island Bay on Wellington's south coast.

Exploring rock pools is a favourite pastime. 'It's just like nature's window.'

A SPECIAL PLACE — TAPUTERANGA MARINE RESERVE

A little further on from Red Rocks, a swathe of hillside has been blasted and carved into the benches and terraces of a now-disused quarry. High on its face, two large yellow triangles announce that this is the western edge of Taputeranga Marine Reserve.

The 854-hectare reserve was created in August 2008 after a number of years in the making and is New Zealand's newest marine reserve. It hangs like a flag from the south coast and is more or less a large rectangle with an irregular top which is the foreshore, stretching approximately five kilometres from the mid-point of the old quarry in the west, through Owhiro Bay, Island Bay and Houghton Bay to the rock pools of Te Raekaihau Point in the east. It abuts intensively populated urban areas — Island Bay particularly, where the reserve surrounds but does not include Taputeranga Island, the rocky outcrop and hill that gives Island Bay its name.

New Zealand currently has over 30 protected marine areas, each with its own special character. Essentially, they are NO TAKE zones, meaning that nothing can be disturbed or removed. Given time, the fish and other marine life in protected areas such as these recover and return to a more natural balance. Many of the more established reserves around New Zealand have become marine wonderlands and tourist attractions in their own right.

Taputeranga's claim to fame is its complex seafloor topography and unusual combination of ocean currents — both the changeable winds above the sea's surface and the warm, cool and outright icy waters below create a huge range of habitats with a corresponding variety of plant and marine life. Over 180 species of fish, including blue cod, variable triple fin and banded wrasse are found here, with the northern limits of some species overlapping the southern limits of others. New Zealand's big-belly seahorse swims among kelp beds and the large slugs known as sea hares browse on seaweed while

> Taputeranga Marine Reserve is not only a secure breeding spot for fish that will eventually enrich the waters outside the reserve, it is a benchmark by which those waters may be measured. It's all part of changing attitudes to the coast.

octopus, rock lobsters and crabs make their homes at the ocean's edge.

As has often happened with marine reserves elsewhere, the initial proposal for the Taputeranga Marine Reserve aroused fierce opposition. Those who had been accustomed to a lifetime's fishing or harvesting from favoured spots were irritated to find themselves displaced. In the end, however, the proposed area was reduced by 130 hectares to accommodate continued access to areas valued by local fishers. It was a matter of striking a balance.

There were compensations. The reserve's creation made some activities off-limits but it made others increasingly rewarding: over 150,000 people in the Wellington area now have access to enhanced diving (including a sunken ex-navy frigate, the F69), snorkelling, swimming, kayaking, photographing, picnicking, playing on beaches and pottering in rock pools.

Al is a convert. 'This used to be my hunting ground and I was a little bit miffed when it was turned into a reserve,' he says. 'But it went through and now when I see the results I think it's one of the greatest things ever. Perfect for education; and with a little bit of luck we will have paua stocks and all these other wonderful shellfish and seafood for the generations to come.' He makes an appreciative stop beside a rock pool: a sea snail hitches a leisurely lift across a lichen-covered rock on the back of a paua, a starfish waves delicate pink legs and small cockabullies weave through a forest of gently swaying seaweed. The water is as clear as glass.

'It's just like nature's window,' Al says. 'It makes me incredibly happy.'

Al is not the only one who is smiling. The reserve is a wonderland for the marine biologists who use the University of Victoria's state-of-the-art Coastal Ecology Laboratory in Island Bay, established in the 1960s and rebuilt in 2009. Researchers and marine biologists are now able to study in a living laboratory with an increasingly pristine environment.

Taputeranga Marine Reserve is not only a secure breeding spot

Ray Ahipene-Mercer, community man and great lover of the coast, says of changing attitudes to the coast: 'It's a very good thing and part of the journey of our country.'

Al with Ray in his 1935 Dodge.

for fish that will eventually enrich the waters outside the reserve, it is a benchmark by which those waters may be measured. It's all part of changing attitudes to the coast.

POINT OF CONTENTION

Changing attitudes is what drives Al's next coaster, Ray Ahipene-Mercer, a man of many talents with a big interest in the community. Ray is a descendant of Wellington iwi Ngai Tara and Ngati Ira, and it goes without saying that his Maori heritage is fundamental to his view of the world. He is an elected member of the Wellington City Council, with a busy portfolio of responsibilities, but as well as that, Ray is a family man, musician, guitar-maker and an environmentalist who has been and remains active in many campaigns. He is also an honorary fisheries ranger and above all he has a real passion for this part of the coast.

Ray meets Al around the headland from the marine reserve at Lyall Bay and drives him east in his immaculate 1935 blue Dodge. 'We're 15 minutes from the Beehive and you can sit out here and civilisation is a long way away,' Ray says. Surfers cruise the waves on the bay's eastern side, against a backdrop of the city's main airport runway, which lies north-to-south across the isthmus dividing the Miramar Peninsula from the rest of the city. Planes big and small, sometimes seemingly only metres above the water as they enter or exit from across the strait or the harbour to the north, are just a part of the scenery. In Wellington, where the winds dominate, this airstrip is notorious for knuckle-whitening arrivals and departures, with planes lurching alarmingly as they touch down and take off. Passengers have been known to applaud safe landings.

But it's not the airport that Al has come to see, rather the headland to its south. This is Moa Point where, for over 90 years, the city's raw sewage was discharged directly into the ocean.

'So this is what was once known as dirty old Moa Point?' Al asks.

'It was indeed, Al,' Ray replies. 'Right out in front of us, this is where it was totally and utterly polluted and everything was sick … it was a real mess. I got involved because I came to live here in 1983 and I couldn't believe such a potentially beautiful part of the coast was out of bounds for swimming, for recreational use, for getting kaimoana. It also impinged on the historical status of the wahi tapu, the old pa site round the corner, so it was a whole mixture of things. I was in disbelief.'

It took 14 years, Ray says, for something to be done about it. In 1984 he and a few buddies and neighbours (including John Blincoe, fellow Wellingtonian and Labour MP from 1990–96) kicked off the Wellington Clean Water Campaign, also known as WC2. Debate about the various options and costs raged for many years before a treatment station was built south-west of the airport above Moa Point Road. Sewage is screened, de-sludged and subjected to a series of processes before being discharged through an 1800-metre outfall

The clear waters of Moa Point today.

into the strait. There are still periodic problems but it's nothing like what it was and the ocean out in front of them is clear. 'It's fantastic today,' Ray says. 'It's back to what it was pre-the late 1800s.'

RANGITATAU PA

That was how Ray's ancestors, the Ngai Tara people, would have known it when they lived in the area. For them, and, for that matter, all Maori, the coast was a place of the utmost importance. It was the first point of contact for seafarers, it was their means of transport and most importantly, it was a place of great bounty, providing them with an essential means of sustenance.

Long before marine reserves were thought of, Maori were practising their own means of protection and conservation through cultural practices such as kaitiakitanga, which saw people or groups providing guardianship over specific areas and resources. It included the practice of rahui, which prohibited the extraction of food and resources for a variety of reasons — from protecting from overuse through to sacred purposes.

It was logical that most Maori settlements were centred on the coast; and at Tarakena Bay, just around from Moa Point, is Rangitatau Pa, Ray's ancestral home. It was once a stronghold associated with the nearby fortified village of Poito. Both were destroyed around 1820 by raiding parties from the north.

'Straight ahead of us is where the actual living dwellings were, the whares over there. The reef provided a safe area for drawing waka up along the sandy beach, and the fortifications for defensive purposes were up on the hill where you have a clear view out to Cook Strait. There was fresh water and there was kaimoana: hapuka out at sea, mussels, crayfish, paua, limpets, kina and karengo, an edible seaweed that was traditionally harvested from the rocks. It was very plentiful here for the family. This is where they lived.'

Ray and Al stroll the small beach in the bay. 'It amazes me how when the tide goes out and takes footprints away, the history still remains,' Al says.

'Indeed it does,' Ray replies. 'It's very apparent after the clean-up that more and more people feel connected, whether Maori or non-Maori. It's a very good thing and it's part of the journey of our country.'

COASTERS WITH WINGS

Ray has also been a spokesman on behalf of another group of coasters — the feathered variety. Like the seals that also choose to haul out along this coast, korora — aka little blue penguins (*Eudyptula minor*, the little diver) — are marine creatures that cannot survive without a base on land for nesting, resting and for times such as during the moult, when they can't go to sea. The smallest living penguins, they are largely nocturnal and can be smelly, rambunctious and sometimes unwelcome neighbours, prone to having parties under the floorboards of sheds and baches along the coast. Who knows how long they have made the commute from water's edge to their havens among the logs, tussocks, nooks and crannies of the lower reaches of the cliffs and hills — certainly, since long before humans arrived to stake a claim to their shores.

Sadly for the birds, when there is a dispute over right of way between humans and these gutsy 1–1.2 kg little coasters, it's the penguins that come off worst. Waterfront roads are particularly perilous, because korora tend to waddle across them in the low light of dusk and dawn, but dogs, cats, pollution and other human activities also take a toll.

Coastal commuter, korora, the little blue penguin.

Ray was especially concerned by the feathered road casualties below his home in Breaker Bay, so he put up signs to let motorists know the birds were there. He also arranged for the construction of artificial nesting sites to entice them to safer places and encouraged people to find ways to value and coexist with their small fellow residents.

The windy city

From Tarakena Bay Al is on his own again, heading east towards the harbour entrance. On his right, Barrett Reef, the treacherous cluster of rocks along the western side of the harbour, is just visible at high tide. At last he turns into the entrance of Wellington harbour, also known as Port Nicholson. There's a stiff breeze blowing off the sea.

It's not for nothing that New Zealand's capital city is known as 'windy'. New Zealand's climate is formed by a combination of the sea, the mountains and the prevailing westerlies — and these winds really come into their own in the Wellington region. The country's three largest islands lie between latitudes 34 and 47°S, within the zone known as the Roaring Forties on account of its frequently strong, if not downright blustery, boisterous and violent winds. With little in the way of land masses to slow them down, especially in the lower latitudes, the winds belt across the southern Indian Ocean and the Tasman Sea, hit the mountains and hills on either side of the Cook Strait and are deflected to blow through it in a north or north-west torrent that increases in speed and strength as it goes.

The Wellington Windsurfing Association, with an interest in such things, describes the city as the 'windiest main centre in New Zealand and . . . possibly the world'. The northerly is most common in spring and summer, while more severe southerlies occur most frequently in winter. The landscape echoes these anarchic airs, with blasted hills, scree and eroded cliff faces. Coastal plants, such as taupata, muehlenbeckia, manuka, kanuka, flax and tussocks grow in strange shapes, stunted, shorn, twisted, tortured and bent.

THE WORST WIND OF ALL

The strongest winds cause mayhem. On 10 April 1968 one of the fiercest storms ever recorded in New Zealand reached its peak in the Cook Strait and brought about the worst maritime disaster in modern New Zealand history. On that day, tropical cyclone Giselle, laden with warm air from the north, collided with an equally severe storm carrying chilled air from Antarctica: the combination was lethal. Throughout Wellington city, roofs were ripped off, trees uprooted and debris sent flying. Oteranga Bay, on the shores of the strait, was hit by a 267-kilometre-per-hour blast — the highest wind gust ever recorded in the region.

Unfortunately, the height of the storm also coincided with the moment when the Union Steam Ship's combined passenger-car ferry *Wahine*, on an overnight trip from Lyttelton, attempted to enter Wellington harbour. With winds gusting up to 160 kilometres an hour and visibility reduced, battered by towering waves and with radar incapacitated, the vessel struck Barrett Reef on the north side of the harbour entrance. Despite the ferry being close to shore, rescue efforts were thwarted by the violence of wind and wave. The ship was abandoned amid chaos; only four lifeboats were launched, some passengers had lost their lifejackets and people

The Wahine *sinking in Wellington harbour.*

Breaker Bay at the entrance to Wellington harbour.

ended up in the sea. Many were blown across the harbour to the rocky coastline at Eastbourne, where access was impeded by slips on the road. There were 734 people on board so it was a miracle that not more were lost, but even so, 51 died from their injuries, exposure, exhaustion or drowning.

INTO THE HARBOUR

The earliest Maori name for Wellington was Te Upoko o te ika a Maui or 'the head of Maui's fish'. It refers to the traditional story in which Polynesian navigator and ace fisherman Maui hooked the monster fish that became the North Island. If you take a look at a map and are feeling imaginative you can see that the North Island is not unlike a giant flatfish, with the harbours and bays of the south end as its nostril and mouth and Lake Taupo as its eye.

That name was largely replaced in the twelfth century when an East Coast man named Tara settled on the harbour's shores, giving his name to both the harbour and the city that later grew around it: Whanganui-a-Tara. His people, Ngai Tara, became the tangata whenua until in later times they were joined by Ngati Ira.

Al continues his journey into the harbour, passing a series of small bays — Palmer, Reef, Flax, Eve and Breaker. He passes Steeple Rock where the *Wahine* finally washed up, and now he's looking at a curving foreshore: this is Worser Bay, after the first harbour pilot, James Heberley, nickname 'Jack Worser'. Rocky outcrops alternate with small sandy beaches and perched on the hills behind is the leafy suburb of Seatoun.

The weather starts to cut up, rain adds sting to the building breeze. Halfway along the beach, just out from the Worser Bay Boating Club buildings, a bunch of kids are sailing P-class dinghies; some are still out on the water, some are hauling out for the day.

'How was that?' Al asks one of the young sailors.

'Pretty good,' the kid says. He's been sailing P-class a few months.

'What do you like about it?' asks Al.

'I kinda like the wind in my face,' the kid says.

It's not what Al was expecting but it's as simple as that: the wind in your face.

THE MODEST MULLET

Getting a feed can be just as simple so Al catches up with a couple of men after his own heart, his greengrocers and old friends, Lucky and Magan Dayal. They're staked out on the jetty at Karaka Bay, the next indentation around the coast. Lucky has been fishing from this spot since he came to Wellington in 1955. Nearly all Wellington's residents live within three kilometres of the coastline and Karaka Bay is typical of most: a beachside settlement where there has always been constant interaction across the coast between the sea and the land.

Today the three of them are after a little something for lunch,

Right: Al prepares mullet, which he considers a delicacy.

Opposite: Al with Magan and Lucky Dayal.

yellow-eyed mullet, *Aldrichetta forsteri*, also sometimes known as sand mullet or — not strictly correct — herring. The mullet feed on algae and small animals such as sandworms and small cockles, and are relatively plentiful in most bays and estuaries around the coast of New Zealand. They grow to 40 centimetres and are a popular catch for children throwing lines off wharves and jetties. Many consider them bait, but Al considers them a delicacy and before long they have half a dozen in the bucket. He holds one of the small silver fish in his hand.

'Look at that, it's a great example of a beautiful yellow-eyed mullet,' he says. 'They're small but they're fat and they're delicious! This is the season and you can pick up a feed very, very quickly. Just a lovely thing to eat, gorgeous.'

As soon as each fish is caught it's killed and put on ice, and after about 20 minutes they each have enough to take home for a feed. Lucky and Magan wander off while Al takes his catch to the water's edge to prepare it for the next coaster he's meeting. After a light scaling, a voice floats down from the jetty above. 'What you got down there, Brownie?' It's Ian Athfield, architect — otherwise known as 'Ath'.

Wellington 25

Designs on the coast

Ian Athfield meets Al at the jetty at Karaka Bay: 'A jetty is the landing spot of any bay and is equally important from the sea as from the land.'

It is people like Ath who call the shots on the way the waterfront looks and works. Right around New Zealand, behind every road, motorway, wharf or coastal housing development, there are layers of architects, designers, engineers, and the behind-the-scenes regulators of what can and cannot be done — town planners. These are the people who are employed by home owners and builders, by businesses and by local and national government to decide where things will go and how things will take shape: all together, they have a huge influence on the appearance of the coast.

Ath's an award-winning architect who has contributed much to the shape of modern Wellington, challenging thinking about the place of urban design in the landscape and the way in which it serves those who live and work in it. An enthusiastic and long-time coaster, Ath has been advisor and contributor to the waterfront development in Wellington and in other cities around New Zealand. Among his achievements he lists the Wellington Public Library and the Civic Square.

Al's keen to hear Ath's thoughts on coastal development and it begins with that great coastal icon, the jetty.

A view of Lambton Quay from 1864.

'A jetty is the landing spot of any bay and is equally important from the sea as from the land. It's where people meet, where they tie up, it's their transition between water and land. It means focusing the community to one particular part of the foreshore and that means the rest of the area is pretty much left to itself. They are a significant part of our background, about our culture and the water's edge. I don't know why we don't have more of them.'

With the fish, bucket and rod they amble along the water's edge. Ath talks about the coastal trends that interest him as an architect and it raises some big questions.

What draws people to stroll along the seaside? How can coastal design enhance people's experiences and get them out of their houses and vehicles into the salt air? In recent years, more and more parts of New Zealand are providing coastal walkways and are finding that they are embraced with a passion. All you have to do, it seems, is put them there and the people will come.

And what about the current obsession with views — with looking at, rather than interacting with, the shore environment? This is causing huge changes, not only to the immediate foreshore, but to the land behind as house after house goes a little higher than the one in front of it, each jostling for a peep of the sea or the most expansive ocean vista. Real estate brochures bristle with photos of infinity pools leading to sandy beaches, while properties in waterfront housing developments are eagerly sought, even in times of recession.

What is the relationship between public and private space on the coast? How does urban design direct and change those attitudes? Most of New Zealand's cities and towns are on or near the sea so these questions have huge relevance to designers, architects and engineers, the people whose plans either make it easier for everyday Kiwis and their families to visit and enjoy the coast, or make it more difficult.

It's a two-way street, with people on one hand influencing the way the coast is shaped while on the other hand, the coast influences the way people live and cultures develop — the places we walk, the way we travel, what we do on weekends, how we view the natural world and how we interact with it.

'You know, the edges of settlements are really important,' Ath says. 'The best custodians of the sea edge are fishermen — just as the best custodians of the countryside are the farmers. That's because they look out on their respective areas and look after them. If you actually

Queens Wharf, Wellington, 1920. 'The toughest part of town was the seafront, and the towns and settlements developed around that.'

Ath and Al sit down to some freshly caught Karaka Bay mullet.

consider the history of the relationships between settlements and the sea, the toughest part of town was the seafront, and the towns and settlements developed around that: on the edge there were the wharves and jetties and fishermen who were tough and who survived tough conditions. It takes pretty gutsy people to live on the edge of the water because complacency is not part of the equation. I think it's really important to respect that.'

Take the kind of settlement that has evolved around Seatoun and Miramar. Ath sees this as a great example of the way that a settlement can grow almost organically and yet be successful, with everything in balance.

'This is unique, where the people live very close to the edge of the water, where everyone has developed their houses differently; there's very little space between the houses but they respect each other, you know, which is really important,' he says. 'And the space between the front of the house and the sea is extremely positive . . . these people have learned to live with the conditions here and have produced a variety of models which suit and respect them. It's something that has developed over a long period of time. Some of these houses have been here for 100 years and some of them have been here for 10 but they all have an attitude and an understanding of the place they are in.'

COOKING UP A FEED

It's time to do something about the mullet. Al invites Ath to come to lunch.

'Mullet is delicious,' Al says, slicing the heads off his catch. 'Most New Zealanders consider them bait but I consider them an absolute delicacy. They're sweet — you don't need a boat, just a handline or a twenty-dollar rod from The Warehouse off your local jetty. They're

Sautéed Herrings with Capers, Lemon Zest and Fresh Herbs

Herring can be found all around New Zealand and in most cases are only your local wharf away. What I love about catching these little delicacies is that you don't need a boat, a charter or even expensive gear to get a feed of wonderful-tasting fresh fish. Purchase a couple of inexpensive rods, a handful of tiny hooks and sinkers along with a little bacon fat for bait. The best burley is stale bread that's been mixed to a paste with a little milk so it sinks when it hits the water. It's a super way to introduce kids to the joys of fishing and cooking, and teach them about sourcing your own food from the ocean. Remember to take along a little ice to keep your precious catch in the freshest condition possible.

Serves 6

Ingredients
18 fresh yellow-eyed mullet, scaled, heads removed and gutted
sea salt and freshly ground black pepper
1 cup flour
canola oil for frying
200g butter
zest of 3 lemons
2 cloves garlic, finely minced
⅓ cup capers, roughly chopped
½ cup chopped parsley leaves
½ cup chopped basil leaves
squeeze of lemon juice
lemon wedges for serving

Method
Preheat the oven to 100°C.

Rinse the herrings in a little salt water then pat dry. With a sharp knife, score a couple of slashes on each side of the fish.

Season the herrings with sea salt and black pepper. Dust with a little of the flour, then pat off the excess.

Put a little canola oil in a skillet or sauté pan and place on medium heat. Once hot, add a few of the herrings at a time. Cook for a couple of minutes on each side until cooked through. Place in an oven dish while you finish cooking the rest, then place in the oven to keep warm while you make the sauce.

Place the pan back on the heat, add the butter, lemon zest, garlic and capers. Fry on medium-low heat for a minute or so before adding the parsley, basil and a squeeze of lemon juice. Remove from the heat.

To serve, divide out the herrings onto warm plates then spoon the rustic butter sauce over. Serve immediately with a wedge of lemon and a bit of crusty bread for dipping.

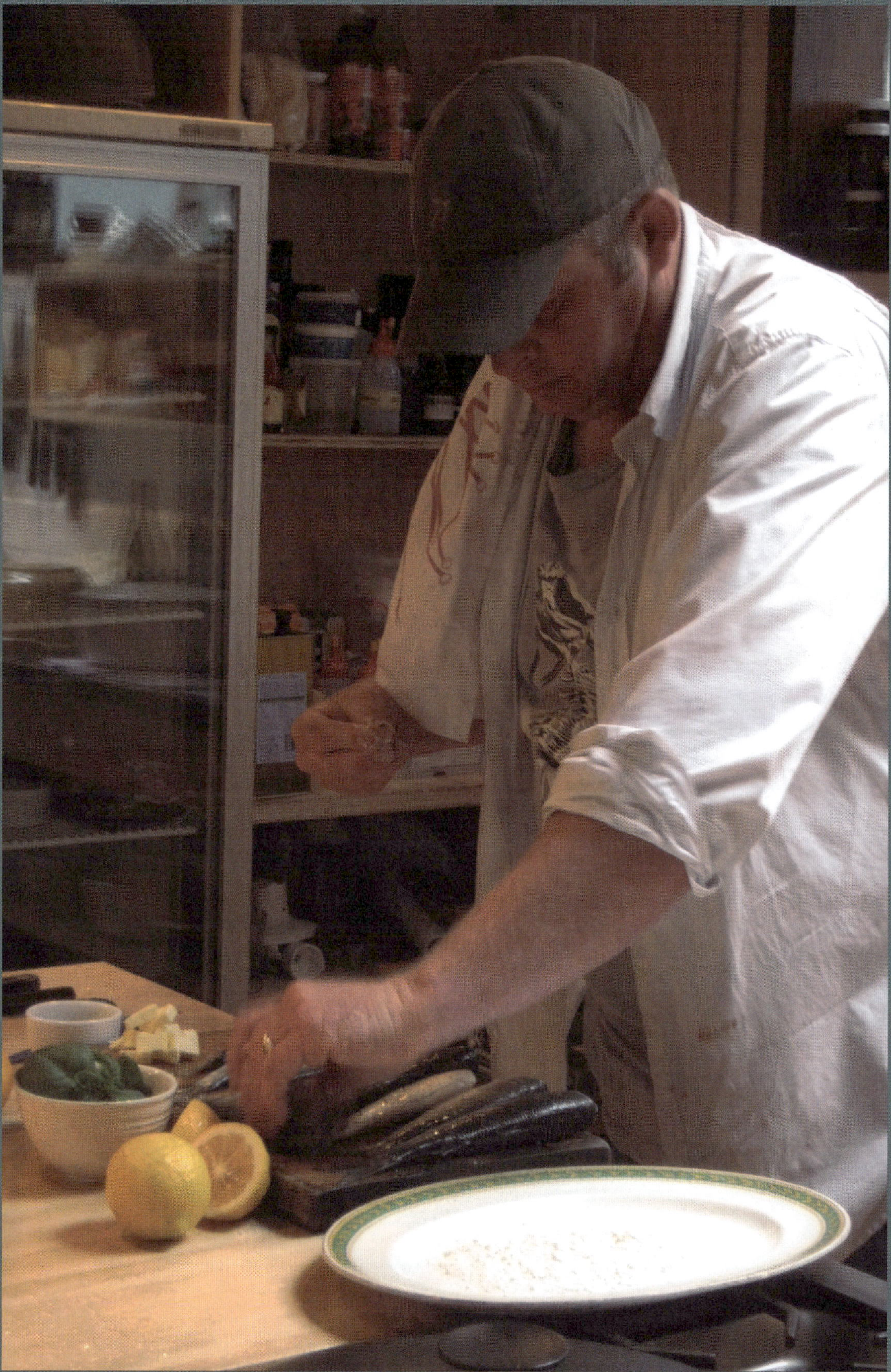

The edge at Evans Bay.

down there just waiting to be caught and eaten. We're going to eat them straight off the bone.'

'An unexpected treat,' says Ath appreciatively as he licks his fingers. 'Exquisite.'

STRONG EDGES

The conversation returns to planning for the waterfront. Al wants to know what Ath thinks are the most important issues regarding the rim of the harbour. What it boils down to, in his view, is respect — for the environment, for each other, for the form and history of the land itself.

'We're fortunate to have a green belt in Wellington,' Ath says. 'We have plenty of undeveloped countryside. Unfortunately, some of our land developers seem to think they can produce flat sites everywhere out of hill sites, but our topography has actually helped us contain the city, which is really important.' Reflecting on Kiwis' changing attitudes towards the environment in general, Ath adds, 'Clean-green is not something you actually travel through in your motorcar, it's something you look out for and protect. And so settlements, cities, towns have to have strong edges, where sheep can graze right up to the last house and strong coastal edges where you get the best fish right at the edge of the coast.'

Al laughs. 'Now you're talking — that's it, eh? Those herrings right on the jetty, right on the edge!'

A city and its waterfront

From Karaka Bay, Al heads towards the northern tip of Miramar Peninsula. Each little bay has its own character: from Scorching, Mahanga, Kau he rounds the point to Shelly and the larger Evans Bay, the northern end of the airport. Then there are more: Kio, Weka, Balaena and Little Karaka bays. At last, Al says, throwing his arms wide as he turns the point that marks the beginning of Oriental Parade and a view of the central city opens before him: 'The big reveal! The most beautiful harbour city in the whole world!'

It's a rich and busy scene. Below the curve of the Kelburn skyline, there's a scatter of houses, and nestled at the foot of the hills, the colourful collection of skyscrapers and buildings of the central business district — houses, apartments, hotels, restaurants, theatres, warehouses, shops, offices. Somewhere behind all that, there's the Beehive and other governmental buildings; this is, after all, the capital city. On the waterfront itself there's the museum Te Papa Tongarewa, a marina and then, moving north, the platforms of the port with its cranes and heavy traffic, rail lines, storage tanks, containers and ships. A pair of kayakers paddle past, walkers promenade and tourists admire the view from seats on the edge of the shore. On a fine day, Wellington city casts a stunning reflection onto its harbour's glassy waters.

A RESTLESS SHORELINE

It's not a fine day, however, when Al meets historian Jock Phillips. Jock is the General Editor of *Te Ara*, the online Encyclopedia of New Zealand that is run by the Ministry for Culture and Heritage — a position he has held since 2002. Prior to that, Jock was New Zealand's Chief Historian for 13 years. He has written or edited 10 books, including *New Zealanders and the Sea* (2009), a comprehensive look at the way our lives and destinies are interwoven with the ocean. If anyone knows anything about the coast and its relationship to our culture, it's Jock.

Jock is waiting for Al in the heart of central Wellington, on

An 1842 painting of Port Nicholson and the town of Wellington indicates how much land has been reclaimed since that time.

the corner of Lambton Quay. The lane behind him is narrow and cobbled, with offices and shops leaning high over it. It's raining and windy and Al is so wet, he jokes that he could almost have come out of the ocean. In fact, had he met Jock in this same spot 160 years ago, he would have come out of the ocean because this was once the waterfront.

'When Europeans got here in 1840, it was exactly at this point that the Kumutoto Stream, which basically drained the whole of the Kelburn hills, came out and ran over the beach to the harbour,' Jock says. 'This would have been a central point for local Maori, a place where they would fish, gather kaimoana and swim.'

European settlers at first planned to locate their new settlement on the Hutt River at the top of the harbour but soon realised that the area was damp and the river was prone to flooding. Which is why, Jock says, they turned their eyes to the land on the southern shores of Port Nicholson or Wellington harbour.

'It was a crazy place to build a city,' he says. 'The land goes straight up behind us and is steep. The only reason they came here was because they needed a port — communities in the nineteenth century lived off the sea. In order to build a city they needed a bit of flat land. The only thing they could do was to fill in the land in front of us and provide a base for these big skyscrapers we see here today.'

Jock Phillips waits for Al where Kumutoto Stream used to enter the harbour.

They began in the 1850s, and a comparison of today's map with the original coastline shows how dramatic the reclamation has been. It's a story common with the ports in most of our major cities but what's unique about Wellington is that it sits somewhat perilously on the fault line between the Pacific and the Australian plates and suffers periodic earthquakes as a consequence. Most notably, in 1855 the settlers' need for additional space was considerably assisted when an earthquake measuring a massive 8.2 on the Richter Scale raised land from the harbour and moved the existing port about 150 metres inland. In all, something like 155 hectares has been added, altering the old coastline beyond all recognition. Today, it can be identified by a series of 14 plaques placed around the city by the Historic Places Trust.

And that's how Lambton Quay came to be a number of streets back from the coast even though it was originally — as the 'quay' in the name indicates — along the waterfront. A succession of quays have been created and then later supplanted: Thorndon Quay is also now back from the water, while Customhouse, Waterloo and Jervois quays claim the right to the sea.

Al and Jock follow the old shoreline down Lambton Quay towards Parliament Buildings. 'Lambton Quay was named after Earl Lambton, one of the New Zealand Company sponsors,' Jock says. 'In front of us would have been the port and behind us you would have seen a whole row of small shops. Our first signs of European settlement would have curved all along here and in early paintings you get this lovely sense of the beach and this row of small shops, pubs and boarding houses.'

EYES TOWARDS THE SEA

The most recent of Wellington's many waterfront transformations began in the 1980s. The business end of the port had moved north and the city awakened to the reality that the waterfront offered a huge opportunity for new direction. Where previously it had been

Wellington 35

Jock and Al look out on a very sodden Days Bay beach.

locked behind Harbour Board gates with shopping and office precincts further inland, a new relationship with the coast now became possible and a dramatic remodelling followed. Parks were created, the promenade above the seawall along Oriental Parade was enhanced, open spaces were created. The whole area invited people in — to look around, spend time, play, contemplate, walk, be. In the words of Wellington poet Lauris Edmond it is the city of action.

At the forefront of this shift in focus was the national museum, Te Papa Tongarewa, relocated from its previous Buckle Street site to its purpose-built five-floor building perched on the waterfront. Opened in 1998, Te Papa Tongarewa celebrates New Zealand art, history and culture. Surrounding it and enticing the public in the waterfront area are many sculptures — from 11 small-scale snatches of poetry typeset in stone on the Wellington Writers' Walk, to a series of larger works, each of which is a response to its seafront location. Kinetic pieces move in the wind, others incorporate water features while still others, such as the bronze 'Kupe Group', featuring that long ago explorer Kupe Raiatea, his wife Te Aparangi and tohunga Pekahourangi, evoke the country's past.

The upper harbour

From the city the coastline tracks north alongside the multilane motorway that is State Highway 1. High above, houses perch on the edge of steep hills, their winding streets following the contours of the land. Wellingtonians are adept at fitting into narrow spaces, at building houses on stilts, at parking cars on platforms, at snuggling into the shape of the land. This is where Ian Athfield has built his home, on the cliff overlooking the western harbour, it cascades down the slope in a series of interconnected white-plastered pavilions, forms, angles, windows and chimneys that has become the signature of his design.

Further round, the coastline leaves the motorway, swinging east into Petone's sandy foreshore that stretches across the head of the harbour for a couple of kilometres before being broken at the eastern end by the Hutt River. From there the coast tracks out the eastern arm of the harbour towards Pencarrow Head, punctuated by a series of small bays and settlements, one of which is Days Bay in Eastbourne.

A DAY AT THE BAY

Al and Jock buy a couple of tickets at Wellington's downtown terminal, board the waiting boat and head up to the top deck. 'This ferry is called the *Cobar Cat*,' Jock observes. 'The original ferry that used to take people from Wellington over to Days Bay round the turn of the century was called the *Cobar*, so it's nice that they've kept that tradition alive.'

As early as 1893 the ferry was a popular form of transport around the harbour, particularly in the weekends when it took many of Wellington's city folk on seaside excursions across the harbour to Days Bay.

The place to be seen in the mid-1890s: Days Bay Seaside Fun Park.

As Al and Jock approach the eastern side of the harbour they see a series of sand and shingle beaches between small headlands, and the forested hills behind. There's a pier in the middle of Days Bay, a road along the beach, clusters of houses, pohutukawa trees and grassy open spaces. The capital with its hustle and bustle now seems far away. This is a small seaside community: the pace and rhythm of life is different here.

In the mid-1890s shipping high-flyer John Williams was also charmed by Days Bay. He paid £1000 and set about turning it into a massive seaside amusement park. He built a pier, laid on a ferry and provided multiple attractions — tennis courts, hockey fields, an 800-seat Brighton-style pavilion and upmarket hotel, a zoo, a castle and, famously, a water-chute. Flat-bottomed boats holding eight people hurtled down a ramp along wooden rails and splashed and bounced their shrieking passengers into an artificial pond. There was candy floss and donkey rides. It was so popular that on fine weekends up to 5000 people took the trip across to the harbour and for them that was what the seaside was about.

'They didn't have a sense of going to the beach like we do, where you go for a swim and this kind of thing,' Jock says. 'Basically, the seaside in English tradition was a commercial proposition. There was quite a different sense of what the beach was about.'

'Essentially a fun park,' Al says.

'Exactly,' Jock says. 'And there wasn't a lot of swimming because there were bylaws that said that you weren't allowed to have mixed bathing. Men and women getting into the sea together was regarded as disgusting. So there was no swimming, but instead people used to promenade up and down the beach.

'It was a big investment,' Jock says, but almost 40 years later, when Robin Hyde wrote *The Godwits Fly*, what she called the 'Day's Bay Wonderland Exhibition' was no more. She described a by-then derelict scene: a small brown artificial lake with swans, and the crumbling water-chute, a closed stucco shell 'adorned with a laughing, moth-eaten tiger' and a double-storeyed bandstand, its stairway blocked because it was 'rotting and dangerous'.

But by then Kiwis' attitude towards the beach was moving on; they were discovering that the trip to the beach didn't need organised entertainment.

Jock and Al stand on the pier overlooking the beach.

'The interesting thing is that from about the 1920s on, New

Zealanders began to realise that the real fun was here on the beach and in the water; they could make their own fun. And for the first time the bylaws allowed them to actually swim, they could lie on the beach and sunbathe, it was Kiwis enjoying a day at the beach.'

'And that's happened all over the country?' asks Al.

'It happened all over the country and it suddenly became part of what the good life was in New Zealand.'

The rain has settled in once again and Jock and Al cut a sodden silhouette against the misty hills. They contemplate the desolate beach.

'Not a huge amount of good life today, I'd have to say. Won't be in my Speedos anytime shortly, that's for sure.'

They laugh heartily and Al farewells Jock to continue his journey out to Pencarrow Head.

The FV Conquest selling the week's catch to keen locals at Lowry Bay.

Wellington 39

Right: The Eastbourne Italian family the Dellabarcas plying their trade at Lowry Bay around 1907.

Below: Dan Dellabarca, fourth generation fisherman whose ancestry traces back to the island of Stramboli, Italy.

Fish on the menu

'FRESH FISH TODAY!' Al's eyes light up at the sign chalked on a blackboard at the south jetty at Whiorau Reserve, Lowry Bay.

'My favourite shop in the whole of Wellington!' he says.

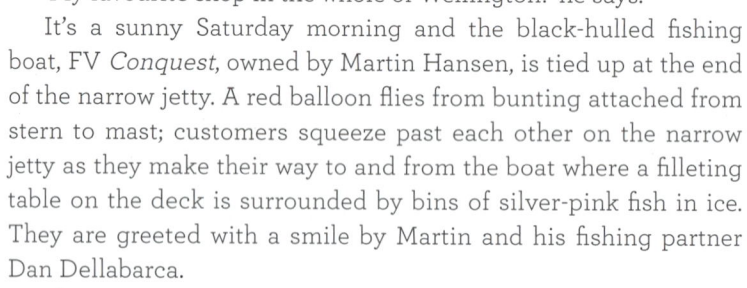

It's a sunny Saturday morning and the black-hulled fishing boat, FV *Conquest*, owned by Martin Hansen, is tied up at the end of the narrow jetty. A red balloon flies from bunting attached from stern to mast; customers squeeze past each other on the narrow jetty as they make their way to and from the boat where a filleting table on the deck is surrounded by bins of silver-pink fish in ice. They are greeted with a smile by Martin and his fishing partner Dan Dellabarca.

The pair have been selling locally caught species such as terakihi, snapper, kingfish, hapuka and trevally direct to shoppers since 2007 and have quickly become a bit of an institution. In the week before each market and depending on weather, they're up before dawn heading out offshore anywhere from Cape Palliser on the eastern head of the harbour as far as Mana Island on the south-western coast. They use longlines or droplines and set nets and then sell their catch direct from the boat at Lowry Bay on Saturdays and at Chaffers Marina in the city on Sundays. To Al selling fish at the wharf makes perfect sense and is what used to happen all over the country in less regulated times.

'There's more red tape than I've ever seen,' Martin says. 'It's killing the fishing industry as a whole because boats and organisations in the industry have to get bigger to survive...'

40 **Coasters**

There have been Italian fishermen at Eastbourne for generations. 'It's in the blood,' says Dan, a fourth-generation fisherman who has taken to the sea since his father and uncle retired. 'I love it, eh.' Their story began with Bartolo Russo, a fisherman from Stramboli, who established a settlement in Rona Bay immediately south of Days Bay sometime in the 1890s. On a trip across to Wellington around 1907, he met Dan's ancestors, the brothers Luigi and Antonio Dellabarca, who were crewing on a visiting ship, and convinced them to immigrate with their families and join him. They returned to Italy and brought back their families and fishing gear. And while their nets didn't take well to the newer and harsher New Zealand coasts, the families did. Dan recalls stories of his grandfather catching fish around the harbour and his grandmother, after filleting the catch with a sharpened butter knife, walking to Eastbourne to sell it.

So selling their fish in this way is not exactly new, but it took a long time for this generation to get it off the ground for all that. 'There's more red tape than I've ever seen,' Martin says. 'It's killing the fishing industry as a whole because boats and organisations in the industry have to get bigger to survive, whereas we want to keep it small, to have a niche market, cut out the middleman and just sell to the public. The system doesn't like it but we do, and the customers do.

Skipper Martin Hansen loves meeting the people that buy his fish: 'They go away feeling like they caught it themselves.'

'Yep,' Martin says. 'It's great not only to fish like we used to, but we get to know our customers and can just about have their fish ready when they're coming up the wharf. And it's a great little social occasion. It's always a good day down here in Lowry Bay — people even come out in southerlies — the sea will be breaking over the wall, but they still come and buy the fish. They go away feeling like they caught it themselves, just like the old days,' he says.

Martin and Dan encourage people to buy their fish whole or, if it has been filleted, to use the frames, heads and the wings. Al agrees, believing that New Zealanders' obsession with filleting fish sees them throwing away some of the best parts.

'This is how we should be buying fish,' Al says. 'This fish will taste twice as good as any fish you would ever buy from a supermarket, and at half the price, and you're getting the whole relationship thing happening as well, filleted in front of your eyes, talk to the guys that caught it, they can talk you through what the different species are about — it's just brilliant.'

BUILDING BOATS ITALIAN-STYLE

Al leaves Martin and Dan to their customers and continues down the coast towards Pencarrow Head. At Rona Bay in Eastbourne he drops in on Dan's uncle, Paddy Dellabarca, who built his first fishing boat, a 35-footer, in his mother's yard when he was 17. He has constructed all the family's boats ever since.

It's obvious even before you enter that this is a boatbuilder's house: it's neatly trimmed in grey and white, the joinery is immaculate, but it's the adornments that are the real giveaway. Balustrades, decks, shutters, the lifebuoy on the front gate, carved dolphins, anchors, a ship's light, a ship's bell, a ship's wheel, a cannon, a model lighthouse and glass buoys in nets.

Al visits Paddy Dellabarca at his home in Rona Bay.

Above: Paddy in 1951 stands in front of the launch he built in his parents' backyard.

'It's pretty nautical, put it that way,' explains Paddy in the understatement of the century. 'It started up in the front with bits and pieces and it grew and grew and everyone was saying what's coming up next?

'I like to have it like a boat — I grew up with boats. They've been my life,' Paddy says as he gives Al a tour of the house. He shows him photographs of the different boats he built and of the family out fishing — there are shots of him as a boy pulling in kingfish from the beach. Paddy talks about his life, both as a boatbuilder and as a fisherman.

Paddy's passion arose from an early age where he spent most school holidays at Island Bay working on the Italian fishing boats. He used to get below deck any chance he got, just to see how a vessel was constructed. He learned to build boats from his dad and anyone else who would teach him. Often they never worked to plans. 'We set a keel down, a bow, a stern and then adjusted and spaced frames to where we wanted them, to the shape we wanted. Building the old plank boat was a work of art, and I loved it.'

Paddy couldn't bear living anywhere away from the sea. 'I can never move away; it's just in your blood,' he says with a smile as he farewells Al.

Below: Paddy Dellabarca says of the coast: 'I could never move away — it's just in your blood.'

Wellington 43

The lady of the lamp

The rocky coast at Pencarrow Head marks the eastern entrance to Wellington harbour.

The last leg of Al's journey around the capital coast takes him through a locked gate on the southern outskirts of Eastbourne and along a gravel road out to Pencarrow Head/Te Raeakiaki on the eastern side of the harbour entrance. The Wellington coastline is living up to its reputation for wind with a northerly screaming off the land.

After a good few kilometres' walk from an empty driftwood-strewn shingle beach, Al climbs a track up the hillside, past golden blooms of gorse to the sun-bleached, grassy world of the tops. Below, the road curves around the base of the cliffs as it has done since he first left Red Rocks. There's a rim of white as waves break and toss against the shore. In the harbour entrance, which feels like a stone's throw from the shore, an outward-bound container ship passes an incoming inter-island ferry, while an aeroplane descends against the backdrop of the western hills. It's blustery up here!

Al's last coaster, Mary Jane Bennett, is no longer with us. She was a remarkable woman whose remarkable story is not widely known, but in her time she knew plenty about that wind. Her great-great-granddaughter, Anne Bennett, is waiting at the foot of the Pencarrow lighthouse, her hair whipping around her face. Several generations of the Bennett family have lived and worked on this remote, wind-battered headland, from Mary Jane to Anne's grandfather, who is buried here.

A map of the New Zealand coastline is studded with lighthouses and light beacons for good reason. In the first 50 years of European settlement, over 1000 ships and 450 lives were lost on rocky outcrops, reefs and headlands, a disaster by any means but even more so for a nation that depended on shipping for trade and immigration. Warning lights were needed urgently and, in the second half of the nineteenth century, there was a flurry of construction of lighthouses. With them came a special way of life and a special breed of coaster that has now all but gone — the lighthouse keeper.

'Mary Jane Bennett came here in 1852 with her husband George,' Anne says. 'They were the first lighthouse keepers for Wellington. A barque had run aground a year earlier with 30 people lost and the people of Wellington were really concerned about this. Governor Grey

Above: Al and Anne make their way to the now decommissioned Pencarrow Head Lighthouse.

Below: Anne Bennett with some of Mary Jane's paintings.

Wellington 45

The first lighthouse at Pencarrow Head, built around 1852.

gave permission for a lighthouse to be put up here — but it wasn't really a lighthouse at first, more like a shack with a light in it.'

'It was nothing like the lighthouses today and life must have been incredibly hard. They would have had to grow their own vegetables, be self-sufficient, shoot and fish. Mary Jane would have had to make her own soap and bread, and there were days when the weather was so terrible they couldn't get a fire going. In some southerlies the family had to take shelter in a cave that George dug out because the shack was in danger of blowing away. Imagine trying to keep six children and a toddler alive and safe in this sort of terrain, as well as having to get up and trim the wick every three hours during the night.'

In 1855, tragedy struck the family. George was returning from Seatoun with two other men when their boat was swamped by the swell. The trio clutched onto rocks for hours but while the others eventually reached land, George was swept off by the rising tide and, unable to swim, was drowned. As with the *Wahine* over 100 years later, rescue was tantalisingly, tragically close. 'We fear that the family would have been watching and seen him clinging to the rock all that time,' Anne says.

Mary Jane carried on alone. She was pregnant with her seventh child and continued to rise and tend to the wick. She proved herself equal to the task and was allowed to stay on in her husband's place under the same terms — except that she was supplied with firewood. She schooled her children, fed and clothed them, walked to Petone for supplies, operated the permanent lighthouse when it was erected in 1858 and, in her spare time, painted delicate watercolours of plants. In 1865, with her oldest girls in their late teens, Mary Jane took the family back to England. 'The boys went to school and the girls got married,' Anne says.

But the pull of New Zealand was too great for three of the boys,

Pencarrow Head lighthouses.

who later returned, including Anne's great-grandfather William, who came back to Pencarrow to work as the lighthouse keeper. His child, Anne's grandfather Percy Bennett, was born and is buried here.

Anne and Al stand out next to the balustrade of the lighthouse. The wind is howling and they both look down on the rugged, magnificent coastline below, imagining the sort of life Mary Jane Bennett, the first woman lighthouse keeper in New Zealand, and probably the world, had lived. 'She was the lady of the light,' Anne says. 'And we are so proud of her.'

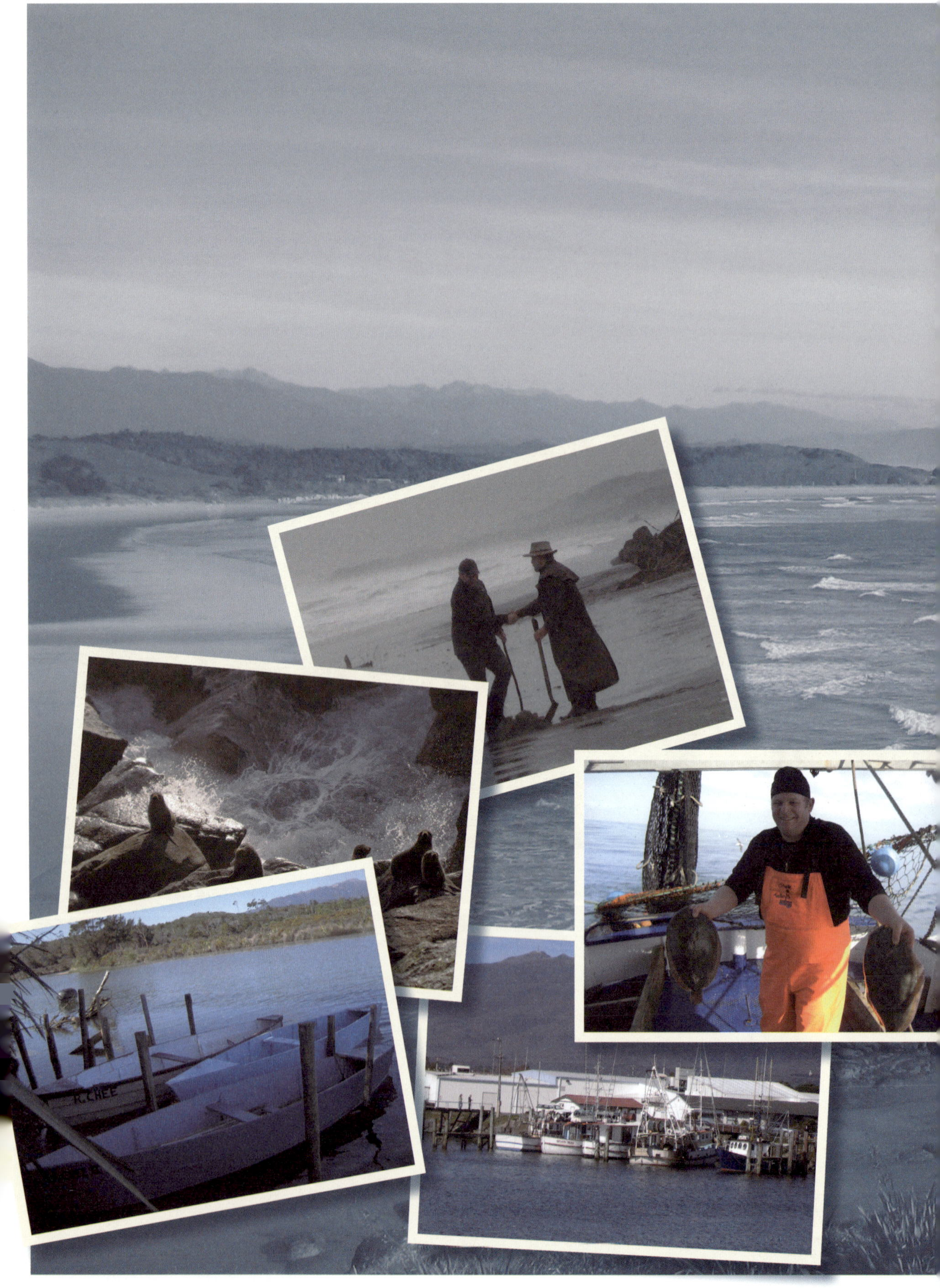
K.CHEE

Welcome to... the West Coast

The Coast of Character

Above: Charleston goldminers — they came from far and wide to find a fortune that few ever did.

Previous page: Heading south down Nine Mile Beach to Charleston.

It's always been the sniff of riches, and the fancy that they're there for the taking, that's drawn people to work the stretch of coast between the mouth of the Buller River and Charleston.

The area has experienced booms of various kinds — pounamu, gold, coal and timber — over time. But anyone expecting this part of the coast to simply roll over and offer up its bounty wouldn't have lasted long. For while it's blessed with resources, the common theme has been the sheer logistical difficulty of making them pay, given the

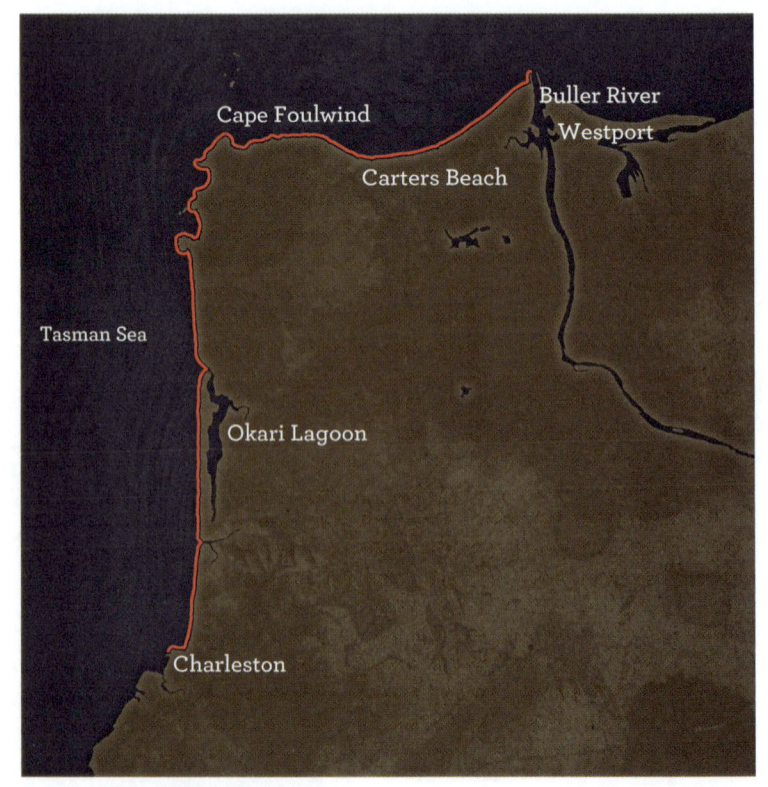

Westport to Charleston

physical difficulty involved in extracting them, and the natural obstacles that exist to commerce here. It's when you consider the hardships people faced in getting there — and in getting stuff out — that you realise how strong the incentive was for early Maori and for the European pioneers. Even in the modern era, with all of the technological advantages that we enjoy, exploiting the wealth of this bit of coast is still a marginal enterprise.

But as Al found when he went for a wander from Westport, at the mouth of the mighty Buller, to Charleston 25 kilometres to the south, all that hardship has left its mark on the people who live here, or at least sorted the men from the boys: you've got to be pretty tough, pretty self-reliant, practical and, beneath it all, a bit of an optimist. It's all too easy to fear the worst living on this bit of coast: it's only those who have been able to see that chink of light who've been able to reach an understanding with it. They're a breed apart, all right. And it's only by getting to know the coast that you really get to know the coasters.

Cliffs just north of Cape Foulwind.

The Buller River was historically the main route to Westport.

The pounamu trail

These days there are a few ways you can get to Westport.

You can get there by road, heading west down the Buller Gorge from the Nelson region to the mouth of the river, where our journey begins. But even today, the narrow, winding road, with some truly thrilling drop-offs down to the swift, icy waters of the Buller, serves to underscore the isolation of the West Coast from the rest of the South Island. Next time you drive it, imagine what it was like rattling along there in a horsedrawn Newman Brothers coach in the days when it was a mud and gravel track.

The route along the course of the Buller was also the principal access for Maori travelling to the coast trading Te Ara Pounamu — the pounamu trail, which led to the South Westland sources of New Zealand jade, or greenstone. There's archaeological evidence of Maori habitation of the Westport area — the site of a fourteenth century village has been explored at Kawatiri on the floodplains to the north of Westport — but it seems these settlements were never especially large and may have been only sporadically occupied.

The fact that Maori came here at all, let alone so often, gives you an indication of how highly pounamu was prized.

According to legend, pounamu was the petrified body of a beautiful woman, who was abducted by the taniwha that guards the Tasman Sea and carried away from her North Island home to South Westland with her outraged husband in hot pursuit. When he found himself cornered, the taniwha transformed his captive into the same substance he was made of — pounamu — and laid her in the bed of the Arahura River. The legend of the pursuit and the luckless lady's fate, like most legends in oral cultures, served Maori as a storehouse of knowledge, and provided a rough route guide to Te Ara Pounamu.

The Maori name for the Buller, Kawatiri — 'deep and swift' — tells its own story. The hard men and women who trod Te Ara Pounamu or who travelled down the coast in taua (war parties) wore paraerae — sandals woven from flax — or quite commonly, bare feet. That makes you think.

It was a footslog, too, for the European explorers Charles Heaphy, Thomas Brunner and James Mackay when they accomplished pioneering surveys of the West Coast. Heaphy and Brunner were the first Europeans to make an overland journey to what became Westport, on an epic bush-bash in 1846. It was Mackay's travelling companion, James Rochfort, who first determined that the mouths of the Grey and Buller rivers were navigable by taking his cutter, the *Supply*, into each in 1858. It was Mackay, too, who in 1860 blazed the trail that became State Highways 6 and 40, the road along the Buller Gorge.

You can also reach Westport from the south by road or by rail. Westport has an airfield that is serviced by Air New Zealand's subsidiary, Eagle Air, but there are only a limited number of destinations. Coasters too ill for the main West Coast hospital at Greymouth are choppered over the mountains to Christchurch, but these links are all contingent, and dependent on the weather.

According to legend, pounamu was the petrified body of a beautiful woman, who was abducted by the taniwha that guards the Tasman Sea and carried away from her North Island home to South Westland.

The Westport bar

And of course, the other, time-honoured, weather-dependent way to get in and out of Westport is by sea. Like the mouth of the Grey down the coast, and several of the other harbours on the west coast of both of New Zealand's main islands, Westport is a bar harbour, which is to say there's a more or less permanent build-up of sand, gravel and silt just to seaward of the mouth of the river. The opposition of the current of the river and the incoming tide heaps up sand and silt at the entrance. Wave action, the stripping of the outgoing tide and the flow of the river ceaselessly sculpt the shoals so that the configuration of the bar is never exactly the same from hour to hour, let alone from day to day. The heavy Tasman swell kicks up in the shallow water to form fearsome breakers, often complicated by wind-whipped chop. Navigating these waters is not for the fainthearted.

Yet in the days before the roads were driven through, navigating the bar was precisely what people were obliged to do when they

Westport harbour, once home to a thriving fishing community. Today there is only a handful of local commercial fishers left.

54 *Coasters*

wanted to get into Westport, or when they wanted to get themselves and their goods out. The bar has gnawed at the edge of the consciousness of Westport's people for the better part of 150 years, and it has been a big influence on their lives and character for at least that long.

A DODGY PIECE OF WATER

Al has an appointment with the Westport bar and Jack Devine is the local trawlerman who's going to help him keep it. Jack lives in Westport, but makes his living on the other side of the bar. He runs a trawler — the *Journeyman*, a little steel-hulled workboat built for the Chatham Islands crayfish boom of the late 1960s and, like many others built for the same purpose, still going strong in the wetfish industry around the country.

'She's a great spot,' Jack tells Al, nodding at the still harbour. 'Nice place to finish up at the end of the day. Pretty quiet these days, though. There's only three or four of us working out of here now, but used to be a hell of a lot more. Time was there'd be 130 boats at the height of the tuna season. You could just about walk across the harbour on them.'

It's an early start, he warns Al. Jack's day on the water often starts the day before, when he begins monitoring the weather bulletins and bar conditions. Before sun-up, he'll make the call on sky and sea: will I get out across the bar? And more importantly: will I get back in again? Jack can hear the bar from where he lives. In the morning, before he goes out, he'll open his kitchen window then sit down for a cup of coffee. If he can hear the roar of the sea on the bar, he'll finish up his coffee, close the window again, and head straight back to bed.

If it's a green light, he'll be slipping the *Journeyman*'s moorings in the pre-dawn twilight. Jack will have checked his motor thoroughly — losing power while negotiating a rough bar could be disastrous — and organised his gear and loaded bins of ice into his holds. He'll file a a Trip Report with the harbourmaster and swing the *Journeyman*'s bow to the gap between the breakwaters, where the Tasman, the inshore trawling ground and the day's fishing prospects await.

The *Journeyman* has a 120 horsepower D-series Ford motor, the power and agility to defy the influences of sea and tide — to a point. She also has a chart plotter and radio communication with the shore

The memorial at the mouth of the Buller remembers the local coasters who lost their lives at sea.

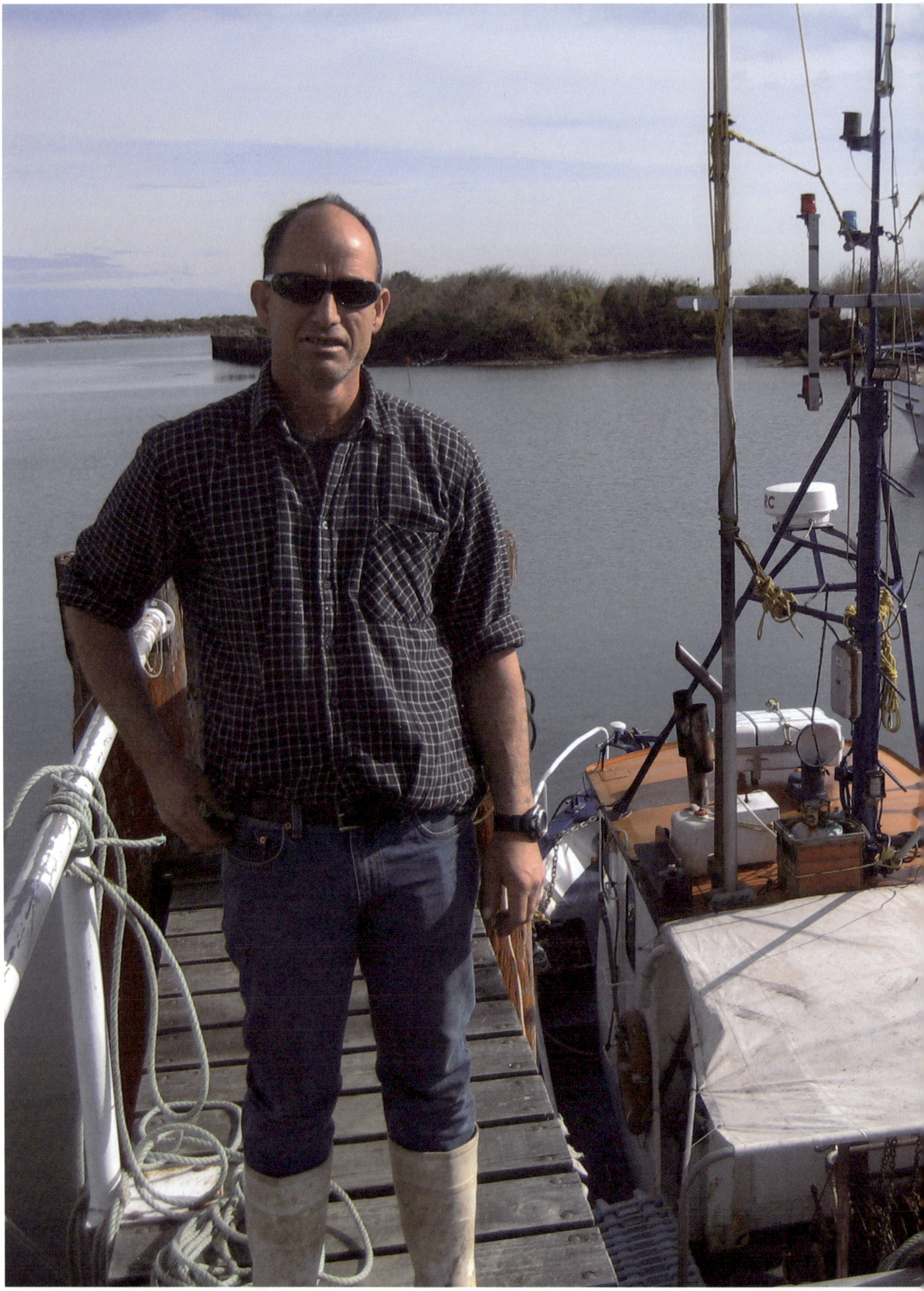

and other vessels. But all of that can count for nothing if the bloke driving it makes the wrong call.

Standing at the entrance to the river at the end of the northern breakwater, Jack points out to where the water changes colour.

'She's a dodgy piece of water when it gets going,' he says, pointing out to Al the play of the water over the bar. 'You can see the line over there, where the colour's different. You've got the river current coming out of here: it's called the set.'

The 'set', the river current, is capable of running at 10 knots, and the incoming swell at five; with turbulent, foaming water apt to go all soggy under the boat and around propellers; with steep, short swells trying to swamp you from behind — or swing you into a broach and tip you up, you need all your wits about you, most days.

'If it's a really bad bar, the skipper will be taking notice of the set coming up — how much current, how high the waves are standing up, the roll, if it's breaking . . . You're just trying to time it, trying to work out where the lulls are. You get as close as you can and if you've got your timing right, you go like hell. It's the greatest adrenaline rush. I've had my knees knocking for half an hour beforehand when I've known I'm going to run a shitty bar.'

Even when all seems well, you can never afford to be complacent.

'Complacency will kill you, all right,' Jack says. 'It can look good for ten to fifteen minutes and then it will just go to custard.'

A WINDJAMMER'S GRAVEYARD

Of course, many of the early vessels plying these waters were more or less at the mercy of wind, sea and tide when things went wrong. Relying entirely on sails for propulsion and steerage, sailing ships of the mid-nineteenth century were challenging to manoeuvre in the best of weathers and ill equipped to deal with unpredictable West Coast river ports. Little wonder the Westport bar was a windjammer's graveyard. The first substantial vessel to fall foul of it was a schooner named the *Eclipse*, which lost the wind just as she was approaching the bar, outward bound, on 30 November 1866. With the anchors she hastily deployed dragging, and attempts to haul her off failing, she was doomed, and was dashed to pieces on the inside of the sandspit to the north of the entrance. Vessel and cargo were a total loss, but at least her crew were saved.

Not everyone has been so lucky. The Westport bar has taken a cruel toll over the years, and plaques dotted all around the town and

Opposite: Jack Devine makes his living on both sides of the Westport bar.

'Complacency will kill you, all right,' Jack says. 'It can look good for 10 to 15 minutes and then it will just go to custard.'

cemented to the memorial on the breakwater commemorate those whose lives were lost out there where the swells roar and murmur over the sandbanks.

The Westport Harbour Board was created at the end of 1884 and the construction of breakwaters began in 1886 in an effort to improve the port and its access. The work was entrusted to an Englishman by the name of John Coode, who had designed the seawall at Brighton in his home country, and another at Port Elizabeth in South Africa. Stone by stone, the walls were built to confine the river to a defined channel in the desired direction under the guidance of the esteemed engineer. The works were designed so that the river has a straight and unimpeded approach to the sea, which enables the current to bear gravel as far out to sea as possible. The mouth faces north, away from the prevailing wind and sea swell, which helps, too. Nevertheless, waves constantly carry fine material over the bar: the harbour silts up fast and requires constant dredging.

The northern tiphead has also provided a vantage, down the years, for relatives of those who were due in during a spell of foul weather to maintain an anxious vigil. Even today, when a storm blows up suddenly and someone's due in, word gets around.

Local vessel Owenga VII *enjoys a calm crossing of the Westport bar.*

They came for gold but stayed for coal. Westport wharf, 1907.

There is, as an old local saying goes, no wrong side of the bar. Even a miserable night or two being tossed on the Tasman is a better bet than adding your name to the dismal roll of the bar's victims. If in doubt, as they say, stay out.

'This,' says Jack, patting the stone of the memorial, 'is where we don't want to be. None of us fishermen want to end up here.'

In for the long haul

Jack is the third generation of his family fishing out of Westport. He made his first crossing of the bar in 1964, when he was six days old. His dad was a trawlerman working from Westport down as far as Jackson Bay and his mum was the crew. So Jack was tucked up in a bassinet and taken along for the day's fun and games. He's grown up on trawlers, with a few stints trucking and working with mining machinery in between.

The West Coast

Above: Jack's father's boat.

Below: Jack made his first crossing of the Westport bar when he was six weeks old.

'Trawling's my bread and butter, but I live for the tuna in the summer. That's further out, and it's all handlines and it's about as exciting as it gets.'

Jack has seen the inshore fishing industry change from one in which a fleet of small-time operators such as himself went out, caught what they needed to turn a profit and came home again, to one where the big boys — large companies with a fleet of big, modern trawlers — have shrunk fish stocks, altering the economics and, Jack believes, the ecology.

'As far as I'm concerned, there shouldn't be any trawler over 48 foot or 180 horse within five miles of shore. They should be out where they were designed to be. It's self-sustaining using these small boats: they can't work all weathers, so that way, the West Coast looks after its own, the fishery gets a rest and you make the most of it when it's there. But the bigger boats can work all weathers.'

The profit motive is opposite to sustainable fishing, he reckons. The bigger boats just aren't so inclined to farm the ocean as the locals who are in it for the long haul, and the inshore fishery is suffering. It wasn't so long ago there would be youngsters lining up on the wharf to be taken on as a deckhand, every one of them dreaming of one day owning his own boat. These days there's no one looking to enter the industry at all. The deckies are all in it for a bit of a thrill, or their fix of the sea. None regards it as a serious career.

60 *Coasters*

'And what about the future?' asks Al.

'Future's pretty grim,' says Jack. 'Can't see my grandkids eating fish and chips. It'll just be chips.'

Nor does Jack hope to make a fortune doing what he does. His trips over the bar are more about getting a feed than getting rich.

'And you never get sick of fishing, do you?' Al says. 'That feeling of anticipation.'

'It's one of the great hunts,' agrees Jack. 'You never know what you're going to get until you get it on the deck.'

Mostly they go after flatfish out here. On a calm day with little swell, when you can be reasonably sure the trawl doors will stay on the bottom, you trawl the sand for flounder and sole, which are well known to the New Zealand fish-buying public and fetch high prices. On a roly-poly day that stirs them off the bottom, you'll go after turbot, which are more of a local delicacy, and others such as gurnard and rig. When it's too bouncy to work the bottom, you'll target mid-water fish like warehou and tarakihi.

Further out, it's all about big factory vessels chasing squid and tuna, and working the deepsea critters — hoki, smooth dory, orange roughy. These get processed at the big Talley's plant in town, which caters to the export market and to big local buyers but at which passers-by can usually pick up a bargain, even though there's no longer a retail outlet. At the height of the season, there'll be two shifts of 75 workers apiece working flat tack to process all that fish.

Jack reckons he doesn't chance his arm on the bar quite so much as he used to, back when he and the others 'were young and foolish and the old finance was pushing, interest rates were high. But a successful day's fishing is when the fish and the fishermen all make it ashore. It's a great life, if it doesn't kill you.'

AL HAS A CRACK AT THE BAR

The big day dawns, and it's a green light. It's Al's turn to have a crack at the bar. He's feeling pretty apprehensive, and the hard knot of anxiety in the pit of his stomach links him to the long line of other mariners who have made this crossing. Luckily, it's a beautiful day. The *Journeyman*'s engine hammers away below deck and the wind

Jack Devine, third generation fisherman. The bigger boats just aren't so inclined to farm the ocean as are the locals who are in it for the long haul.

'It's one of the great hunts,' agrees Jack. 'You never know what you're going to get until you get it on the deck.'

whips the mingled tang of salt and diesel into the deckhouse. On days like this, the sun paints your way toward the Tasman with your own shadow. Contrary to widely held belief, Westport gets plenty of benign weather. A lot of the time, you'll steam out between the breakwaters in an oily calm as though the only bar in the harbour were the one where you'll be having a well-earned drink after your day out. But you certainly don't count on those days. And you can't even count on those days lasting.

Even on a good day, as you're readying the trawl, tying the 'money knot' in the bottom of the net — 'you never tie it before you leave the wharf: it's bad luck,' Jack explains — heaving your nets over the side, enjoying a cuppa while your vessel earns her keep burbling over the grounds for two or three hours, you keep a weather eye and you always remember, whatever you're doing, to keep one hand for the ship.

'The last thing I ever want to do is fall over the side and watch it steaming away from me,' says Jack.

'Yeah, it'd be tough,' says Al.

'Yeah, it's happened to a few guys over the years.'

All going well — you've remembered to tie the knot, you haven't donated your net to a totara log that's taken a fancy to it down on the seabed — you winch up the nets and even after all these years, there's

Al in his element. 'There's only one thing that is going to get me over the bar and that's a fish I love, turbot.'

still a tightening of your gut as the head of the net appears and a thrill as you see the quick splash and the flash of colour there — turbot, sole, brill, perhaps, or cod, depending on what you're targeting, and the bycatch of crabs, eels and maybe even the odd cray.

'Turbot, look at that!' Jack shouts.

'Boy, turbot, look at them all,' says Al, smiling.

Then it's all action, because once the fish are aboard, a lot depends on how they're handled. The condition of your catch, the price it will fetch at market and your reputation all depend on processing the fish fast — gutting them with swift flicks of your keen knife — and chilling them down.

Plenty of coasters have been head down and hard at it splitting fish as a cloudbank has reared in the west, stealing up to chase them home and — if it wins the race — to raise a welcoming committee of demons on the bar.

Above: Turbot, a traditional West Coast delicacy.

Below: Al and Jack work to get the fish on ice and cooled down as soon as possible. 'Every hour they're off ice is equal to a day.'

The West Coast 63

Turbot and Whitebait Butty

There is something very special about catching, cooking and eating fish just hours out of the water. Tied up to the Westport wharf, one frypan, one gas ring, cramped in the smallest of galley kitchens. A knob of butter, glistening turbot fillet, the whitebait still wriggling and a loaf of fresh white bread. In my eyes, this truly is as good as it gets. Magnificent in its simplicity, this sandwich is unquestionably my favourite in the whole world, and to devour it at the source transcends this humble kaimoana gobstopper into another culinary stratosphere!
Serves 6

Ingredients
butter for spreading and frying
1 loaf sliced white bread
mayonnaise for spreading
2 eggs
½ tablespoon flour
500g whitebait
sea salt and freshly ground black pepper
500g fresh turbot fillets
2 lemons

Method
Preheat the oven to 100°C.

Butter the bread and smear each slice with a good lick of quality mayonnaise.

Separate the eggs, putting the whites in one bowl and the yolks in another. Add the flour to the egg yolks and whisk to a paste. Mix in the whitebait, season with sea salt and black pepper then set aside.

Heat a skillet or sauté pan over medium heat. Season the turbot fillets with sea salt and black pepper. Add a little butter to the pan and cook the turbot in batches for a couple of minutes on each side until slightly golden and cooked through. Place in the oven to keep warm.

Whisk the egg whites until just stiff then fold into the whitebait batter.

Heat the skillet or pan again over medium heat. Add a little butter then drop in spoonfuls of the fritter mix. Cook until golden on each side and cooked through. Keep the fritters warm in the oven until you have finished cooking the rest in batches.

To serve, simply place a fritter or 2 on a slice of the prepared bread, top with some turbot then squeeze over a hit of lemon juice. Finish with a pinch of sea salt and grind of pepper and top with another prepared slice of bread. Repeat with the remaining ingredients then you are good to go!

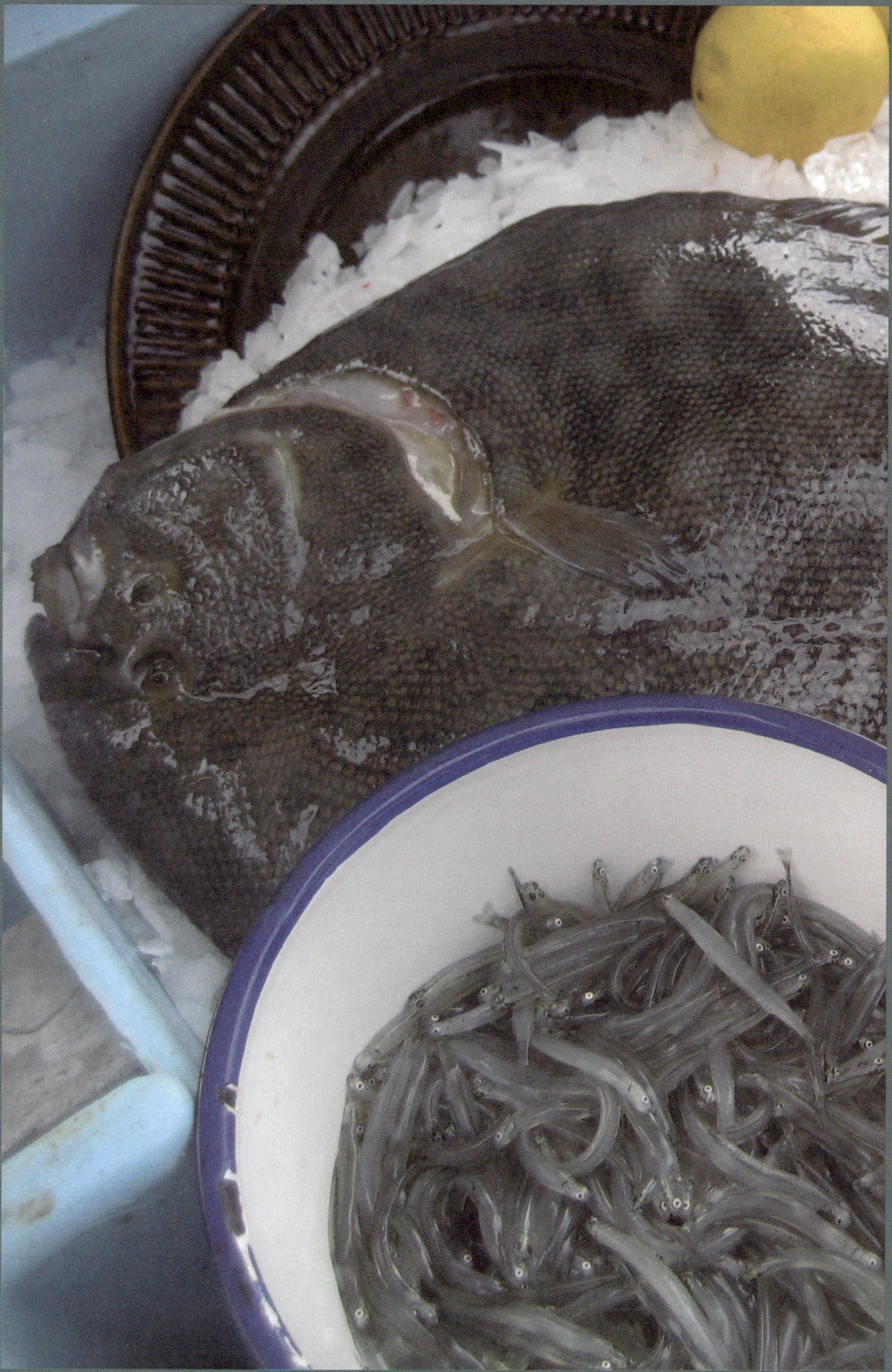

David Barnes, the former harbourmaster, who began his career on the sea when he was thirteen and a half.

Keeping the port in line

One man who knows the Westport bar as well as anyone alive is David Barnes, ebullient district councillor, former harbourmaster and passionate amateur historian. David arrived at Westport in 1995 after a career at sea that began when he was 13½, at which age he began his apprenticeship aboard the training ship HMS *Worcester*, moored in the Thames. Barnesy arrived in New Zealand in 1974, and worked for the Union Steam Ship Company, mostly on tankers plying the coastal trade. The scope and variety of the job of Westport harbourmaster appealed to him, and it so happened the demands of the position neatly fitted the assortment of skills and experience he had acquired in his long career at sea. He got the job.

There was, Barnesy tells Al, a settling-in period when he first arrived on the Coast. Coasters are known as a hospitable bunch, but they're also tight-knit, and their respect and acceptance is earned rather than gifted willy-nilly. He brought an outsider's eye, and 'tanker discipline' to his job managing the port. Things on general cargo vessels and colliers, the coal carrying workhorses of the shipping trade, can get pretty loose, but aboard a tanker, he reckons, with thousands of litres of flammable liquid sloshing about the hold, there's no room for any of that. Barnesy wasn't long in the job at Westport before he got wise to the tricks of the trade — the corners cut, the ruses and the fiddles. When a collier's crew wanted an extra day enjoying the conviviality of the astonishing profusion of Westport pubs, for example, they'd simply arrange for one of the coal trucks loading their vessel to derail. The clean-up would set back loading at least a day.

It will come as no surprise to anyone who knows Westport that his biggest battles were fought with the fishermen and with the whitebaiters. The baiters will go to extraordinary lengths to secure a good 'possie', and despite the comings and goings of big vessels such as Westport's regular caller, the *Milburn Carrier II*, they would clamber in under the piles of the wharf and even make little 'structural modifications' to accommodate their stand, their nets and themselves. Trouble was, you couldn't just tell them to clear out as they'd been doing this for generations. In the end, a compromise was reached: baiters who claimed the right to fish from beneath the wharf undertook to the port authority to hang out a yellow flag to show they were there, and if for operational reasons they were told to get out, they promised to get the hell out.

And as for the fishermen, it was always going to be a clash of wills. The Westport harbourmaster has the right to close the bar to shipping: in the old days, a signal would be run up a mast on shore to indicate whether the bar was safe to cross or not. Everyone who's ever been in the job has done it more often than the fishermen thought necessary.

There are, Barnesy tells Al, three myths about the Westport bar. Myth number one: I have a good bar boat. Myth number two: I have years of experience. Myth number three: it's bad out here, so I'd better get back across the bar.

No boat is safe on a rough bar, he says, and nor will years of experience amount to anything when the laws of physics take over. Above all, when in doubt, stay out.

As harbourmaster Barnesy always felt there was a distance between him and the local fishermen. When the widow of one of the fishermen lost on the bar came to him and pointed out that Westport lacked anywhere she or others could go to mourn her loss, Barnesy was quick to ensure a memorial was constructed on the tiphead to commemorate the fishermen and other mariners who wouldn't be coming home. That gesture touched the locals, Barnesy reckons. Every loss at sea in so close-knit a community leaves a scar. Giving all that grief a focus helps to soothe the wounds.

HI-TECH SOLUTIONS

Technology has made the bar more workable than it was for most of its long history. These days, the harbourmaster has a fancy electronic rig aboard the port's workboat, the *James Gower*, that uses differential GPS and an echo sounder to do the hydrographic work that was once performed by men swinging a shot line to take the soundings and using a sextant to fix positions. Today this data is fed into a computer that paints a picture of the bottom and the bar at the push of a button. He can do in a couple of hours what used to take a couple of days to accomplish with the old methods.

The digital maps of the bar are supplied to ships, and can be uploaded to their electronic chart plotters. That means their masters can see their position relative to features of the bar and the sea floor in real time.

But Al finds out that some things are still done the old-fashioned

Like an airport control tower, the harbourmaster's building is the place from which traffic in and out of the port is directed.

Above: The biggest vessel regularly entering Westport is the Milburn Carrier II.

Below: Acting harbourmaster Nico Weeda.

way as he catches up with Nico Weeda, Westport's acting harbourmaster. Every time a vessel's due in port, Nico will drive to the tiphead at the entrance to the river and observe the bar. He does the trip each day, and as the vessel makes her approach, he'll make radio contact with her master and they'll formulate a plan of attack.

Just before a ship sails, Nico will collect the master and the two of them will drive out to the tiphead and sit in the car and watch the bar. He sits with Al and shows him what this part of the job's all about.

'Basically, we're looking for anything that makes the bar dangerous: the heart of the swell, the set — that's the current going across the bar, that may set the ship off her course,' Nico says.

If one of them is at all nervous about a crossing, they'll call it off. Nico knows the local conditions; the master knows his vessel and what she can and can't do. Even when their opinions differ, there's never any argument.

Today, Westport's most frequent callers are the two Holcim cement carriers, the *Westport* and *Milburn Carrier II*. Large enough to negotiate the bar in all but the roughest of conditions, their deep draughts and snug fit into the river mouth call for regular land-based

68 *Coasters*

assistance, and whatever the conditions, it's always a dramatic sight — to see these big boats enter the tiny river port.

The main problem for large shipping here is draught. Westport harbour is limited to five metres. The bar height changes all the time, and depending on the amount of water in the river, it can lose up to a metre in height overnight. On the other hand, when the river's low and there's a big sea running, the bar builds up, with the fine material washed over the shingle by wave action accumulating very quickly. That's why, among the many and varied tasks in the harbourmaster's job description — port operations manager, enforcer of marine bylaws and safety regulations, civil engineer — directing dredging operations is one of the most important.

Dredge master Jeff Walker.

A CONSTANT BATTLE

Few people in history have felt they could control Westport's bar. One of them is Jeff Walker, who's the skipper of the *Kawatiri*, the Westport dredge. Most days, he'll work on the bar to keep the entrance open and to the necessary depth to accommodate the usual traffic.

'Once they've done their survey, and they have all the soundings for us, they send us a digital chart which we put onto our hydro [hydrographical chart plotter], and that shows us the high spots where we need to dredge. With GPS, we can get within a metre of where we need to go and just take the high spots when we need to. We can take 600 cubic metres per load, which is about 1200 tonnes of sand. That takes us about an hour. In a normal day for us, we can take five loads. Still, about half of what we dredge comes back the same day. It's a constant battle.'

As Al watches, fascinated, Jeff fiddles with a few knobs and levers on a console in the bridge, and the dredge arm swings out and plunges the draghead into the water.

It works like a giant vacuum cleaner, sucking the silt from the bottom and dumping it in the hold. From the port, it's taken to a spoil ground around a mile out to the north-east of the harbour entrance. The littoral drift does the rest, taking the sand further up the coast.

It's a necessary operation: back in the days before such physical manipulation of the bar was possible, boats could spend days, even weeks, in the harbour waiting for the river and the sea to organise a navigable bar for them. But before the road links and the railway — the branch line from Christchurch didn't reach Westport until 1942

Above: The Westport dredge Kawatiri.

Below: There's nothing too sophisticated about a dredge, but the simple process of sucking up sand and dumping it at sea provides a lifeline to this coastal town.

— people shifting themselves and things in and out from Westport had no choice but to play by the bar's rules.

Even with all the power and the technology at his disposal, Jeff Walker can only sculpt the bar within certain limits. When things turn pear-shaped and the bar cuts up, even the *Kawatiri* stays home.

'You've got to keep your wits about you,' Jeff says. 'When things go bad they go bad fast.'

Beachcombing on Carters Beach

If you'd slogged your way to Westport on foot or risked your life on a vessel inbound over the bar, you'd be pleased to find the going easier as you headed south. Carters Beach, which stretches the better part of 11 kilometres from the mouth of the Buller to Cape Foulwind, is like a four-lane highway — broad, flat and black, thanks to the fine ironsand of which it's made. It's a wonderful walk, with the Tasman grumbling to your right, the dunes giving way to the flax and the cabbage trees on swampy Addisons Flat to the left. You can walk barefoot with an easy rhythm, perhaps pocking the sand every stride with a sturdy bit of driftwood culled from the beach for a walking stick. There's no shortage of walking sticks, especially after a storm, with the great rivers nearby — the Buller and the Grey, and the lesser Okari between the two — carrying windfall timber down to the sea.

You can't imagine a better place for a spot of beachcombing, or nutting something out, or just breathing the salt and seaweed tang deep.

LAND UPLIFTED HIGH

The first European to set eyes on New Zealand described what he saw in a sentence that translates from the Dutch as 'land uplifted high'. Abel Tasman got that more right than he could have known. He was looking at the Southern Alps from the sea in the latitude of the Pancake Rocks, and what he was describing was a landform that was the product of a process known as 'geological uplift'. This occurs where two tectonic plates slap into one another, with one forced beneath the other and the overriding plate buckled up into a mountain range — land uplifted high, indeed.

Over the millennia, the backbone of the South Island, the Southern Alps, have copped their fair share of rugged weather. Periodic glaciation — freezing — and the slow, inexorable grind of glaciers flowing seaward have left their mark; so, too, has the relentless battering from the prevailing westerlies, hurling rain off the sea, with the trickle and rattle of streams carving channels in the rock and the great rivers laying down deep fans of alluvial silt and gravel.

These are the processes that gave us the West Coast, which is essentially a narrow shelf of alluvial rubble extending from the foot of the Alps to the Tasman Sea, apart from points where the old bones of the land poke through. The swampy ground was once a lowland podocarp forest, dominated by the towering and ruinously beautiful kahikatea and studded with groves of nikau, although today's remnants are but a small fraction of what there once was.

Tipping up a piece of the Earth's crust has the effect of exposing ancient geological layers, which are shot through with minerals. There was pounamu in the south, of course, and gold and coal in the north. Not surprisingly, the human history of the West Coast has mostly been one of exploitation of this natural wealth. After pounamu came gold, discovered in 1861 after the government offered a £1000 bounty to anyone who could turn up a find, to spark a rush of Otago proportions. The West Coast goldrush lasted from 1865 to 1867, and for a time, the Coast boasted fully 21 per cent of New Zealand's European population.

Then, when the gold was paid out, interest turned to coal, and since 1864 when the first mine opened, over three million tonnes of the stuff have been ripped from the ground by 100 mining companies. Two companies still work the 13 active coalfields on the Coast: Solid Energy has several mines, including the open-cast Stockton just 35 kilometres north of Westport; and Pike River operates a large underground mine working the Brunner coal seams, south-east of Cape Foulwind.

It was coal that built Westport, while the goldrushes mostly passed it by: the Merchandise Wharf was built in 1877 to facilitate the first outward shipment of coal from the Waimangaroa mine, about 25 kilometres to the north of the town. Coal shipments were steady from then on, fed by a network of railway lines. It wasn't until

The Southern Alps, as viewed from the coast at Punakaiki.

the completion of the Westport branch railway in 1942 that all the coal mined around Westport bypassed the town. The town grew on the back of a coaltruck.

CEMENTING IN THE LANDSCAPE

Other commodities have had their time, too. The lowland podocarp forest that once blanketed the Coast was progressively felled and milled, the last commercial logging operations winding up only a few years ago. And the Coast's abundant limestone resource has been quarried and used to make cement since settler days, too.

Just before he reaches the end of Carters Beach, Al climbs the dunes to find the Holcim Cement Works. Well, you don't really 'find' it: you can't miss it. It's been plonked with a singular lack of sensitivity right in the middle of the landscape, jutting from the flats just inland from the rugged beauty of Cape Foulwind. Aesthetics didn't really cross the minds of coasters in 1958, when the plant opened its doors: 'Let's make cement,' they said. 'The limestone's over there, so let's make the cement here.'

In 1963, the plant's owners, the New Zealand Cement Company, merged with the oldest cement producer in the country, the Milburn Lime and Cement Company of Otago. A Swiss company took a controlling interest in 1977 and bought the local interests out in 1999, and the name was changed to that of its new owner, Holcim Cement Ltd.

Above left: For years the Westport harbour provided the main lifeline to the outside world.

Above right: A full set of coal tubs at the mouth of the Denniston mine.

There was pounamu in the south and gold and coal in the north. Not surprisingly, the human history of the West Coast has mostly been one of exploitation of this natural wealth.

You can't imagine a better place for a spot of beachcombing, or nutting something out, or just breathing the salt and seaweed tang deep.

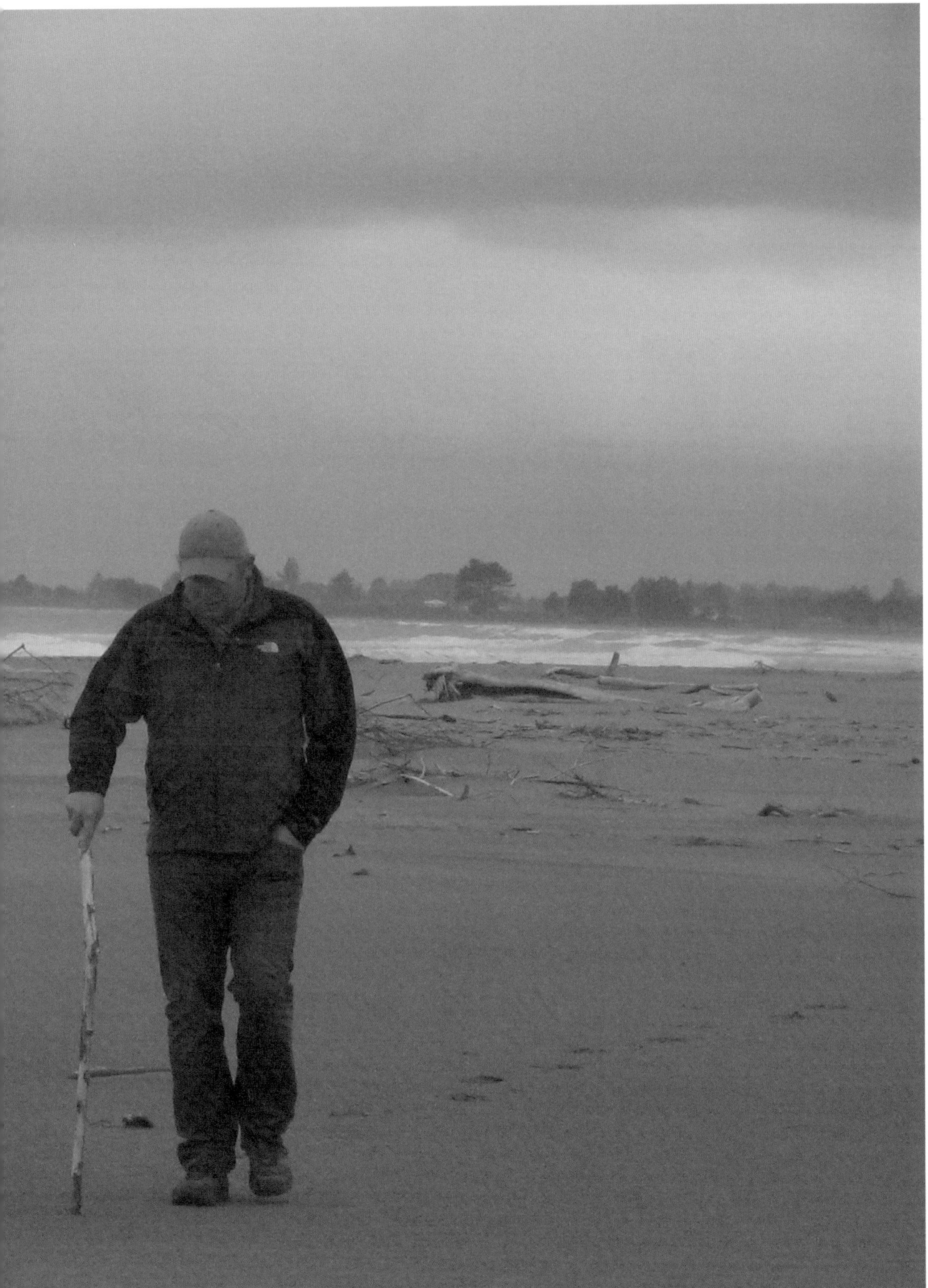

Above: Flat burning coal sourced locally heats the rotating kilns.

Below: The cement works just inland from Carters Beach has been part of the coastal skyline since 1958.

These days, the plant works around the clock, 24 hours a day, according to long-time plant employee Brian Thomas, producing 500,000 tonnes of cement a year. Brian explains that cement is produced by heating limestone (which is actually the concentrated remnant of the shells and the delicate calcium carbonate skeletons of ancient shellfish and plankton) and adding marl (a lime-rich form of clay). Each of the key ingredients needed for cement manufacture — limestone, marl and the coal needed to produce heat — are available locally, making the Cape Foulwind factory site just about perfect.

'Man, this is impressive!' Al yells, over the noise of a giant slurry mixer. 'It's like an oversized cake mixer!'

The plant has three vast, roaring rotary kilns tended by a busy fleet of vehicles: so busy, in fact, that the plant has its own set of traffic lights, the first to be installed on the Coast. Standing near the kilns, Al is awed by the heat emanating from them.

'It's like a rocket,' he reckons.

'Price of electricity wasn't an issue when the plant was built,' Brian says. 'We use a bit of recovered oil as well as coal in the burners. Helps the environment out there.'

The huge stacks billowing steam into the air are clearly visible from Westport, let alone from Cape Foulwind. The environment, like the price of electricity, is only a recent consideration.

'Come this Guy Fawkes, we'll have been here 51 years,' Brian says. 'Done the community a lot of good in that time.'

'A lot of the country is built on product that is coming out of this plant. The buildings, all the cities, the towns, the homes, the houses,' he tells Al.

But for all that, the Holcim works looks likely to be shut down and the operation moved to a new plant in Oamaru, which is similarly blessed with locally available raw materials. Given the local abundance of raw materials, the sole reason the Westport plant can't expand would seem to be the difficulties in delivering an increased output to the outside world. The company presently uses two vessels to distribute its product to eight terminals around the country. The larger of the two, the *Milburn Carrier II*, was never designed to work a bar harbour and due to her draught can only operate to a maximum 50 per cent capacity in the Westport trade.

The plant's closure would ultimately mean the loss or relocation of 130 employees, including Brian, who is the third generation of his family to work for the company. And with Holcim Cement providing the bulk of the funds for port operations at Westport, including dredging the bar, the future for this river port is also in question.

'And cement from here has built the nation,' says Al. 'Next time I mix up some concrete, I'll have a whole new respect.'

Cape Foulwind rocks

Leaving behind the rumble of the cement works, Al resumes his walk along Carters Beach and before long finds his way blocked by an untidy heap of granite slabs. That's Cape Foulwind.

You might at first think it gets its name from the smell that assaults your nostrils as you approach — seal colonies have an aroma all their own — but in fact, the name was given by Captain James Cook, who encountered a bit of a blow here on his visit in 1770 and was driven far out into the Tasman Sea. Abel Tasman, who wasn't

Above: Cement being batch brewed at the Westport works 24 hours a day. From the slurry it is cooked in giant spinning ovens.

Above: Three generations of Brian Thomas' family have worked at the cement works.

The West Coast

Local DOC historian John Green tells Al that the project to quarry stone for the Westport harbour breakwater lasted for years — 'There were generations working on it.'

Opposite: Cape Foulwind's granite boulders are a formidable match for the Tasman's pounding waves.

above commemorating his bad experiences in his cartography — just look at Murderers Bay — must have had a happier time here a century earlier, as he called it Rocky Point.

And rocky it is. The Cape granite is the land's old bones, formed where magma — molten rock — has cooled slowly far beneath the earth. It's very much older than the limestones and mudstones that comprise much of the rest of the Coast's landforms.

Its permanence, the shade offered by the nooks and crannies, the cooling-off opportunities in the rockpools in the jumbled mass of rocks, all make Foulwind prime real estate for the New Zealand fur seal seeking a haul-out, according to long-term coaster and passionate local historian John Green of the Department of Conservation. After being all but wiped out first by Maori, who regarded the kekeno as an important food source, and then by Europeans, who prized the skin and the oil that could be made from their blubber, the fur seal has made a solid comeback. The Foulwind colony, for one, has bounced back.

If you're here in late summer, it's all happening, as John explains.

'At this time of year, you have the yearlings about to be weaned off. They'll leave this place and head out to haul-outs, and meanwhile the big bulls will come in and the cycle will start again.'

They're big animals — beautiful, sleek-looking and with soulful brown eyes — but you don't want to get too close.

'Don't get between them and the sea, that's the golden rule,' John says.

'What can they do?' asks Al.

'They can carry some nasty diseases. There's one called "seal finger". If you have a little cut and you get that virus in there, it just blows your whole hand up, your whole arm blows up like a bike tube, and you've got it for 10 years before you get rid of it. And they carry tuberculosis, too, so you should keep your distance.'

THROUGH GRANITE TO GET GRANITE

The visitor clambering over the rocks and treating seals with a whole new respect after acquiring this particular nugget of information will be amazed to find that Cape Foulwind was, for a time, the westernmost extremity of New Zealand's rail network, with a branch line reaching from Westport to a terminus just short of the point itself.

Over the years John has heard many a tale of train trips to

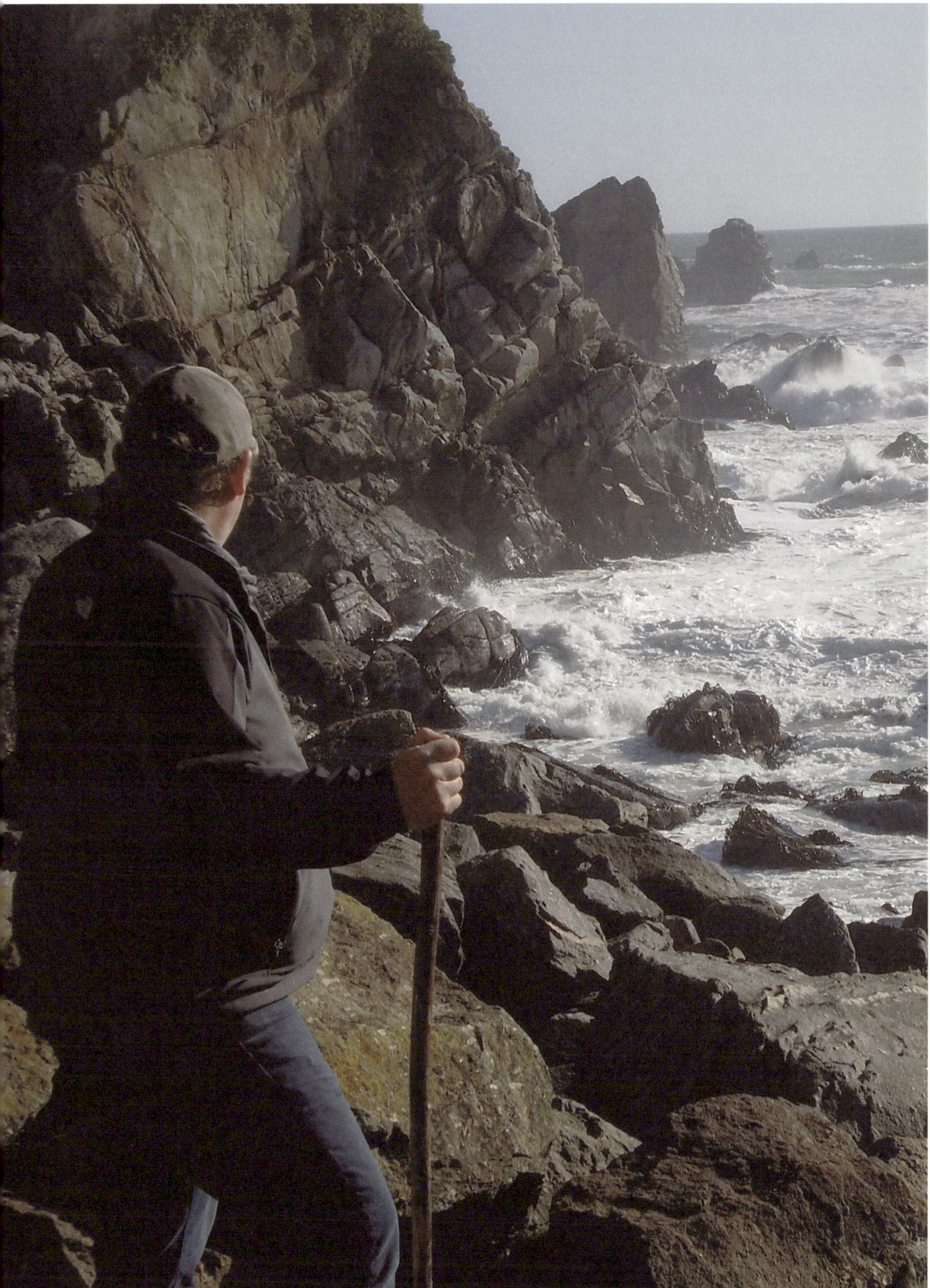

Above: A New Zealand fur seal eyes Al on his journey around Cape Foulwind.

Right: John Green fills Al in on the locals.

80 **Coasters**

The seal colony at Cape Foulwind is making a comeback after being all but wiped out, hunted first by Maori, who used seals as a food source, and then the Europeans who hunted them for their oil and skin.

The West Coast 81

Right bang in the middle of the seal colony, the tunnel to nowhere.

Cape Foulwind on Sundays. These were big community days out and picnics were the most popular pastime. 'Everyone would dress up and catch the train — there were six stations between Westport and Cape Foulwind — for picnics, and there were always races for kids, greasy pig chasing, men at the bar, women setting out food on blankets. These picnics remained a "big do" right up until the 1950s.'

It's from the cape that the granite used for ongoing construction of the Westport Harbour's tipheads was quarried. The first blast at the quarry, which took place near the lighthouse in 1886, was reportedly a great success, bringing down an estimated mass of 35,000 tons of stone. Quarrying at the cape was on a large scale — by 1895 one million tons of granite had been taken out, run down the seven mile line and deposited at the port breakwater. It was an on-again, off-again enterprise, resuming on a large scale in 1927 until a major breakwater extension was completed in 1931, and again for a final round of river protection works — including 90-metre extensions to both breakwaters — in 1965. As a result, there is a very large nick out of the Cape Foulwind headland.

'This project lasted for years — there were generations actually working on it,' John tells Al.

'I keep seeing things that I can't believe they achieved back then', Al replies.

'Well it's the nature of the Coasters I think; if the job had to be done they just got stuck in and did it.'

And they didn't just chip away at one headland to do it: they actually drove a two-kilometre tunnel through that headland to get at another headland. The scale of the engineering enterprise is impressive: this isn't easy material to drill or dig.

'One story that's locally known,' John says, 'is that they didn't really need to go through to the second headland. There was enough rock back here. But the guy who was in charge of the job wanted to build a tunnel to get his tunnel-building ticket, which is supposed to have been a big deal back then.'

Only West Coasters would tunnel through granite to get at granite.

SURF HEAVEN

From the south flank of Cape Foulwind, Al finds himself overlooking another gorgeous, pristine sweep of beach — Tauranga Bay. In the right conditions, this is one of the country's best surf spots, with the rocky headland transforming the inexorable Tasman Sea swell into a pretty left-hand point break. Surfers in this area have a problem unusual for New Zealand board riders: they're often obliged to wait for the swell to die down before they can wax up their boards and get amongst it.

And perched at the southern end, with the best view in the house of surfers wiping out in the Tauranga Bay break, is the Bay House Café. The board and batten building, nestled out of the way amongst the flax on the headland, had already served a long career as a notorious surfer hangout and the scene of many après-surf parties every bit as wild as the water by 2003, when acclaimed chef Luke Macann shifted in and turned it over to its present purpose. It was a roaring success from the outset. Part of it was the food, but a big part of it had to do with the location, too: as one local put it, 'they could serve fried cardboard and people would still eat there'.

In many ways, the Bay House Café represents a shift that's happening on the Coast, away from the 'extraction' industries that first brought people here and that have subsequently shaped both land and population, toward the 'attraction industry', where the Coast itself with 'all its beauty and drama and opportunity for adventure' can be mined, figuratively speaking, for wealth. Tourism is on the increase, but things are in a transitional period at present, with an uneasy tension existing between the two competing philosophies.

Whitebaiting kings

Keep going south, and you reach Nine Mile Beach (which is really only 12 kilometres — seven miles — long, but who's counting). Your progress will be halted about halfway along by the point at which the Okari Lagoon breaches to the sea, a point that changes constantly with the contours of the beach. You have to skirt the lagoon inland, and unless you've got access to a boat, you'll get pretty wet if you mean to get across.

There are plenty of boats about, for the most part, little plywood punts and canoes — bearing an unsettling resemblance to coffins, as Al's next coaster, Darryl Kerr, points out to him. They belong to whitebaiters like himself, who pole them upstream, gondolier-style, to their stands and to the baches that many of them keep just so

Next page: The Tasman Sea meets the cliffs just north of Cape Foulwind.

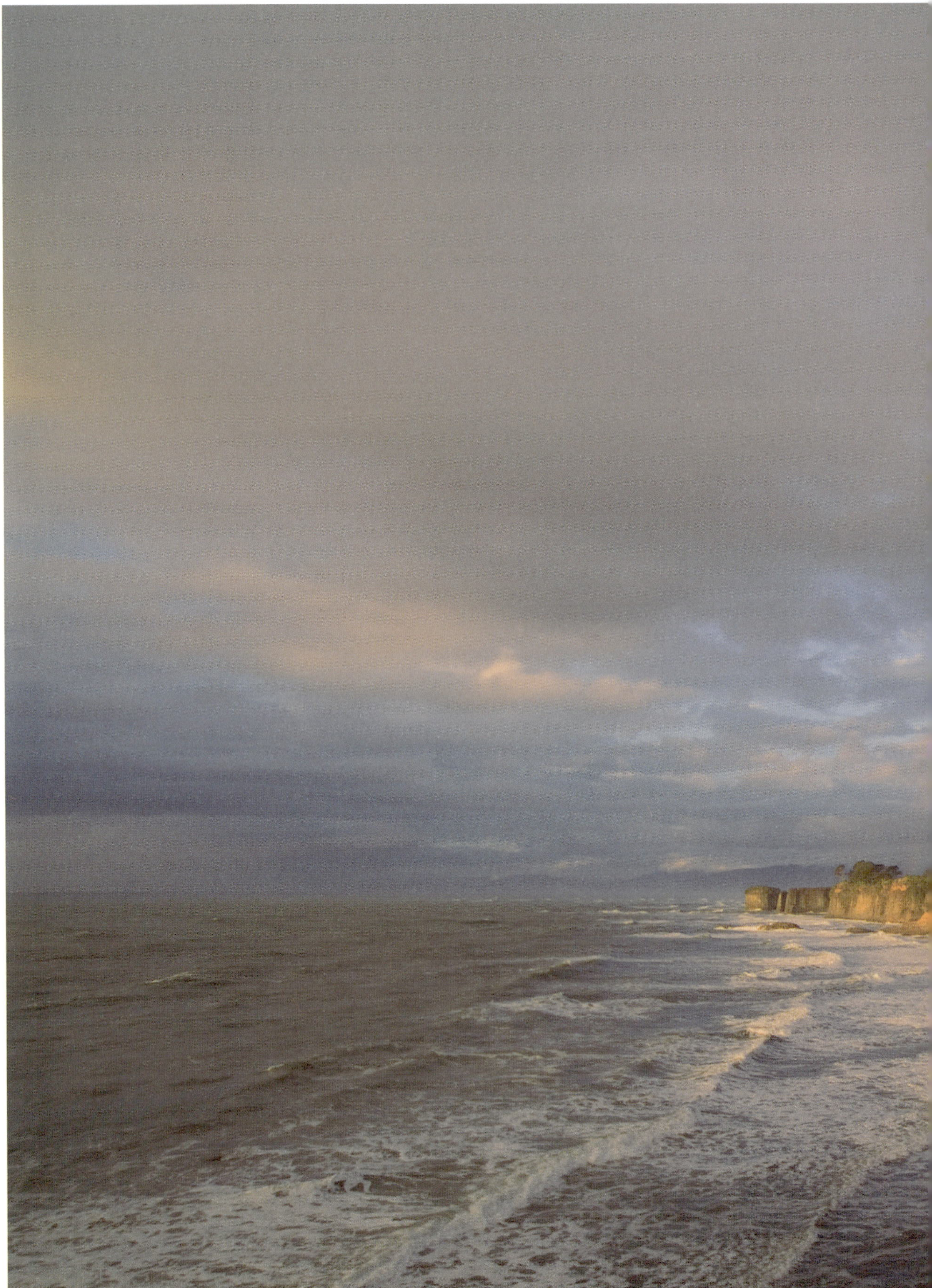

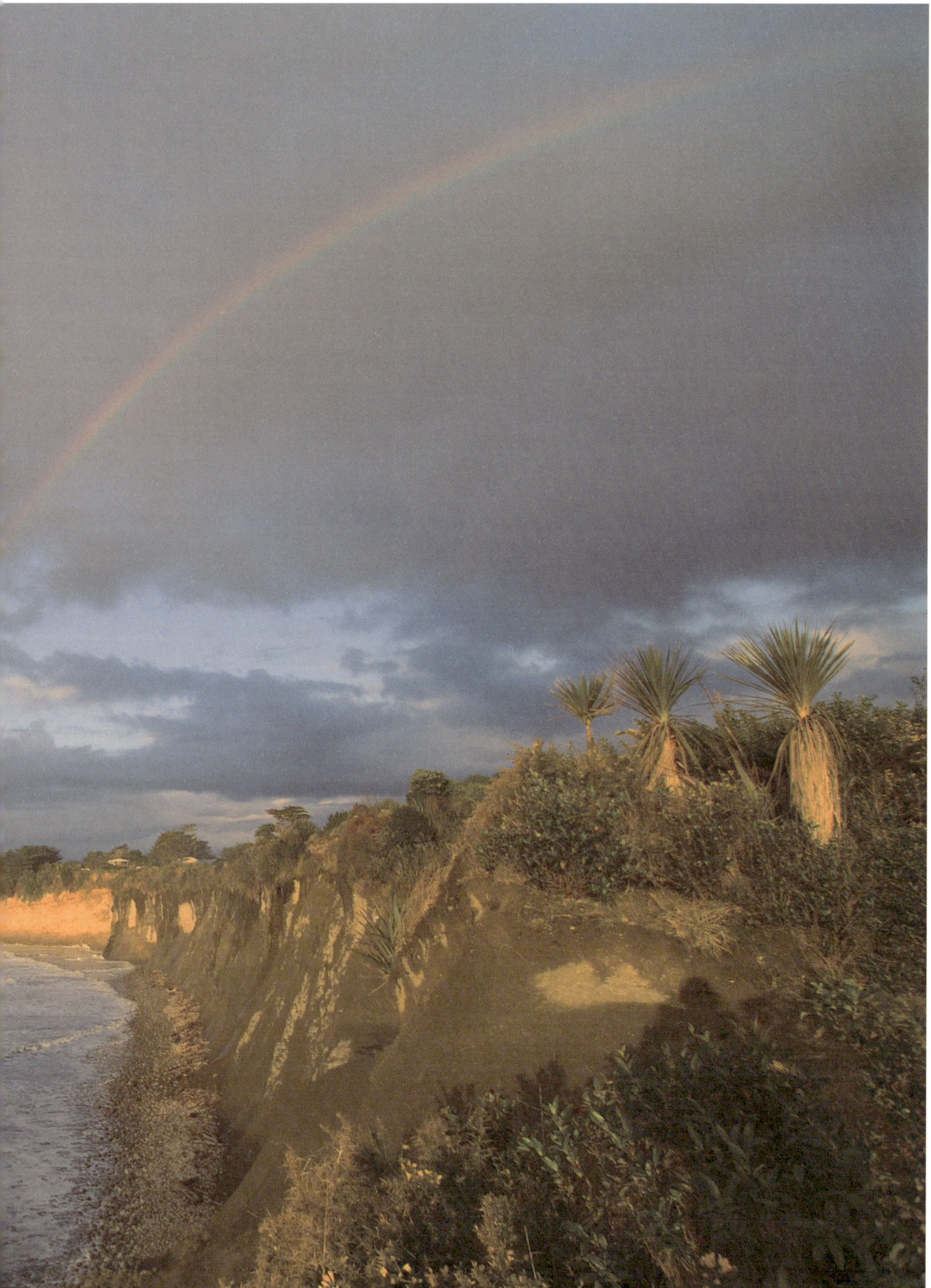

Darryl Kerr offers Al a unique way to cross the Okari lagoon.

they don't have to go too far away at the end of a day chasing bait. Some of these would be among the most desirable holiday homes in New Zealand if the secret got out — and if the access was better. Most are as hard by the waterfront as it's possible to get — some are even floating. It's pretty extraordinary the lengths people will go to get amongst the whitebait, but that's Coasters for you, throughout history: if they want it and mean to have it, trifling matters such as logistics aren't going to stop them.

Whitebaiting is synonymous with the West Coast. And while Coasters are pretty laid-back as a rule, Darryl reckons nothing will get their goat to quite the same degree as anyone attempting to interfere with their right to catch whitebait, or with the stand or 'possie' that they occupy in the whitebait season. A good possie will be jealously guarded and even passed down from generation to generation. Stands on the Okari are particularly sought after, Darryl reckons, as the remote Okari River is a whitebaiter's paradise.

In theory, whitebaiting is simple, he explains. In late winter and early spring, the little fish — there are three main species

86 *Coasters*

encompassed by the general term 'whitebait': inanga, koaro and banded kokopu — are on a mission to get from the sea to the headwaters of the river or stream where they were spawned so that they can spawn in their turn. They travel in shoals or 'runs' as the baiters call them. All you have to do is put a net in the way of a run and you're in fritters, right?

Well, not really. For one thing, they're as cunning as ship rats. They seem to sense the presence of a net long before they get to it, and will swerve to avoid it. They seem to notice when you put things in the river (such as indicator boards, which are white planks placed on the riverbed that show up the fish as they swim over it). They're no pushover.

For another thing, they're getting scarcer. While there are restrictions on what you can and can't do to catch them — you can't build a funnel-shaped dam across a river and stick a net at the business end, for example — so that they get a sporting chance of winning through to replenish the population, their numbers are declining. The loss of suitable spawning habitat (they prefer rivers and streams that are overhung by trees and grasses) and river water quality due to farming, forestry and mining operations are believed to be the main culprits.

Charleston

Once you're across the Okari, you can pick up Nine Mile Beach again for the walk to Charleston at its southern end. Along this stretch, Al runs into the stooped, bearded figure of Val Currie, who's widely reckoned to be the last of the gold prospectors in

The West Coast 87

Val Currie, a man with gold fever. 'I was born with it, inherited it from great, great and great.'

this district. Val fossicks on the beach for the fine gold dust that can be panned from the iron sand, or retreats up the streams and rivers inland where gold flakes and nuggets can occasionally be found in the stony streambeds — if you know where to look and how to go about getting it.

Val does know. He reckons he was born with gold fever, inherited from his 'great and great and great'. Val shows Al how beach mining was done in the old days — 'you're looking for the black sand, the blacker the better' — and how it was done up in the creekbeds in the days when the goldrushes transformed the nearby township of Charleston from a population of 1200 in 1866 to around 14,000 in 1870 according to same estimates. Sand and gravel dug from the watercourses — which are actually a 600-year-old sea beach, Val explains — are patiently washed in a broad, shallow tin pan or in a shovel, each little wash of the water dragging more of the lighter material off and the gentle to and fro motion encouraging the heavier material to settle to the bottom. Eventually, you're down to the heaviest material of all — the iron sand and, when that's washed away, the glint of 'the colour', the thrilling yellow gleam of gold.

'Woohoo! Look at that, will you!' hollers Al.

Val looks up from the shining crescent with the same sparkle in his eye. Doesn't matter how many times he's seen it: he's got the fever, all right.

Up in the bush at Mitchells Gully is a claim Val's family have worked since the goldrush days. They've restored the stamping battery that was used to crush gold-bearing gravels to powder that could then be panned or mixed with mercury to extract the gold.

'Mercury's got an affinity with gold. They used to run the fines over mercury-coated copper plates. The sand would be washed away, and the gold left behind.'

The clattering, pounding stamper is driven by a waterwheel, harnessing the power of the stream as it rushes down its stony bed.

CONSTANT BAY

Gold was first discovered on the beach just north of Charleston in 1866 by the explorer and prospector William Fox, who had been Charles Heaphy's companion on the first expedition down the

Classic boom and bust — Charleston in its heyday was one of the largest towns on the Coast.

Coastal traders supplying Charleston had to navigate the dangerously narrow entrance to Constant Bay.

Buller. Fox found the fine grains the sand yielded too hard to keep, so he headed to South Westland to find out how they were making beach mining pay there. While he was away, one of his companions, Timothy Linehan, registered a claim to the area he called 'Parkeese' (after the Maori name Pakihi meaning bog or barren land), and the rush was on.

'About 100 families were here within a few months,' Val says.

Story has it that the inhabitants were cut off by bad weather and the people were starving. 'There wasn't enough food to go around. But Captain Charles Bonner became aware of their plight and despite advice to the contrary, loaded his small ship, the *Constant*, with food and a volunteer crew to brave the storms and enter the small harbour, now known as Constant Bay.

'Charles Bonner got his ketch, the *Constant*, into the bay down there' — Val points to Constant Bay, little more than a rocky cleft, really — 'and landed a ton of flour. The people were so grateful they were going to rename Parkeese "Charlie's One Ton of Flour Town", but it was a bit of a mouthful. So they called it "Charlie's Town".'

This came in time to be shortened to Charleston and is but a ghost of the bustling mining town of Charlie's time.

Val Currie's restored stamping battery near Charleston.

GOLD STAMPERS

Beach mining was tough, because although there was — and still is — a vast quantity present, the yields are too poor to reward the effort required to extract it. Similarly, alluvial gold was never found in the Charleston area in the kinds of concentrations it was in Otago, where it was possible to set yourself up for life with a single lucky strike. The West Coast alluvial flats were known to the miners who worked them as 'tucker ground' — good for paying your way come mealtime, but not so good for lining your pockets.

It was when the diggers attacked the gold-bearing rock and machinery was applied — there were 600 stampers like the one at Mitchells Gully operating around Charleston at the peak — that the true rewards were gleaned, but the level of capital required to buy and run such machines spelt the effective end of the lone prospector. Still, the boom had made Charleston. At one point, this tiny town and Brighton, about 10 kilometres to the south, boasted around 90 hotels between them, endlessly pouring drinks and even importing

The West Coast

Constant Bay from the air.

Australian dancing girls to variously slake and whet the appetites of the hard-living miners.

'Those girls got married off pretty quick. There was a ratio of about five miners to one girl.'

Charleston had the first concrete buildings in New Zealand and the first concrete-piled suspension bridge, built in 1867. When Wellington's postmaster was moved there, he regarded it as a promotion.

These days, Charleston is another West Coast town that has made the conversion from a site of extraction to a centre of attraction. The mines, the natural caves and the rock-climbing opportunities offered by the rocky landforms around the town all draw their share of visitors, even if not quite in the numbers that once came. The permanent population ranges from 300 in the summer down to 150-odd in the winter. A hundred and fifty, as Val Currie puts it, and one old grump.

You'd go a long way before you could find a better example of the way in which the land shapes the lives and characters of the people who live there. The isolation of the West Coast has made those who have chosen to stay necessarily rugged and self-reliant. And, as in any community that faces adversity, along the stretch just south of the Buller, there's a real sense of pride about being a Coaster — a distinctly stick-together, united-we-stand kind of thing.

In this part of the world life has never been easy, and rags-to-riches stories are few and far between. Pounamu, gold, coal, timber, cement, fish — none have been won without danger and grinding hardship. And perhaps that's why the Coasters are so sceptical of the prospects of tourism to provide the region with a new economic base: it just seems too easy. You don't have to work like a bastard and risk life and limb to earn money out of it? Sounds too good to be true.

Welcome to... the Bay of Islands

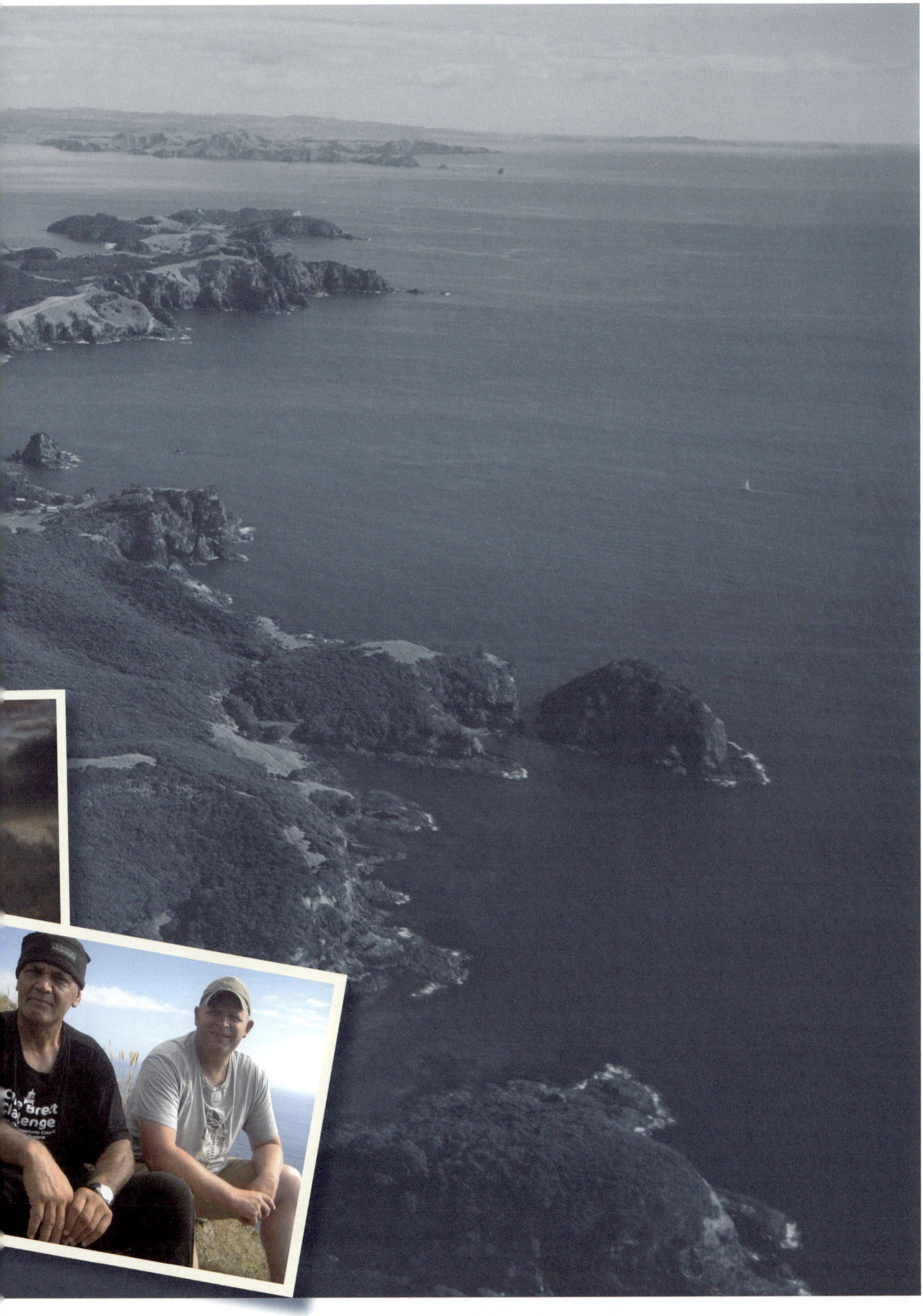

The Historic Coast

The coast is a paepae, or threshold — the area in front of the marae upon which the tangata whenua (people of the land) and manuhiri (guests) meet in stylised confrontation. In the same way, the coast is a place where different elements meet and negotiate their proximity. The coast can be a collision zone, full of drama and fury. It can be a tranquil place, where water gently laps the sand. The stretch of coast ahead of Al, from Cape Brett to Russell, is both.

Some of the areas of Aotearoa settled by Maori — think Otago, Westland and even Wellington — have you feeling for our first coasters: Polynesians more accustomed to palm-fringed tropical beaches than frigid, shingle shorelines. However, one could assume the canny crew settling this stretch of the shoreline weren't too unhappy with their choice. Ipipiri, the Bay of Islands, is a large,

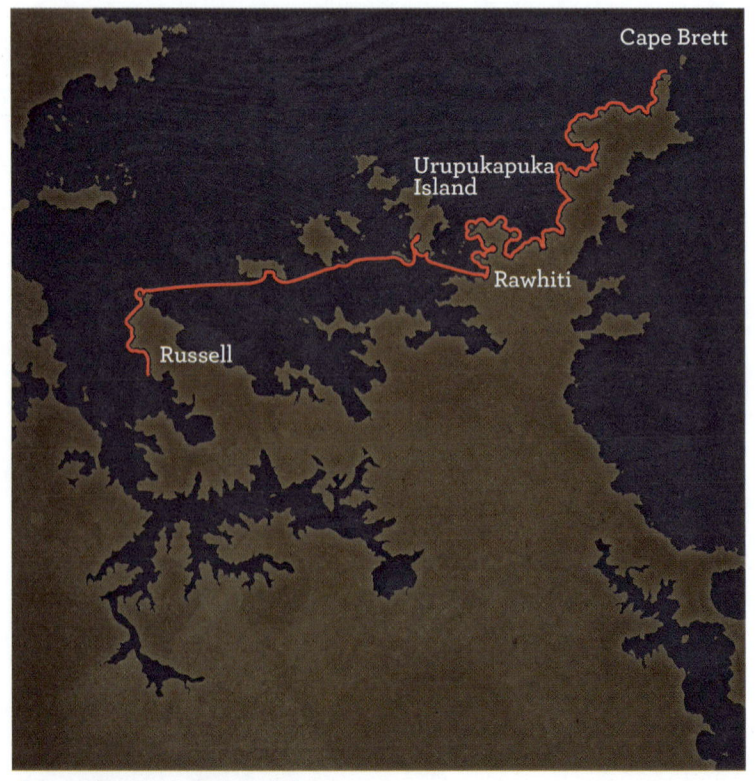

Above: Riding the bow.

Previous page: Bay of Islands from the air.

Cape Brett to Russell

96 Coasters

natural harbour on the balmy east coast of Northland, and there are around 150 islands of varying sizes encompassed in its commodious embrace. It's rich in sealife, and in pre-European times, the forested hinterland was equally as abundant in birdlife. Consequently, it was densely settled by Maori. It was also the first site at which Europeans chose to settle, and so it's here that the tricky business of building a single nation out of two peoples began. There was diffidence and difficulty, even conflict, but ultimately, there was coexistence. That's why the Bay of Islands is sometimes called 'the cradle of the nation'.

Al's journey begins at the lighthouse at the tip of Cape Brett, the gateway to the Bay. From here he walks the ancient Nga Puhi trail along the Cape's backbone, before exploring Urupukapuka Island's rich archaeological history. He then sets sail to Russell on a gaff-rigged schooner and rounds off his journey by participating in the annual Tall Ships race — complete with its traditional hangi — the sharing of food with which negotiations between people were always sealed, according to Maori custom. And sharing is what this journey is all about. Along the way, Al shares the ride with coasters, locals who can impart their knowledge of the area's rich history with him, and share some of the pride they feel living in its shadow.

Ipipiri, the Bay of Islands, is a large natural bay embracing almost 150 islands — in the foreground is Moturua.

The Bay of Islands

There's something poignant about the beam of a lighthouse when you're standing beneath it in the darkness: it's a reminder of how precarious the lives of those at sea are.

Above: The lighthouse at Cape Brett is the only one in New Zealand with all internal workings intact.

Opposite: The beginning of Al's journey — dawn at Cape Brett.

FOLLOW THE LIGHT

Facing east from the Cape Brett light, all you see is the great, blue Pacific stretching all the way to South America. That is, except for Piercy Island — Motukokako — which sits across a narrow channel just below the headland. Cook named this little islet after Admiral Piercy Brett of the Royal Navy on 27 November 1769. The little pun on that gent's first name (the island is pierced through by a sea arch, popularly known as the Hole in the Rock) is one of the dour explorer's few recorded jokes, and shows how light his mood must have become as he sailed this enchanting coastline.

The 14-metre-high lighthouse was completed in 1910, and was tended by a lighthouse keeper who lived at the isolated spot with his family until a smaller, automated light was installed alongside the old tower in 1978. It must have been a hard, lonely existence out here: supplies and mail arrived by launch and were landed on a crane that reached precariously out over the heaving water and hauled 150 metres up a pair of rails to the settlement. Apart from the telegraph and the launch, there was little contact with the outside world.

The Cape Brett light was one of three major navigational signals guiding shipping on its run down the east coast. Illumination was provided by a kerosene lamp up until 1955, when an electric lamp was installed, along with a diesel-electric generator and, later, mains power from Rawhiti.

There's something poignant about the beam of a lighthouse when you're standing beneath it in the darkness: it's a reminder of how precarious the lives of those at sea are, particularly when they near the coast. And Cape Brett memorialises this precariousness in another way, too: it's the scene of our first actual shipwreck. The *Parramatta*, a Sydney schooner, visited the Bay of Islands in 1808 and engaged a group of local Maori to load her cargo, likely timber and flax. But after keeping their side of the bargain, the Maori were

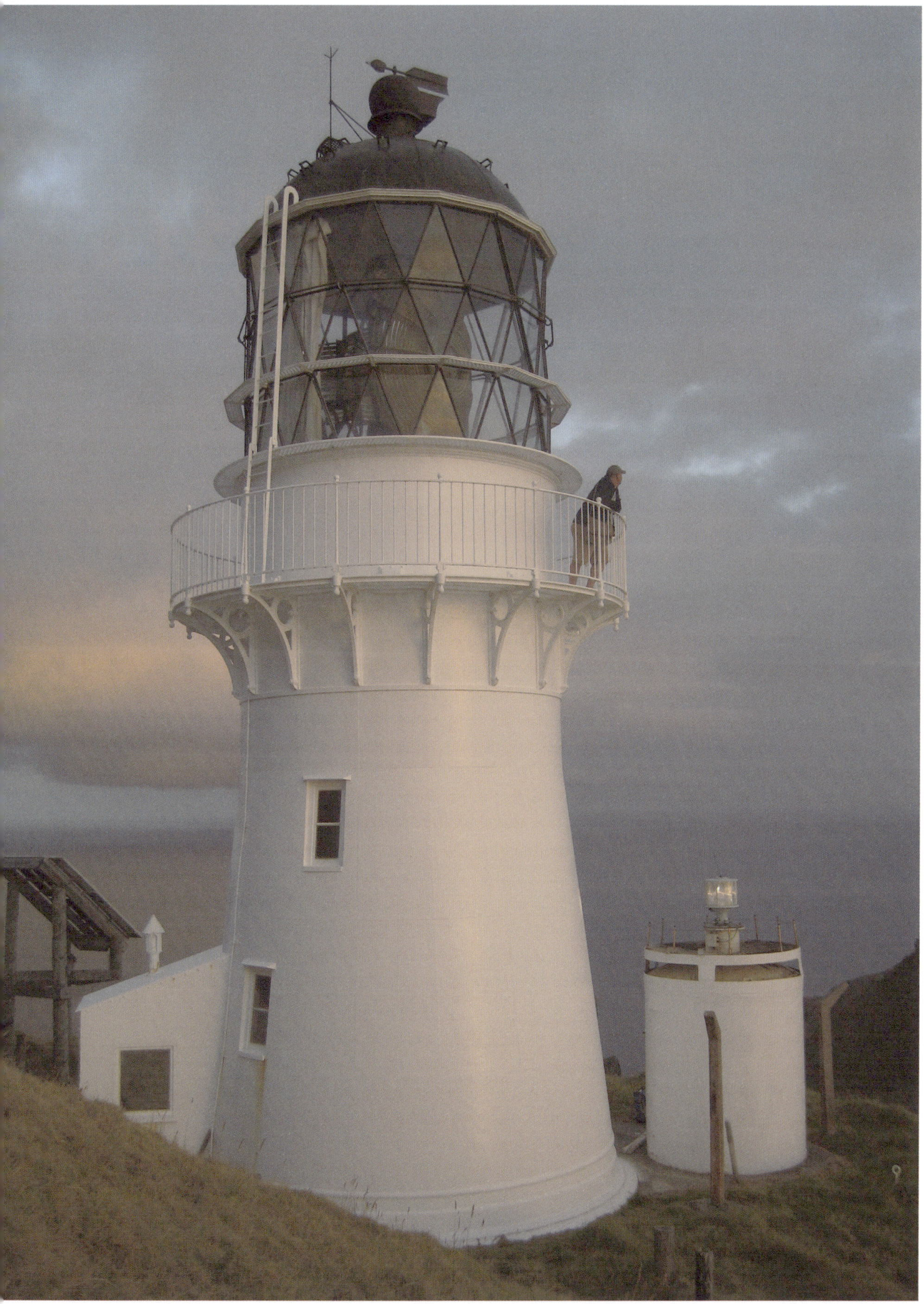

thrown overboard by the *Parramatta*'s unscrupulous master, Captain Glynn. Then, to add insult to injury, they were shot at. But in a twist of fate the *Parramatta* met a gale as she set sail for Sydney. She was driven ashore, and as they decided between death by drowning or at the hands of the vengeful Maori, Glynn and his crew must have bitterly regretted their lack of business ethics.

Such were the uneasy beginnings of the relationship between Maori and Pakeha.

Local knowledge

Long before the *Parramatta* — or Cook's *Endeavour*, for that matter — came to Ipipiri, which means 'many places', it had been settled by Maori.

As the day dawns over the start of his journey, here to shake Al's hand and mingle warm breath in a hongi, is coaster Richard Witehira, known to all and sundry as 'Blandy'. Blandy can give you a good account of the pre-European history of this area: he's Nga Puhi, and whakapapas to the tall timber in the ancestral forest of the Bay of Islands, including the notorious warrior chief Hone Heke and right back to Rakaumangamanga itself.

'Rakaumangamanga's our sacred mountain. And it's significant in the rest of Polynesia, too,' Blandy tells Al. 'It marks the southern point of the Polynesian triangle. As I understand it, while the Europeans weren't sailing too far because they were afraid they'd fall off the edge of the world, my tipunas were roaming all over the expanse of the Pacific, working out where they fitted in. Kupe marked out the Polynesian triangle, the area where Polynesians lived, and Rakaumangamanga is the southernmost point. Rapanui [Easter Island] and Hawai'i were the others.'

Blandy is the head guide on the Cape Brett walking track, the fruit of a joint initiative between Patukeha and Ngati Kuta, the two hapu with mana whenua over Cape Brett, and the Department of Conservation to upgrade the ancient tribal walkway. Blandy's grandfather used to ride horses along it on food-gathering expeditions, the same kind of expeditions that Nga Puhi had mounted along the Cape since they settled the area. The walkway took a year and a half to complete, employed 17 people and was finished in 1993.

'Now you're sharing it,' says Al.

Blandy Witehira can give you a good account of the pre-European history of this area: he's Nga Puhi, and whakapapas to the tall timber in the ancestral forest of the Bay of Islands, including the warrior chief Hone Heke and right back to Rakaumangamanga itself.

'Sharing it,' nods Blandy. 'Opening it up to show the world. People from all over the world come to walk it. Germans, Dutch, English, Australians, Americans . . . Hundreds a week at this time of year [high summer].'

'What do they get out of it, Blandy?' asks Al.

'Well, if they learned a bit of Maori history, that would be a bonus. But I guess beautiful scenery, a beautiful walk. It's one of the hardest walks in New Zealand, but everyone I've come across loves the views. Best views in the world, I reckon, but then I'm bound to say that. This is where I'm from.'

Al and Blandy set off along the track, with their destination — Oke Bay, near Rawhiti — several hours' tough slog away. As the track strikes off along the ridge beneath the sacred mountain's shadow, they walk through low scrub, mostly manuka with wind-flattened tops. Bees are busy among the flowers as the heat of the day rises.

Cook estimated there were 20,000 Maori living on the peninsula in 1769. With abundant kaimoana and prolific birdlife in the bush, it

Above: Blandy and Al take time out from the steep Cape Brett Walkway, for which Blandy is head guide.

Next page: The Hole in the Rock with Cape Brett in the background.

The Bay of Islands

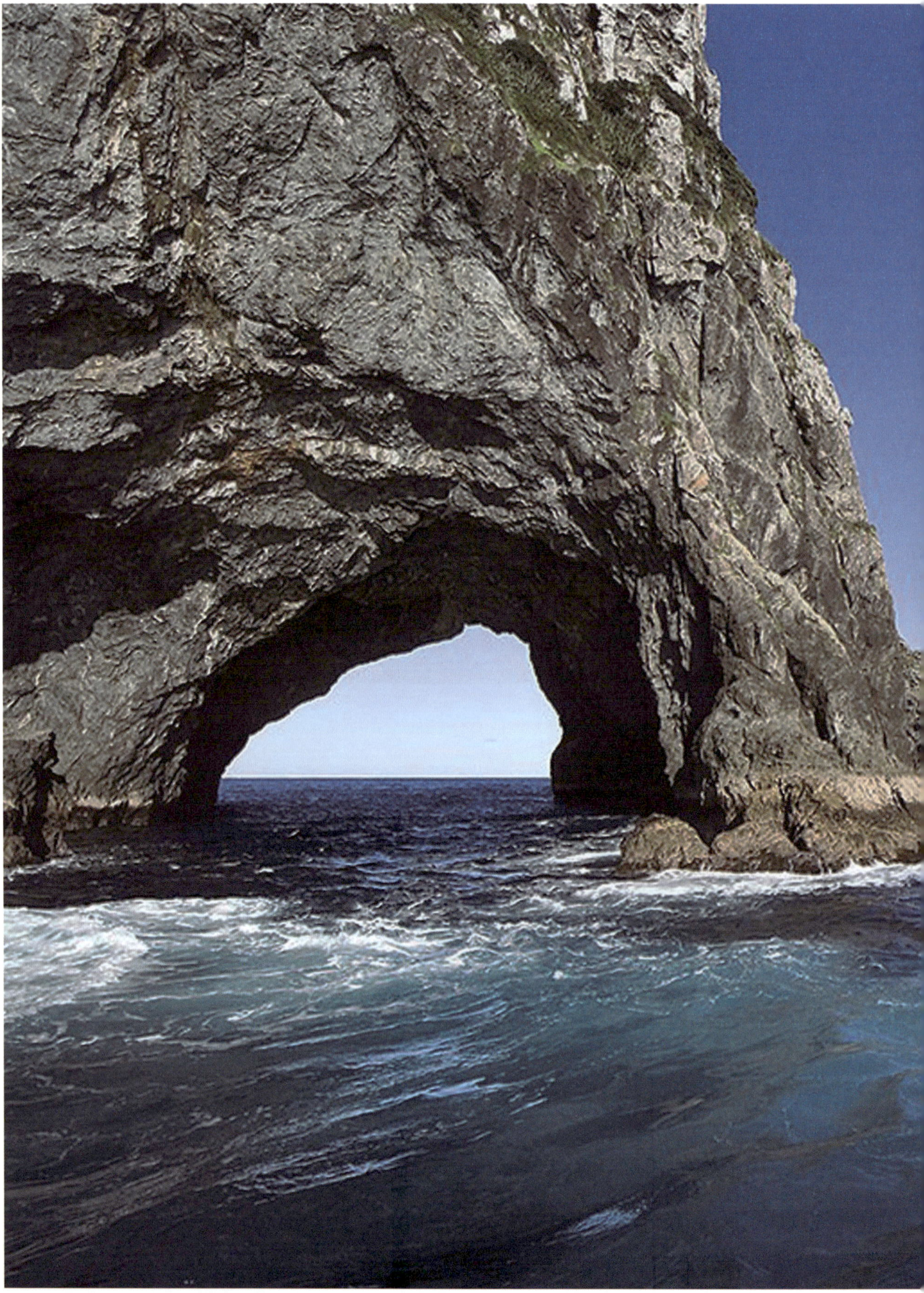

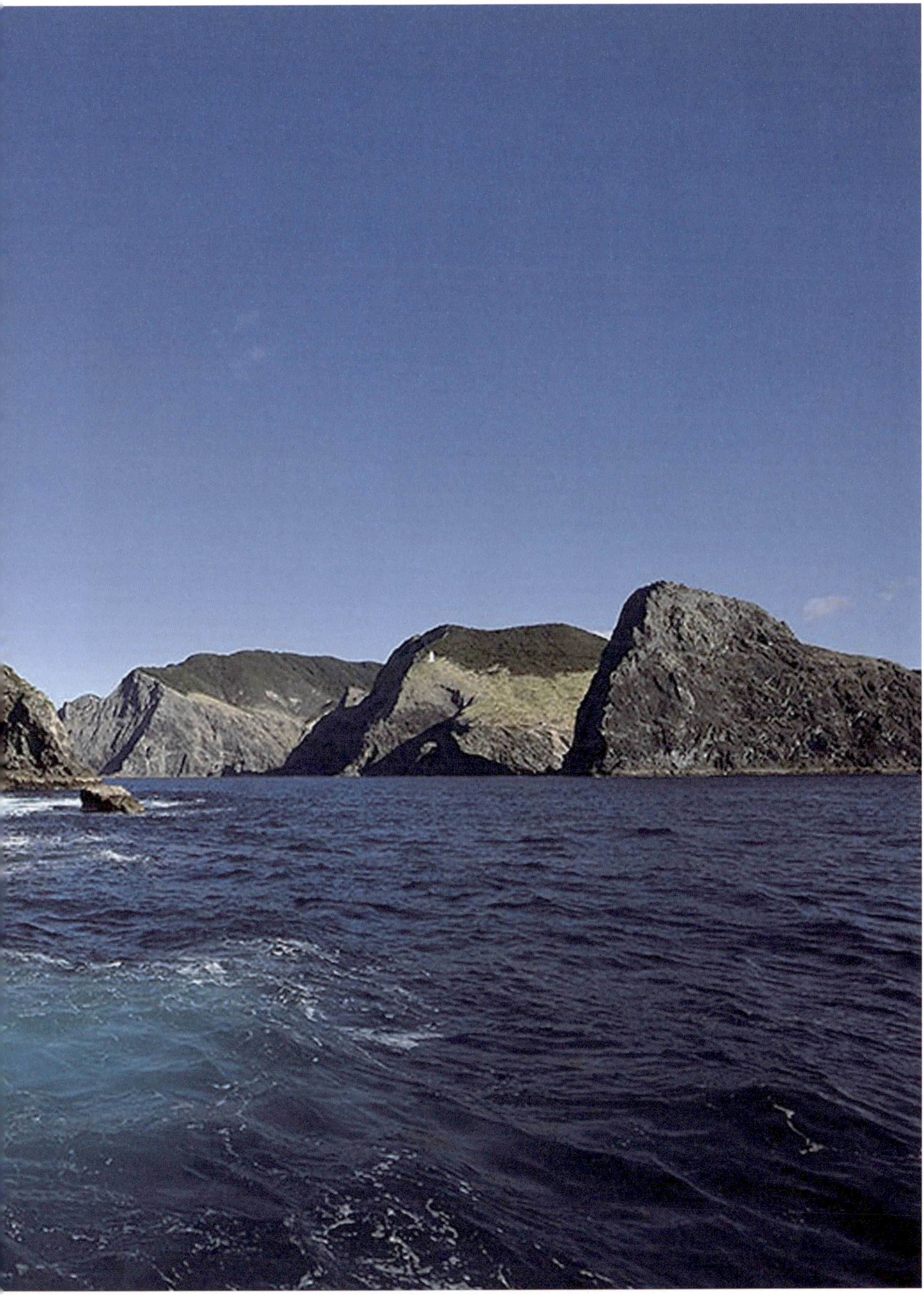

A pair of walkers passes by during filming for Coasters on the Cape Brett Walkway.

was a regular food basket in peacetime. And the high cliffs and narrow approaches made it a natural defensive position when the clouds of war gathered. It's pretty easy to understand its appeal for Nga Puhi.

Today, though, the bush cover is mostly regenerating. The lush cover of pre-European times was cleared in the early twentieth century and the land turned over to a marginal dairying enterprise. Here and there, the silvered limbs of dead rata and puriri protrude. Blandy points to one of these.

'This area was known for its blossom in the old days. Now look at the trees.'

They pause to take in the panoramic views of the Bay and its islands to the north. Al welcomes the rest — Blandy, in his fifties, has hardly raised a sweat. He's ex-army, after all, and he delights in doing this walk as often as his guiding services are required.

As they stand there, another pair of walkers happen by, smiling and calling a greeting as they pass, gazing appreciatively out at the vista. Al can sense Blandy's pride.

Al stops for a brew at the work camp for the Cape Brett Peninsula pest-eradication programme.

RESTORING THE LIFE-FORCE

It's hard yakka along the switchbacked ridge in the heat of the Northland summer. They have several hours of it, before Al and Blandy drop in on a team who are working on a pest-eradication programme for the peninsula. Tommy Rewha and Kanye Lawrence brew up a cuppa and they sit drinking it on the verandah of the hut where they're based.

'This is the first year of a five-year programme,' Blandy explains. 'Basically, the aim this first year is to get pest numbers down to a two per cent residual trap catch and maintain it at that. Then we'll re-establish habitat, and then we'll release native birds back into the wild. The boys here are split into teams. One team cuts tracks and puts up bait stations and traps. The other one is dedicated to killing anything that moves that's not indigenous or human.'

Al laughs.

It wasn't just the settlers' axes that laid the bush low and silenced the birdlife on Cape Brett. Introduced pests did their bit, and have seen to it that neither the bush nor the birdlife has had

The skeletons of dead trees show the devastating impact of possum browsing our native bush.

a chance to re-establish itself. Possums are the main enemy, and they're everywhere. But there are rats as well, and stoats, feral cats, and even the odd dog and goat. The Cape has been isolated with an electric fence that stretches right across the landmass. The eradication programme has been methodically working to clear the seaward side of nasties. The goats have been eradicated, and other pest populations heavily reduced.

'Once we get rid of the mustelids and the possums, the diversity of the forest will come back,' Blandy says. 'That's the moemoea — the dream and aspiration — of the old people: to re-establish the birds, the manu here. They used to be quite prevalent. This stream is called Waitui — there's a whole lot of trees up here on either side of the creek where the tuis come to nest and feed. Another puke further along the Cape is called Pukehuia, hill of the huia. Well, it's too late for the huia, but our dream is to bring back the mauri, the life-force, of the forest. That'll be good for the land, and good for our people too. Over 300,000 tourists come through our tribal area. We want to capitalise on that opportunity. Give these fellas a job, anyway.'

He gestures at the boys.

'Gives us the opportunity to learn about our maunga, too. I enjoy it. I love it out here,' says Kanye. He was born in Auckland, but his mum brought him back to Rawhiti to live when he was three.

'It's all right, eh,' agrees Tommy. 'Come out here all day, help out around camp. It's all right.'

Back on the track and there's a few more ups and downs before they finally arrive at Rawhiti, marking the end of the Cape Brett Walkway. The marae, under the joint guardianship of Patukeha and Ngati Kuta, fronts the water, and it's the centre of this remote rural community. When Al and Blandy arrive, kids are kicking a ball on the lawn in front of the old marae buildings, which date back to 1910. Blandy explains that the tekoteko at the top of the wharenui is a depiction of Tangaroa, the god of the sea, and the one who looks after coasters.

Sitting and gazing out at the sparkling waters of the Bay, with the happy shouts of the children around you, you'd have to reckon he's doing a pretty good job.

The tekoteko at the top of the wharenui at Rawhiti marae — a depiction of Tangaroa, the god of the sea.

FILLING UP BEFORE MOVING ON

The Bay of Islands is a system of drowned river valleys. In times gone by, with lower sea levels, it would likely have resembled the Marlborough Sounds. Today, it's a 16-kilometre-wide bay that divides into several inlets at its inland limits. Out in the Bay itself, there's a maze of islands and islets — over 150 by the official count — which makes it one of the best recreational boating grounds in the world.

The next leg of Al's journey takes him by tinny, courtesy of Blandy's cousin Rana out to Urupukapuka, the largest of the islands formed when the area was inundated at the end of the last ice age. As their little boat hits the beach and Al helps to pull it up the sugary white sand of Entico Bay or Otiao, it's easy to see what a great spot for beaching waka this would have been. Practically everything about Urupukapuka suited the Maori, particularly the kaimoana — and they've got a good feed of it today.

After being replenished with fresh kina, scallops and pupu, Al farewells Blandy and Rana and heads to the other side of the island.

The Bay of Islands

Mussel and Pupu Boil-Up

Cooking seafood needn't and shouldn't be complicated. The terrific thing about shellfish is, each variety has its own unique and often subtle flavour. The day we made this on the bow of the aluminium dingy, we were eating much of the gathered seafood raw, before any of it even hit the pot. I had only eaten pupu once before and these, along with the huge Coromandel mussels, were simply delicious steamed open and cooked in a little white wine and garlic. As seen in the recipe below, there is no real recipe using weights and measures for this sort of dish. It is just whatever shellfish is available then 'free-styling' as you go. What is most important is to start with the shellfish that will take longest to cook then follow with the rest.

Ingredients
live mussels
live pupu
white wine
chicken or fish stock
minced garlic
fresh chilli, roughly chopped
butter
fresh parsley, roughly chopped

Method
Scrub the mussel and pupu shells until free of sand and grit. Place the mussels in a large saucepan over high heat. Pour in a cup or 2 of wine and stock. Toss in the garlic and chilli. Place a lid on and cook for 5 minutes before adding the pupu. Check after a couple of minutes then, as the mussels open, add a couple of knobs of butter and the parsley. Pour into bowls along with some cooking liquid and serve with good-quality crusty bread for dipping.

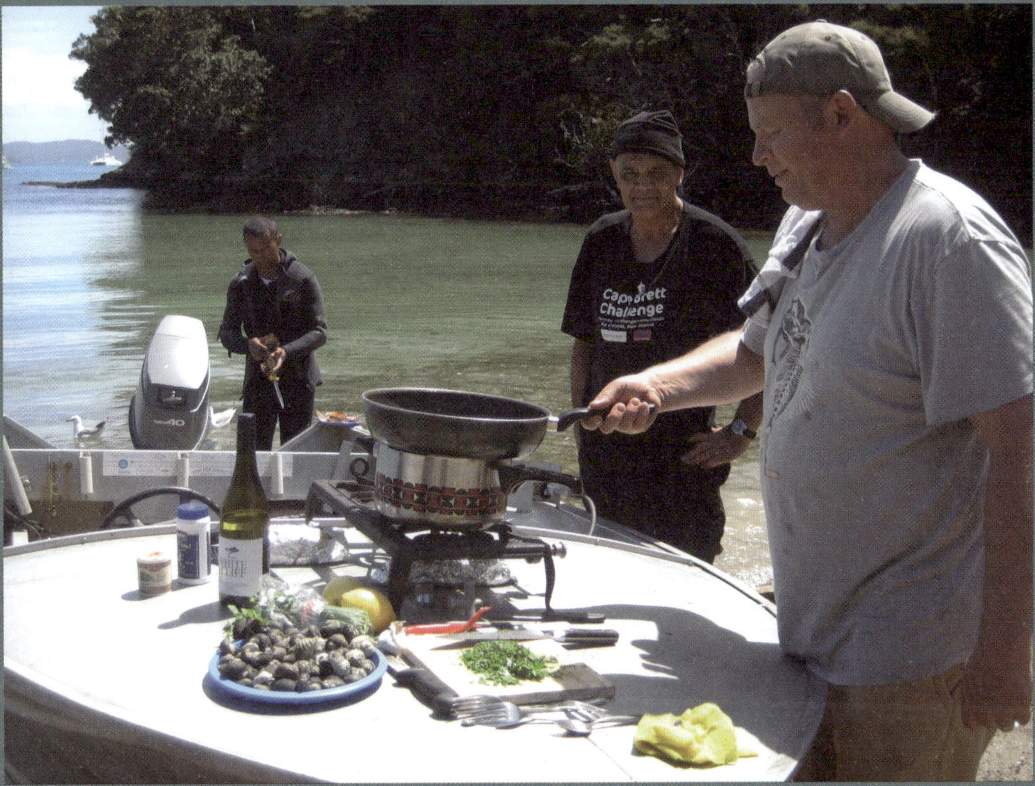
Challenge

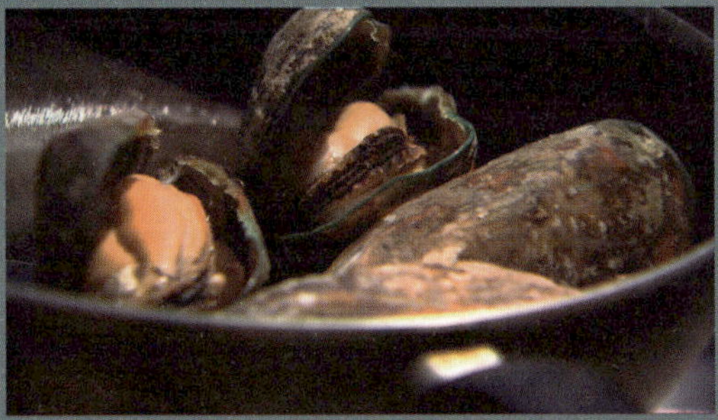

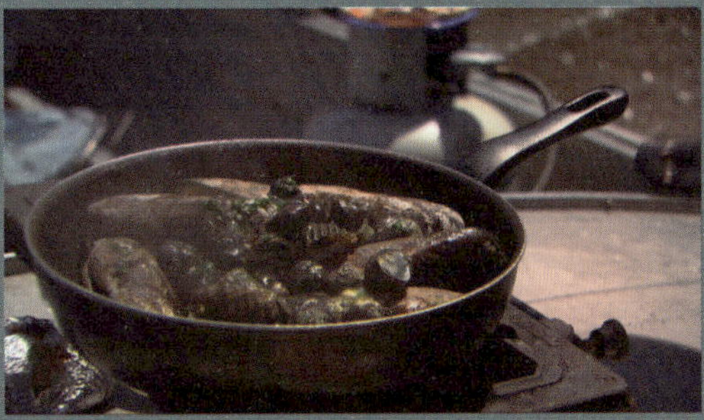

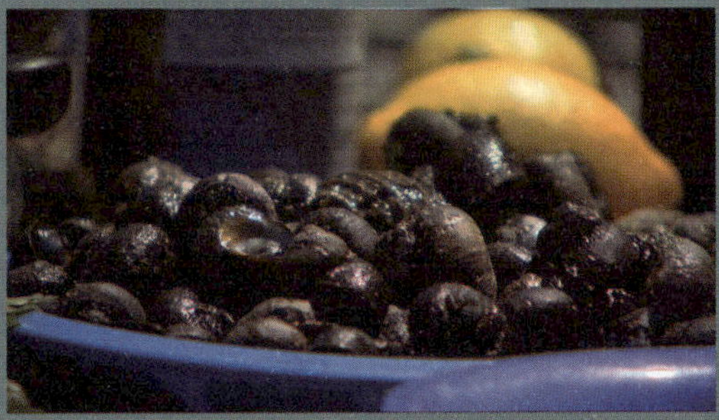

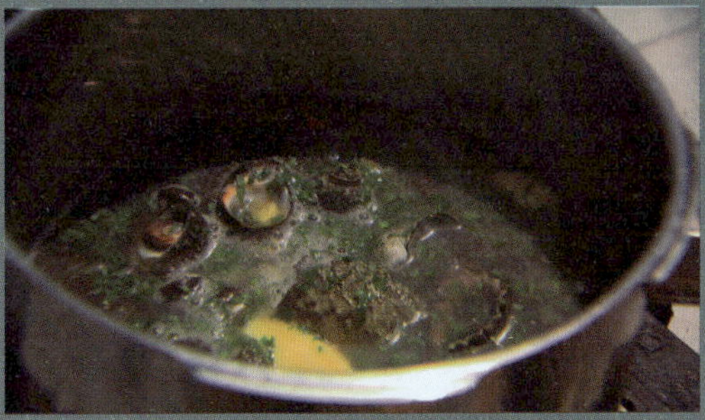

Camping and conservation

Urupukapuka Island was sold by Maori into European hands in the late nineteenth century, and farmed until it was acquired by the Crown in 1970. In 1927, the American angler and writer Zane Grey based himself on the island at Otehei Bay, and got amongst the legendary gamefishing opportunities that the Northland coast provides. He made the Bay of Islands internationally famous with the fishing resort he built there, and with tales of his exploits.

It's the height of summer, and there's plenty of warmth in the sun as Al reaches the crest of the hill overlooking Urupukapuka Bay. There are people everywhere, enjoying the Kiwi notion of the good life. Watercraft of every description are tootling about. Kids are shrieking, splashing and skimming stones. Some of the adults are joining in the fun; others are chilling out in the shade with a book. It's idyllic.

> All of the predatory species are good swimmers, and it's important if the islands are to be kept in their pest-free state that the mainland populations are kept down, too.

A friendly reminder for visitors to the island.

'Now that,' nods Al, 'is why we live in New Zealand.'

His visit has coincided with a fun day organised by the Department of Conservation for campers on the island, designed to raise awareness of the area's biodiversity and to encourage visitors to support the aims of Project Island Song, the pest-eradication programme run jointly by DOC, the local iwi and volunteers from the Guardians of the Bay of Islands. The Department lays on a barbecue and all kinds of activities for the kids. It's a well-attended event.

The trapping and poisoning operation that Blandy runs on the mainland is a complement to Project Island Song, explains Al's next coaster, Andrew Blanshard, a DOC historian and archaeologist, who has been helping out with the fun day. The islands in the chain between Russell and Cape Brett, including Urupukapuka, underwent an intensive eradication programme from June 2009, and will be declared pest-free after two years — all going well. But all of the predatory species are good swimmers, and it's important if the islands are to be kept in their pest-free state that the mainland populations are kept down, too.

Above: DOC's Urupukapuka Bay campsite is a great destination for a family summer holiday.

Below: Andrew Blanshard and Al head off to explore Urupukapuka's archaeological trail.

Another way pests can arrive is in the same way they got here in the first place: as stowaways from much further afield.

'Since June, we've had nothing on the island until December 30,' explains Andrew, 'when a rat was found under a tent. It probably came here by one of the 60-odd boats that visit each day in the summer. That's what the fun day is all about. It's to make people aware. We're encouraging people who visit the island to stop and check before they come out. Renovating the islands is a huge job, but we've managed it in other island situations around New Zealand, so we're confident we can do it. It'll mean a whole lot more birdlife for people to enjoy.'

DIGGING UP THE HISTORY

Al and Andrew head up a steep path from the campground to explore one of the features of present-day Urupukapuka, a well-developed interpretive trail linking and explaining the island's many points of archaeological interest. The path takes around two hours to walk, and it's popular with campers. Al and Andrew's journey covers a small part of it — over the hill to Zane's old hangout, Otehei Bay. Andrew Blanshard trained as an archaeologist and worked for a number of years in the UK. But New Zealand — and the Bay of Islands in particular — drew him back. He loves it here.

The Bay of Islands

Above: Urupukapuka Bay was once the site of a Nga Puhi village. Urupukapuka Island has over 100 archaeological sites.

Opposite: The R. Tucker Thompson, a replica gaff-rigged schooner.

'We've done a lot of archaeological work all through here,' he tells Al, sweeping his arm around the Urupukapuka landscape laid out below them. 'We've surveyed, and found over 100 archaeological sites. And within that, we've got over 1600 individual features, which makes it one of the most densely populated archaeological sites in the country.'

They reach a point on a hillside with a view down to the campground. 'This,' Andrew points to the grassy area they're standing on, 'is a terrace knoll, a place that would have been used for storing food grown on the slopes and brought up here to store. You're actually standing in a large storage pit. It would have been half a metre to a metre deep with a roof on top. You would have been storing your kumara over the winter so they survived for planting in the next season. The living areas were primarily on the flat ridges and down in the bays themselves. You can imagine the waka pulled up on the beach down there . . .'

Looking down, you can imagine it, and the whares roofed with fronds.

'We've got village sites, and pa sites, and terraced areas where they stored food. We've got gardens for kumara and taro . . . The kaimoana here was just amazing! It's recorded that they had nets that were nine metres deep and over a kilometre long, all made of flax. That's a big net, even by today's standards.'

As Andrew and Al pick their way down to a small bay on the other side of the hill, Andrew continues.

'It would have been a highly structured community, especially

112 **Coasters**

in the later period. Different communities had different resources, so trading was essential. As the population grew, the inter-relationships between the whanau and the hapu became very important.'

Al stops and looks out to sea. 'And then, hello, along comes this tall ship...'

'Yep. In 1769, along comes Captain Cook in the *Endeavour* and the world changes.'

Sailing into the past

At the jetty at Otehei Bay, a Zodiac is waiting for Andrew and Al, and further out in the bay is their ride to Russell, the *R. Tucker Thompson*. A gaff-rigged schooner of the type that plied New Zealand's coastal trade in the Age of Sail, she's fully evocative of that day the world changed, back in 1769. Al can't take his eyes off her as the crewman takes him and Andrew out to meet her.

Russell Harris, the skipper, a larger-than-life coaster if ever there was one, is at the graceful vessel's rail to greet them.

Russell Harris, skipper, builder and former owner of the R. Tucker Thompson — which has now been placed into the ownership of a Northland trust — says of her: 'Easily managed, fast, sea kindly — all relative of course. Can't really compare her to the fancy yachts today.'

> The awesome colour and light and shape of this beautiful landscape — such a harmony. It's unequalled anywhere in the world. So when I can take people from all over the world and show them this . . . for me, it's just wonderful.

Russell shares duties at the helm with Al.

'Welcome aboard, Brownie,' he says. 'May I see your credentials, please?'

There can be no doubting Russell's credentials. As he likes to put it, he sold his farm and ran away to sea, and has never once regretted it. He was looking around for a challenge when he met free-spirited, American-born yachting enthusiast, Robert Tucker Thompson — known to all as Tucker — while they were both working on the rigging of a replica of the *Bounty*. He was interested to learn about Tucker's backyard project — a working replica of an American halibut schooner — and when he heard that Tucker had died (at the tragically young age of 49), leaving the vessel in an advanced state of incompletion, he didn't hesitate too long. He pitched in with Tucker's son Tod to finish her off. They were short of money, but blessed with a large number of willing helpers and a considerable amount of skill in improvisation. The ship, named in honour of the man whose dream she was, was launched in 1985. She had become Russell Harris' ruling passion.

In 2007, the vessel was placed in the ownership of a Northland trust, which uses her to give sail training to youth, as well as running sailing excursions in the Bay of Islands. Russell calls to his crew, who get busy with the bewildering array of ropework. Canvas flogs in the breeze and then billows full. The sails are set, and the fine hull begins to slip through the water.

'You see?' Russell says. 'Easily managed, fast, sea kindly — all relative, of course. Can't really compare her to the fancy yachts today.'

A sail aboard the *Tucker* is an introduction not only to the Bay of Islands, but also to a bygone era.

'I love showing people New Zealand,' says Russell, who's taken tourists out in the boat for 25 years. 'I would get people in from the urban sprawls of the vast cities who haven't seen anything like this,' he sweeps his arm out around the vista of islands and glittering sea. 'When we come around the corner, you just see their jaws dropping. The awesome colour and light and shape of this beautiful landscape — such a harmony. It's unequalled anywhere in the world. So when I can take people from all over the world and show them this... for me, it's just wonderful. I don't want them sitting in a plastic seat looking through glass and being shouted at through a microphone. I want them to feel a bit of what Cook felt.'

'It's infectious, mate,' Al assures him.

'You would have seen ships like this all around here. The Williams family built a little schooner like this called the *Herald* along the beach at Paihia in 1826. If you put a picture of the *Herald* and one of the *Tucker* on top of each other, you find very little difference.'

'What were they mostly used for?' Al asks.

'Carrying Bibles,' chuckles Russell. 'And fishing, of course. The Gisborne Maoris owned a fleet of such ships. They grew potatoes and kumara down the east coast and fed the burgeoning European populations in towns up and down the coast, running a fleet of little ships like this.'

As they run in toward the inner Bay of Islands, Russell takes Al

Riding the bow into Russell.

Right: In full sail, the R. Tucker Thompson makes a dramatic spectacle.

Below: This painting, by Louis John Steele and Kennett Watkins in 1890, is called The arrival of Captain Cook, an incident in the Bay of Islands.

down to the foremast, and shows him the profusion of ropework used to raise, set and control sail.

'I'll show you how it all works,' he promises.

'Righto,' Al says. 'Can't promise to be the best, but I'll give it a crack.'

Under Russell's amused direction, Al gets to work.

'This is what we call "sweating the halyard",' Russell tells him.

'Sweating the halyard?' pants Al, hauling hard on the rope, which pulls the sail taut.

WHEN TWO WORLDS MEET

The *R. Tucker Thompson* glides westward, passing Motukiekie and raising Motuarohia, or Roberton Island.

Al takes a breather and rejoins Andrew Blanshard, who has been watching his exertions from the starboard rail.

'That's Cook's Cove on Motuarohia,' says Andrew, pointing. 'When Cook arrived in the Bay, he came around the outside of the islands and anchored just off here and straight away there were about 30 or 40 waka around him with 300–400 people in them. Some of them came aboard, and there was a bit of trading, a few gifts, a few things back and forward. There were a few issues, too, but nothing major. Cook was concerned that it was a bit shallow, so he took the ship further out to anchor. He went ashore in a little boat and landed on the beach right over there. Another bunch of people — about 600 — appeared from nowhere and surrounded him.'

Al squints at the sandy beach of the cove, imagining the scene.

'They performed a haka on the beach,' Andrew goes on. 'Cook drew a line in the sand, like he did in a lot of places: just come this far, and no closer. There were issues again. The shore party was definitely feeling threatened, and the crew who'd stayed behind aboard the *Endeavour* brought her around so that she could fire a broadside over the top of the heads of the Maoris. I think they fired four of the big guns, which dispersed the crowds pretty quick. The shore party were able to get back to the ship. Bit of an exciting day for Cook.'

'Bit of an exciting day for everyone involved, I'd say,' nods Al.

It was a nervous start, all right, but things settled down. Cook stayed in the Bay for couple of weeks. He did some cartographical work, while Joseph Banks and the botanists surveyed the flora and fauna. There was some trading with the Maori, conducted with a kind of wary respect on both sides.

Al and Andrew are quiet, looking at the sparkling water, and it's hard to imagine a more peaceful scene. A small puff of wind overtakes the *R. Tucker Thompson*, and she shivers and lifts her head.

Al takes a breather and learns a bit of local history with Andrew Blanshard.

The Bay of Islands

The visit of Captain Cook, and later the Frenchman, Marion du Fresne — whose encounter with the Maori was very cordial until a series of cultural misunderstandings led to his death at the hands of the locals — broke the ground. Once New Zealand was on the map, other Europeans soon followed. By the 1790s, the whalers and sealers working the Southern Ocean started using the Bay of Islands. They formed strong trading links with the local hapu and iwi, exchanging iron, metal, muskets and hatchets for fresh water, food and timber for masts and spars. The Maori were astute traders, and customer-driven, too: once they'd worked out that the Europeans wanted the white-fleshed potatoes they'd brought with them, they started growing them instead of kumara. Similarly, noting that salted pork was a staple, they took to pig farming. By the turn of the 1800s, you'd find a couple of dozen ships in the Bay at any one time.

'So Maori and Europeans were starting to get along?' Al says.

'Mostly,' Andrew nods. 'But it was all unregulated. The missions — Samuel Marsden was the first — had a civilising influence, but there was still a fair bit of strife.'

'Disrespect and misunderstanding . . .'

'Yeah, that sort of thing. There was a fair bit of trade in native girls with the whalers, and there were issues with people not paying and so on. It all reached a point where the local chiefs, Hongi Hika and some of the more important rangatira of the area, realised a more formal relationship was needed, and that was the beginning of the move into the Treaty of Waitangi.'

Kororareka / Russell

Al and Andrew stand and look at the approaching headland, with the flagstaff above what used to be known as Kororareka visible over Oneroa Bay. The *R. Tucker Thompson* has a fair breeze to lay Tapeka Point, which will take her around and on to Russell.

The township of Russell is the site of the first European settlement in New Zealand. Kororareka was a rough clutch of buildings servicing the unregulated trade between Maori and the whalers and sealers — in other words, a hive of grog-swilling, gambling and prostitution, where quarrels and violence were commonplace. Little wonder it was known as 'the hell hole of the Pacific'.

Not that you'd think it today, looking at the genteel little town nestled into the hillside above the shingle beach. The *R. Tucker Thompson* cuts quite a figure as she makes her graceful entrance, and she's not alone. Other windjammers are in, flags fluttering gaily in their rigging. The harbour is packed with pleasure-craft, and the town is buzzing. It's a big day tomorrow: the annual Bay of Islands Tall Ships Race.

The *R. Tucker Thompson* is aided alongside the wharf by the willing, leathery hands of other old salts, skippers and crew of the *R. Tucker Thompson*'s rivals in the race. Good-natured banter passes to and fro: it's a close-knit fraternity, the group of people who keep alive the memory of the age of sail. For every disparaging remark, there's a gaze of real affection for the *R. Tucker Thompson*.

Al farewells Andrew Blanshard and Russell Harris for now, and heads up Flagstaff Hill. Blandy's waiting for him up here. This spot has a special significance for him.

'I'm a direct descendant of Hone Heke, the first chief to sign the Treaty of Waitangi,' he explains. 'He was also the first to take up the gun against the British. He cut this flagstaff down three times before the British put a steel collar around it. He knew as soon as he saw how things were going after signing.'

He and Al admire the peerless vista of the Bay of Islands laid out to the east, and the spectacle the tall ships make in the bay below.

'Still, the race is good kaupapa,' Blandy says. 'Brings everyone together. I believe we've all got to live together.'

Above: The Duke of Marlborough Hotel, the first licensed premise in New Zealand, is still standing today.

Below: The Duke of Malborough Hotel

Next page: Russell township from the air, with Cape Brett in the distance.

The Bay of Islands

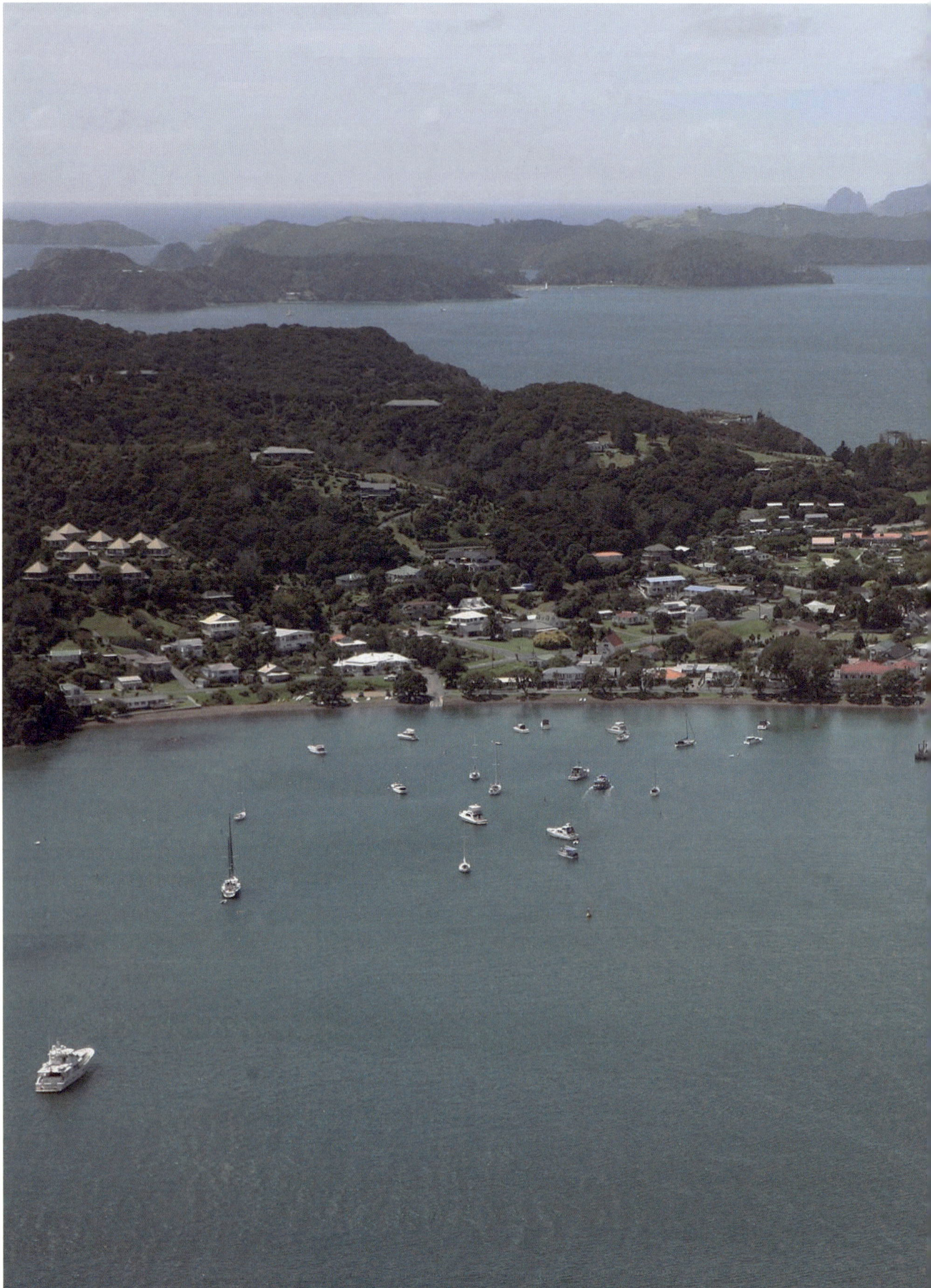

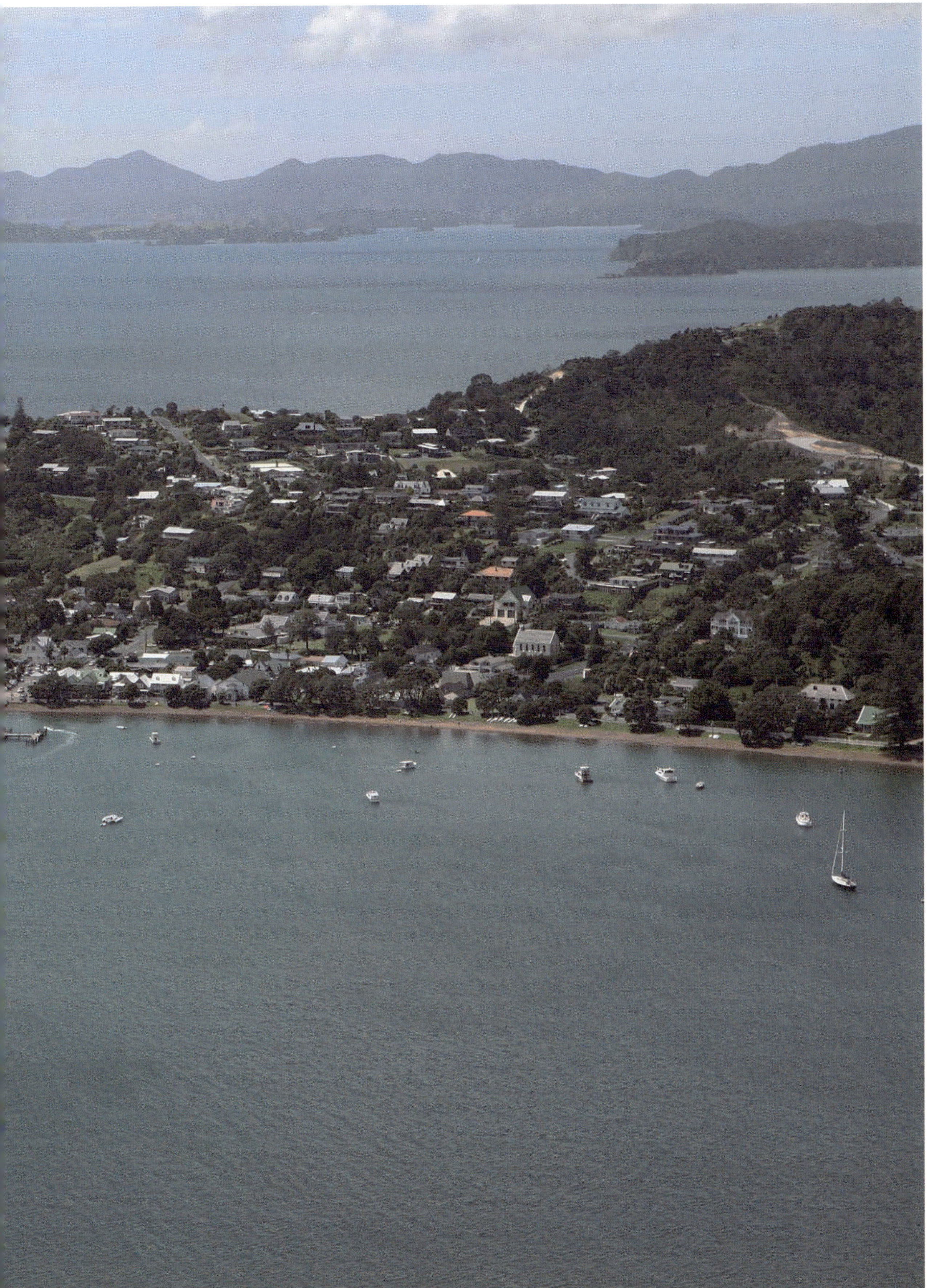

The barman sets a tall glass of cold beer in front of him.
'Hardly the hell hole of the Pacific these days,' Al says.

'I'll drink to that,' Al nods. True to his word, as soon as he's back downtown, he makes a beeline from the wharf to the gorgeous, gabled Duke of Marlborough hotel, the first licensed premises in the country. It's cool inside, and quiet, the rich carpets muffling the sound. Al looks around appreciatively at the wood-panelled walls hung with old photographs and paintings depicting scenes from the Bay's past.

The barman sets a tall glass of cold beer in front of him.
'Hardly the hell hole of the Pacific these days,' Al says.

THE TREATY AND THE FLAGSTAFF WAR

It was the lawlessness in Aotearoa, as made notorious in Kororareka, which convinced everyone that some form of authority was needed to bring things under control. William Hobson was dispatched from the nearest British colony, New South Wales, to enter into a treaty with Maori, whereby New Zealand would be annexed by Britain and the protection of British law extended to Maori and Pakeha alike. Hobson arrived at the beginning of 1840, and read the series of proclamations that would be formalised as the Treaty of Waitangi in Kororareka's Christ Church on 30 January. The Treaty itself was presented to an assembly of Maori chiefs across the Bay at Waitangi on 5 February. Opinion was divided amongst the Maori on whether they should sign. But the first to sign on 6 February was young Hone Heke — Blandy's tipuna — influential Nga Puhi warrior, entrepreneur and convert to Christianity; and the fact that a man of his mana set his name to it may have persuaded many of the others to follow suit. As copies of the Treaty were made and taken on a roadshow around the rest of the North Island, New Zealand was formally annexed by Great Britain on 21 May.

Maori disappointment with the Treaty was almost immediate, even if the major misunderstandings that arose from it would only become clear in later years. The tensions around it in the first few years after annexation were more local and economic than political and national in character. The British capital was moved from Okiato (seven kilometres south of Russell) to Auckland in

1841, severely depleting trade through the Bay of Islands, which seemed a betrayal of the trust to Nga Puhi, who had prospered on its back — and which angered Heke in particular. With the country finally under the control of a formal government, more and more European settlers were beginning to arrive, and it became clear to Maori that the rights to use the land that the Treaty had granted the Europeans were regarded as something more permanent by the Europeans.

Heke was influenced by anti-British sentiment expressed to him by the French Catholic bishop, Jean Baptiste Pompallier, and by the American consuls; they convinced him that the Union Jack fluttering proudly on the mast on Flagstaff Hill — a mast that he had personally presented to Hobson — was an emblem of the British intention to enslave the Maori. So when an insult offered by the Maori wife of a Kororareka butcher named Lord reached Heke's ears in late 1844, he decided the white man had to go. Leading a band of warriors into town he abducted Lord's wife. They jeered and flaunted their weapons at the townspeople and, almost as an afterthought, they felled the flagstaff as a calculated insult to British mana.

The government responded by sending troops to try to keep a lid on things, but the flagstaff was felled twice more in the space of six months. Tensions escalated, and when Heke's men chopped the flagstaff down for the fourth time on 11 March 1845, also killing the detachment of troops assigned to defend it, the entire European population of Kororareka was evacuated to Auckland and the town shelled by the aptly named British warship HMS *Hazard*. Most of the town was then razed by Heke, although he spared the houses of missionaries and the church. Shrapnel damage from the *Hazard*'s bombardment can still be seen on the walls of the church.

This episode sparked the so-called Flagstaff War, the first of the New Zealand Wars, in which Heke and another Nga Puhi rangatira, Kawiti, fought a series of battles against the British army and its Maori allies before it ended in a stalemate and peace in early 1846. It was the end of the episode, but just the beginning of the trouble and strife that have surrounded the Treaty ever since.

Making a single nation of two peoples was never going to be easy.

Top: Flagstaff Hill has special significance to Blandy.

Above: Heke fells the flagstaff at Kororareka, Arthur David McCormick, 1908.

The Bay of Islands 123

Russell Boating Club hosts the sailing social event of the year.

The Tall Ships Race has been a highlight on the Bay of Islands' social calendar since it began about 35 years ago.

A race for the feast

A couple of bays around from downtown Russell, Al finds the Russell Boating Club, where preparations for the following day's big race are in full swing. A gang of people are busily peeling spuds and kumara, chopping up meat and combining bread, melted butter, herbs, grated carrots and onion into stuffing balls.

Al goggles at the heap of bread destined for the stuffing.

'Give me some stats,' Al asks one of the workers.

'Eighty loaves of bread, two sacks of onions,' she replies. 'We'll make about 1000 stuffing balls. We're a bit behind schedule at the moment, because we've run out of herbs. But we'll get there. We'll work late tonight.'

The building was originally a fish factory, then briefly a boat-building shed, before a group of enthusiasts got their hands on it for their boating club. It was out of a club brainstorming session,

Al helps Murray Tauri and Anthony George prepare mussels for the hangi.

looking for ways to boost membership and promote the existing members' interest in traditional sailing techniques, that the Tall Ships Race was born. Someone had the 'outrageous idea' that an annual race for 'two-stickers' — boats with more than one mast — be inaugurated. That was the beginning of it. The boating club and other people in the community threw themselves into it heart and soul. It's grown enormously in that time, and changed from a serious contest to more of a social event. These days, it's necessarily an 'invitation only' affair, such is its standing within the traditional sailing fraternity.

And as traditional as the race itself is the hangi which caps the day of sailing and precedes a night of celebrating. For years it was overseen by Joe Cotton, a club stalwart — commodore for a while — and ace hangi master. Joe was as passionate about his Nga Puhi heritage as he was about sailing, and he saw in the Tall Ships Race and its aftermath a way to bring them both together.

Joe passed away a couple of years ago and his daughter Nicole, who heads the food preparation team, leads Al to a corner of the clubrooms where Joe's portrait keeps an eye on the proceedings.

'Nice that he's still present. Bet he looks down on all this pretty happy,' says Al. Nicole smiles in agreement, 'We'll do 1000 people tomorrow,' she says.

The Bay of Islands

Right: As traditional as the race is the hangi, for which preparations are well underway. This stack took several days to build.

Below: Joe Cotton's portrait looks over the activity at the hangi pit.

'So the hangi is a big thing in Russell?'

'It seems the easiest way to feed a big group of people.'

Nicole points Al to a grass clearing 50 metres from the clubrooms where Nicole's husband, Anthony George, is busy with a chainsaw putting the finishing touches to the huge mound of firewood sitting over the hangi pit. Anthony has taken over Joe's duties as hangi master.

The hangi, of course, is an ancient ritual. The act of sharing food sets the seal on ceremonies of every kind: when the manuhiri — the guests — accept the hospitality of the tangata whenua, (their hosts), they cease to be tauiwi (strangers) and earn the right to cross the paepae and sit with the people of the land.

The debates and the grand ceremony that marked the signing of the Treaty of Waitangi in 1840 were followed by just such a feast. As Maori and Pakeha ate together, it was symbolic of the spirit of the words that Hobson intoned as each chief signed the Treaty: He iwi tahi tatou — we are all now one people. When the ovens were opened, the cloud of steam must have mushroomed upwards like optimism; when Maori shared their food with Pakeha, it was an act of acceptance, as though they had symbolically allowed the newcomers from the sea to cross the beach.

STOKING THE OVEN

When Al returns to the boat club the next morning, the hangi site is still a hive of activity. Under a huge marquee, food is being packed into tinfoil parcels, and outside firemen are hosing down the grass ahead of the lighting of the fire at 10:45. The Russell Boating Club clubrooms are awash with high-spirited sailors, awaiting the briefing before the big race and the delivery of the sailing instructions.

The race briefing — a festive, jocular sort of affair — takes place bang on nine, and Al duly receives the envelope for the *R. Tucker Thompson*. But before he joins her down at the wharf, he's got another duty to perform. Joe Cotton's portrait now hangs from a tree overlooking the fire pit, and under Joe's watchful eye and after kaumatua Cliff Whiting has recited a karakia, a piece of newspaper is lit and handed to Al. He touches it to the mound of firewood in several places, and the dry crackle and the haze of fragrant blue smoke announces that the fire has caught.

Al steps back beside Anthony. 'A big day for you, mate. Do you ever flick the lid off and think, ooh, the chicken needs a bit longer? Anything like that?' he asks.

'Nah, never happened, mate,' Anthony replies. 'There's enough heat in those stones to see everything gets done. Doesn't stop you getting worried, though.'

They stand and watch the hypnotic spectacle of the flames for a minute or two before Al rouses himself from his reverie.

'Got a race to win,' he tells Anthony.

'Good luck!'

As the smoke wreathes his portrait, you'd almost fancy old Joe's smile widens.

Al is given the honour of lighting the mound of firewood for the hangi.

The Bay of Islands

IT'S NOT ALL ABOUT WINNING

Al boards the *R. Tucker Thompson* for the last leg of his journey. As the entrants line up for the start of the Tall Ships Race, the sight of the sails billowing before the breeze is an unforgettable spectacle and a living reminder of what the Bay of Islands must have looked like in those early days of first contact.

Russell and Al stand next to the helm as they jockey with the others for position on the start line. 'Five minutes!' someone yells.

'Main competition's over there,' Russell points. 'That's the *Breeze*, built by Ralph Sewell in the Coromandel about 27 years ago. Another perfect model of a little working ship, probably much like the *Herald*, the ship the Williams family built in Paihia. She's similar to us, but with subtle differences. She and the *Soren Larsen* are both brigantines. See? They've both got topsails, gaff, big main above the gaff. But they've got staysails instead of foresails like we have.'

Russell takes the helm from Al for the final, pre-start manoeuvring. He starts the run for the start line. The whole fleet converging in this small stretch of water is a majestic sight and as they near the start line, the tension noticeably rises.

Russell calls a few orders to the crew, who heave on the ropes.

There's a plume of blue smoke and they're off and racing. After a flurry of initial activity that sees the more modern boats surging ahead, it becomes pretty plain that the *R. Tucker Thompson* won't be taking out line honours this year.

'None of these boats were exactly built for speed,' observes Al ruefully.

'Well, they were built for speed, but you're talking about a different clock,' Russell shrugs. 'Still, we'll never get the best out of these vessels. We can make copies as close as you like, but the blokes who sailed them back then — they knew so much more about the wind, tides and sea than we ever will. It's the old story: a wee bit

Al takes the helm

The whole fleet converging in this small stretch of water is a majestic sight and as they near the start line, the tension noticeably rises.

The race is underway.

of new technology wipes out thousands of years of old technology. As much as we try to emulate the sailing ships, we can't really do it as it was done.'

As the race progresses, the different boats find their course. Many pass close by and all hands are called to deck to exchange volleys of friendly abuse and a flurry of waterbombs. It dawns on Al that winning isn't really what the Tall Ships Race is about. Win or lose, it's not a bad way to spend a day and for the coasters who have travelled from far and wide to get here, well worth the effort. With the wind against them, the *R. Tucker Thompson* never makes the top mark and, later in the afternoon, turns to find a fair breeze for home. Al takes the wheel again, revelling in the sensation.

'Some of those fast boats will already be back enjoying a beer by now,' says Russell. 'Steering the ship, it's like life,' he says, by way of advice. 'You're looking ahead into the horizon, fixing your gaze on something in the distance. Don't be a city person and look down in front of you.'

The Bay of Islands 129

The Spirit of New Zealand heads for the finish line.

HANGI TIME!

There's nothing like a great feed after a brilliant day out on the water. Or that's what Al's thinking, anyway, as he stands with the rest of the crowd — skippers, crews, club members and those who are just here to be in on the fun — as the results of the race are announced and prizes handed out. Al has spotted Blandy in the crowd, and Andrew Blanshard. Russell and his crew are here, of course, and so are others whom Al's met along his way, too.

Once the formalities are over, the announcement everyone has been waiting for is made.

'Hangi time!'

Outside, everyone gathers to watch as a group of men set to with shovels to unearth the hangi. Traditionally, a hangi consisted of a pit lined with stones that were heated to white-hot. Food in kete (flax baskets) was laid over the stones and sprinkled with water. More flax

130 *Coasters*

mats were laid over the kete, more water sprinkled and the whole thing buried. A few hours later, it was all dug up, the food done to a turn by the trapped steam.

These days, wire baskets and tinfoil replace the kete, and sacks and sheets of iron stand in for the flax mats. But the principle is the same, and all going according to plan, so is the distinctive, earthy flavour that the hangi imparts to the food.

'It's time for the big reveal, mate,' Al says to Tony George. 'How you feeling?'

'Bit nervous,' admits Tony. 'Lot of people to feed.'

The spades hit the iron and soon the sheets are lifted off. The first waft of fragrant steam sets everyone's mouths watering, and there is an appreciative round of applause.

The sacks come off next, layer by layer. At the first glimpse of the foil-wrapped parcels, there's a cheer.

Al joins the line and gathers his parcel of food and opens it reverently.

Perfectly cooked. What a relief for Tony and his crew.

Al eats, and closes his eyes in pleasure.

'That's the way to do mussels. And look, we've got the stuffing, the pumpkin, the pork, chicken, mutton, peas . . . This is how they do it up here in the North.'

Hungry onlookers await the moment of truth

The Bay of Islands 131

The steam rises over the crowd, young and old, men and women, Maori and Pakeha, tangata whenua and tauiwi. No matter what happened out on the water today — who won or who scored a direct hit with a water balloon — and no matter what happened on this coast in the past, you'd struggle to find divisions anywhere in this happy throng.

KEEPING YOUR EYES ON THE HORIZON

It is sort of fitting that the birthplace of this nation was at Ipipiri, the southernmost pole of the Polynesian empire, and the point at which Europeans and Maori first made prolonged contact. Like other parts of our coast, it's still resonating both from the impact of the first visitors — the vegetation and the wildlife are only now starting on the road back to what they were before human beings and their hangers-on arrived — and from the collision between peoples. The relationship between Maori and Pakeha has been marked with uneasy moments right from the beginning. Misunderstandings were inevitable, and occasionally catastrophic. The consequences are still with us after the better part of 250 years. But for all that, it's a functioning relationship. The trick, as Russell Harris, will tell you, is for all parties to keep their eyes on the horizon.

The coast is a paepae, after all. All kinds of emotions have been expressed in the Bay of Islands, but ultimately it is a place where people have confronted one another across a distance — the space between a tall ship and a waka, the gap marked by a line in the sand, a cultural and linguistic gulf, a table on which lay a scroll of paper, a quill and an inkpot — and yet have eventually found a way to share. That's what Andrew Blanshard's history lesson will teach you. That's what Blandy and his hapu are doing with their taonga on Cape Brett. And that's what Al feels he's celebrating at journey's end, as he participates in the unifying ritual of the hangi after the fun and drama of the Tall Ships Race.

He iwi tahi tatou — we are all one people.

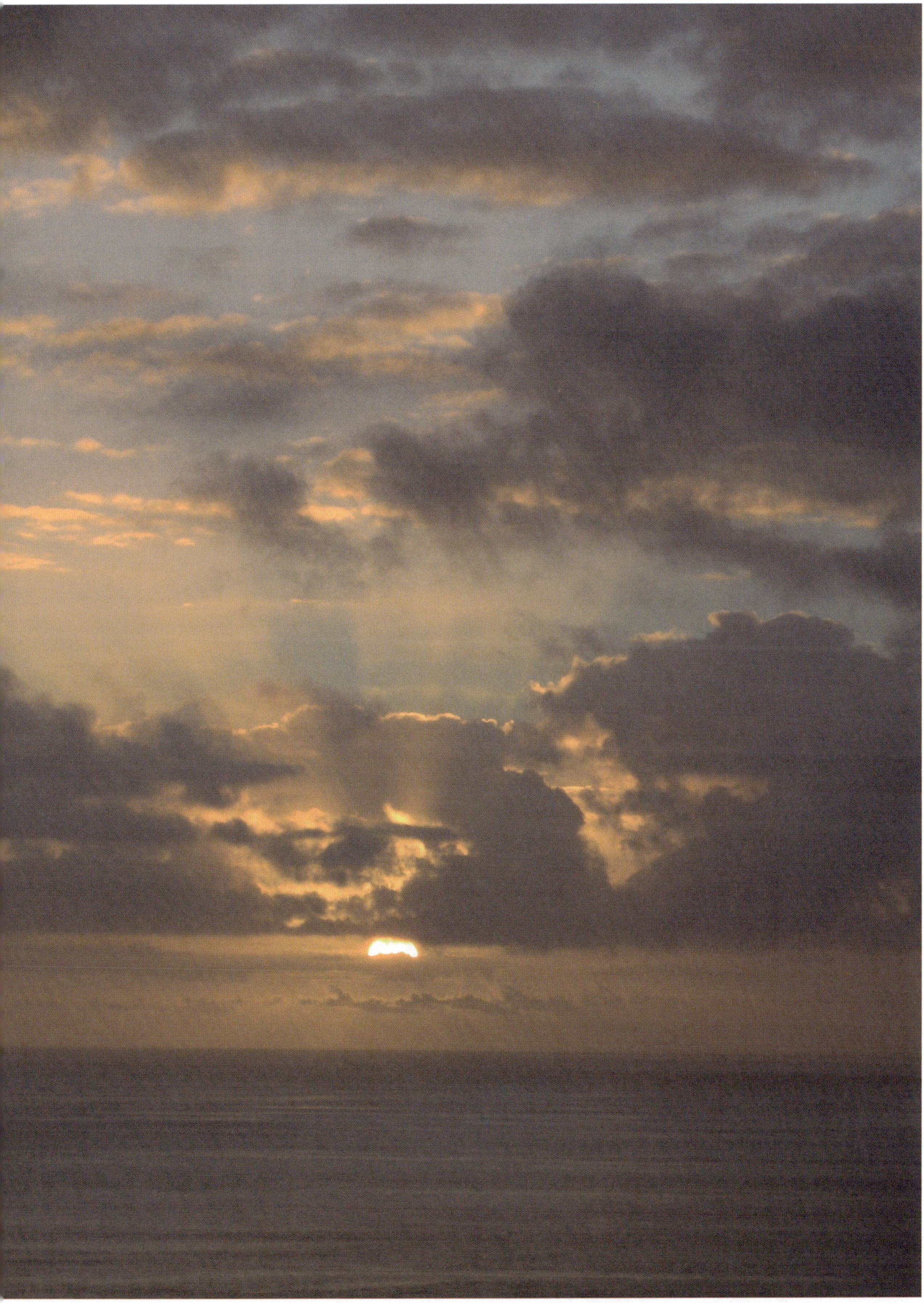

Welcome to... Doubtful

Sound

The Protected Coast

Al's coasting adventure takes him far from civilisation into the heart of Fiordland, one of the most isolated places in New Zealand.

Previous page: Doubtful Sound from Wilmot Pass.

He travels by boat to the rugged south-west coast of the South Island, from the wild waters of the open Tasman Sea into the sheltered arms of Doubtful Sound, the second longest of the 14 fiords in Fiordland National Park, and the deepest. It's a labyrinth of inlets and branching waterways, passing through massive jagged peaks clad in dense rainforest.

As Al travels inland, past towering Secretary Island at the entrance to the head at Deep Cove, he meets some dedicated coasters who have visited this spectacular, isolated wilderness, and returned inspired to protect it. Trappers, divers, eco-tour operators and wildlife researchers — none live here but all share a special connection with the breathtakingly beautiful landscapes of Fiordland.

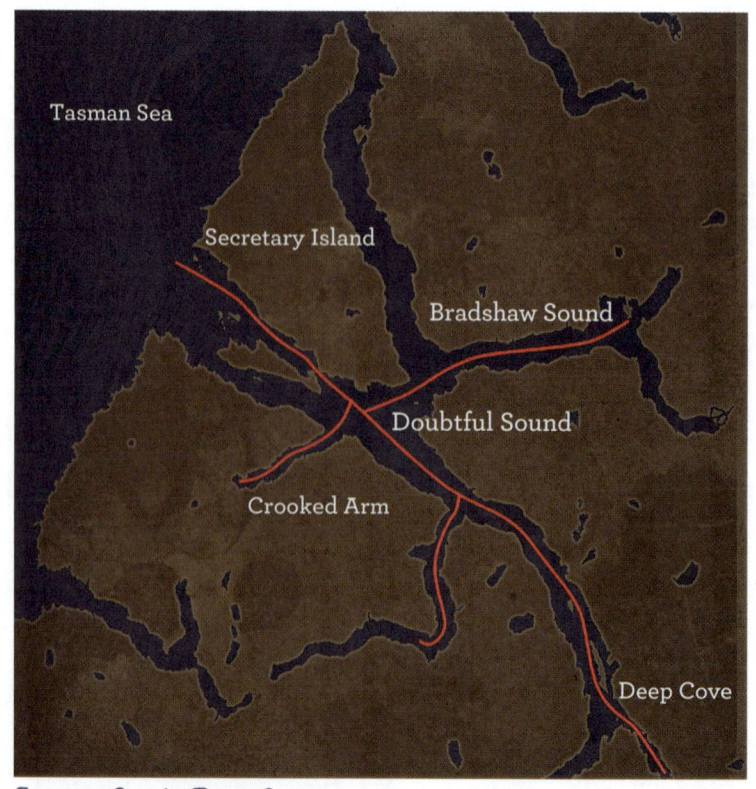

Tasman Sea to Deep Cove

The 1.2 million-hectare Fiordland National Park was established in 1952. It is our largest national park, and is so vast and impenetrable that it is one of the few places in New Zealand — or perhaps the world — where it is possible to imagine that your footprints are the first. Far from the influence of humanity, Fiordland is dominated by two things: the mountains and the weather.

MIGHTY PEAKS AND DROWNED VALLEYS

According to Maori legend, the sounds were created by the atua (or god) Tu Te Raki Whanoa, who used his enchanted adze and magical incantations to carve them from the coast for use as places of refuge for waka abroad on stormy southern seas. Perhaps Tu was a

Fiordland National Park, the largest in New Zealand.

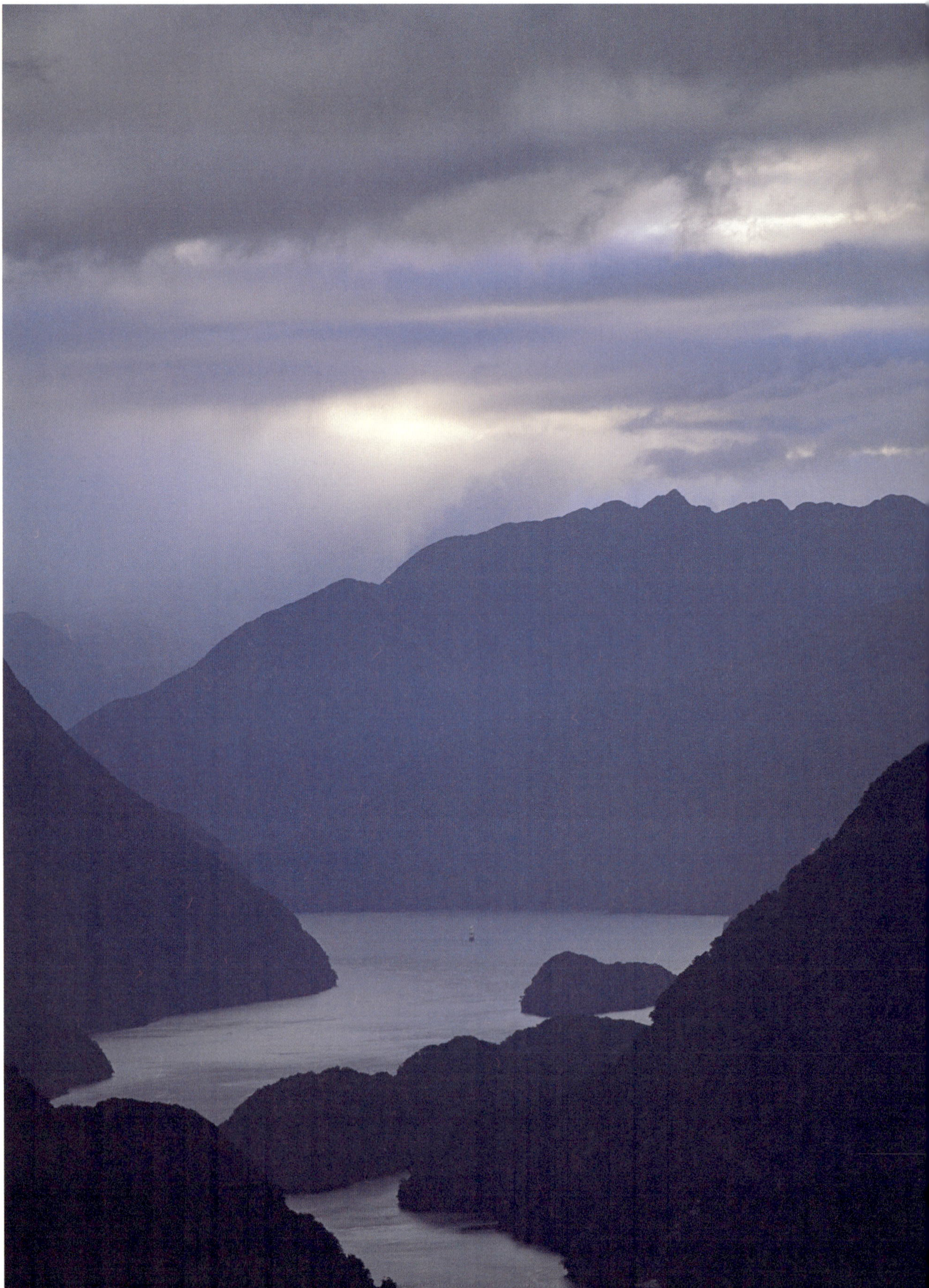

personification of the forces of nature — the enormous subterranean pressures that pushed and pulled, twisted and fractured ancient rocks of Gondwana into the crumpled mountains you see today. Massive glaciers bulldozed and chiselled U-shaped troughs, and when the ice melted at the end of the last ice age, the troughs formed inland lakes of stunning beauty while along the coast, the seas rushed in to form the deep indentations in the coastline that are known as fiords.

The result is a landscape of snow-capped peaks, magnificent forested hills, towering cliffs, glaciers, lakes, rivers and tussock grasslands — all running down to the rocky coastline. In 1986, in recognition of its exceptional land forms, plants and animals, many of which are found nowhere else in the world, the national park was placed on the UNESCO World Heritage list and in 1990, along with Aoraki/Mount Cook, Westland/Tai Poutini and Mount Aspiring national parks, it became part of Te Wahipounamu World Heritage Area.

Opposite: A sailing ship dwarfed by Doubtful Sound's mountains.

WATER, WATER, EVERYWHERE

It doesn't matter where you go in Fiordland everything comes back to the weather. It is the overriding, all-consuming refrain, the chorus to which you return again and again. Of course, the coast *anywhere* involves the marriage of sea and land, but here it is the water that has the upper hand. Fiordland is the wettest place in New Zealand and one of the wettest places in the world. Much of the access to the coast is only via the sea.

And it all comes back to those mountains. The mountains, in combination with the sun, winds and seas, are the engine room of this environment. The sun converts the waters of the Tasman Sea and the Southern Ocean into moisture and the winds drive it west until it collides with the coast and the mountains. The water vapour barrels skyward, hits the cold air above the peaks and there you have it: mist, clouds and finally rain, buckets of it. It is said that there is rain in Fiordland on average 200 days a year. In parts there is upwards of seven metres of rainfall, most of it falling on the western side of the mountains. The crests and hills are often ghostly with mist, while during and after rain the walls of the fiords are streaked white with countless cascades. The water erodes the hills and loosens the cliff faces, leaving the sides of the fiords scarred by slips. Even when it is not raining and the falls subside to a trickle, the bush is rarely dry. Water drips continuously from leaf to leaf, from twig to branch, through mosses and ferns and forest-floor humus, taking on the colour of tea as it picks up tannins and acids from the decaying forest.

The rain, the inhospitable terrain and the ever-present, all-consuming sandflies have made Fiordland an unattractive place to live permanently, but people have always visited. Early Maori harvested its seas, took pounamu (New Zealand jade) from the rivers, and named the region Atawhenua, the Shadowlands, referring perhaps to the remarkable light and shade and the reflections for which it is renowned. This place of many moods has special meaning for the South Island iwi, Ngai Tahu, whose culture and identity are interwoven with its mountains, hills, rivers, lakes and valleys.

THE SOUND OF SILENCE

When he sailed past the entrance to Doubtful Sound in March 1770, James Cook was urged by some on board to take a look but decided against it. He wrote: 'A little before Noon we passed a little Narrow opening in the land, where there appear'd to be a very Snug Harbour, form'd by an Island . . . inland, behind this Opening, were Mountains, the summits of which were Cover'd with Snow that seem'd to have fallen lately, and this is not to be wondered at, for we have found it very cold for these 2 days past. The land on each side the Entrance of this Harbour riseth almost perpendicular from the Sea to a very considerable Height; and this was the reason why I did not attempt to go in with the Ship, because I saw clearly that no winds could blow there but what was right in or right out, that is, Westerly or Easterly; and it certainly would have been highly imprudent in me to have put into a place where we could not have got out but with a wind that we have lately found to blow but one day in a Month.'

Cook called the sound 'Doubtful Harbour', a reflection of his hesitation in going there, but its Maori name is more evocative: 'Patea', or 'sound of silence', the pun and paradox of this translation aptly describe its scale, grandeur and stillness.

Doubtful Sound is the second largest of the sounds, after Dusky.

> Cook called the sound 'Doubtful Harbour', a reflection of his hesitation in going there, but its Maori name is more evocative: Patea, or 'sound of silence'.

It is long and narrow, lying like a strangely distorted twig diagonally across the map from north-west to south-east, extending 40.4 kilometres from the outer coast to the arm of Deep Cove at its head. It branches into narrow arms on the south-west of the main fiord: First Arm or Taiparipoto (short), Crooked Arm or Taiparinui (big), Hall Arm or Taipariroa (long) and Deep Cove or Taiparitiki (little). Doubtful connects to, and includes as part of a larger complex, Thompson and Bradshaw Sounds, which lie to the north.

Doubtful's entrance is guarded or protected by the large triangular-shaped Secretary Island, with the smaller Bauza Island tucked beside it. Bauza was named by the Spaniard Alessandro Malaspina, who visited Doubtful Sound to conduct scientific experiments in 1793. Unlike Cook, he entered the fiord and charted the entrance, leaving

Pendulo Reach in Doubtful Sound, one of the few Spanish names on the New Zealand map.

The DOC launch Southern Winds *near the entrance to Doubtful Sound.*

Mark Peychers, ex-fisherman, contract DOC skipper and founding member of the Fiordland Marine Guardians.

the only Spanish names on the New Zealand map: Bauza Island plus Febrero Point, the Nee Islets, Pendulo Reach and Malaspina Reach are all the Spaniard's legacy.

It's here at the entrance to the sound that we first meet Al. He's standing on the deck of the Department of Conservation launch *Southern Winds* as it steams from the open sea into the sound south of Secretary Island. 'We're at the entrance to Doubtful Sound,' says Al. 'It's huge, quite intimidating. I can't wait to just get in there and have a look!'

THE SOUND AND THE SEALS

The *Southern Winds* is skippered by coaster Mark Peychers, who was a commercial fisherman in these waters for 28 years, but who is now leading some of the conservation initiatives in Fiordland. It's an unusually calm day and in no time they are under giant granite cliffs. Mark pulls back on the throttle. 'The deepest part of Fiordland is just here at the entrance,' he says, then gesturing to the peaks towering above them, 'what you can see above the waterline is what it's like underneath. It gets up to 430 metres deep.'

Above: Protected since 1978, the New Zealand fur seal is making a comeback.

A little further on they pass a colony of New Zealand fur seals lazing on the rocks on the Nee Islets. These large, sleek mammals are found in colonies around the coastline of the offshore islands and mainland New Zealand as well as South Australia.

Fur seals were hunted in pre-European times by Maori, who used their meat, skin, bones and teeth. Like whales, seals were also valuable commodities elsewhere in the world. However, they were under pressure from hunting and numbers were beginning to decline so when explorers like Tasman, Cook and D'Urville reported large populations in places like Doubtful Sound, it was game on. In the early 1800s they were slaughtered around the New Zealand coast in their thousands.

One of those responsible was Captain John Grono, settler, sailor, adventurer and all-round entrepreneur, who is thought to have been the next to call into Doubtful Sound after Malaspina. In 1809 he established a sealing station on Secretary Island in what is still known as Grono Bay, targeting the seals on nearby Nee and Shelter Islands. In 1813 he exported 14,000 seal pelts from the fiord. His lasting thumbprint in this place has nothing to do with the seals, however: Grono named a number of Fiordland landmarks, among them Elizabeth Island near the head to the sound, after his wife, and one of the area's most well known, Milford Sound.

Harvesting seals on that scale was unsustainable. Within

Below: Mark shows Al the fur seal colony on Shelter Island near the mouth of Doubtful Sound.

Doubtful Sound

Mark in his commercial fishing days. 'The Guardians was set up because of concern about the depletion of local fish stocks.'

decades, as they had done elsewhere in the world, numbers dwindled to the extent that hunting lost its point. The fur seals are now fully protected under the Marine Mammals Act of 1978 and numbers have recovered to the extent that today there are thought to be upwards of 60,000 around New Zealand's coastal regions.

The fence at the top of the cliff

In 1995 Mark's long association and strong bond with this part of the coast led to his involvement with the Fiordland Marine Guardians. 'The Guardians was set up because of concern about the depletion of local fish stocks in Doubtful Sound and Milford,' he says. 'It started off with just fisheries and then we realised we would have to look after the environment because it's an important factor.'

A diverse group of people came together — commercial and recreational fishers, charter boat and tourism operators, environmentalists, marine scientists, community representatives and tangata

In the early days of commercial crayfishing only the tails were kept.

whenua. All were concerned not just about fish stocks but also about managing the fiords in an integrated manner, and with the need to include local communities in decision-making. Initially they called themselves Guardians of Fiordland's Fisheries Inc and later the Guardians of Fiordland's Fisheries and Marine Environment Inc. The initiative has been a huge success.

'It's been a model for resource management around New Zealand,' Mark says. 'Everyone's bought into the process and it's been really satisfying being a part of it.'

The group adopted the common-sense approach that the only effective and worthwhile solutions had to come from within. 'It was local solutions for local problems,' Mark says. 'What's different about the Guardians is that it's a bottom-up approach. Instead of being told by government or someone in Wellington how to do things, we thought "we're not going to wait for that to happen, we're going to come up with our own solutions". What we presented to them was "these are the problems and this is the way that we believe it should be sorted". We gave them a solution to the problem, if you like.'

In particular, the members of the group realised they would have to make sacrifices, to give up things they had previously held dear in order to benefit the marine environment and the fisheries, a process they called 'gifts and gains'. One of their innovations was to designate small, specific areas of special significance — areas that have become known as 'china shops'. Their Fiordland Marine Conservation Strategy was subsequently adopted and implemented by government, and the fisheries regulations were amended to exclude commercial fishing from large areas of the internal waters of Fiordland, but non-commercial harvesting was still allowed.

'Where we are now is inside the commercial exclusion area,' Mark says. 'It's what we call the "habitat line". It draws a line between the

Today commercial fishing is only permitted outside the sounds.

outer coast and the inner fiord. On the outer coast it's more plant-based, which is hugely productive, with a lot of finfish out there and lobster. Once you move into the inner fiords it's more animal-based communities that don't support large numbers of finfish and lobster, so we've got different limits on the inside of these lines to what we have on the outside of the lines.'

Currently there is a ban on blue cod fishing, recreational included, in Doubtful Sound and in Milford because of uncertainty about the state of the fishery, but, as Mark says, 'the rest of it, it's business as usual'.

Mark believes that the key to the group's success was that no one came to the table with a predetermined outcome. 'We were there to look out for what's best for Fiordland, and what's best for Fiordland would be best for everyone. We wanted to put a fence on the top of the cliff instead of the ambulance at the bottom. These are finite resources; they are easily depleted and when you get into a bad state of affairs it takes quite draconian measures to bring them back again, so the idea is not to let fish stocks get into a bad state in the first place. What we've got here now, we want for our grandchildren and their kids — for them to come and have the same experience and catch a fish for a feed and not for the freezer.'

'Why do you want to freeze fish anyway?' he asks. 'You want to eat it fresh, as you know, being a chef. Go catch it fresh and only take enough for a feed, that way there will be enough for everyone tomorrow.'

Al couldn't agree more. 'It all makes perfect sense.' And with that thought in mind, Mark and Al motor off to see if they can get themselves a fresh feed of crayfish — or rock lobster, as these large marine crustaceans are known elsewhere in the world.

Mark and Al sort the menu. 'What we've got here now we want for our grandchildren and their kids — for them to come and have the same experience.'

ENOUGH FOR A FEED

The only fishing in the sound now is recreational; no bulk harvesting is one of the Guardians' strategies. 'There's no conflict between users,' Mark says. 'When you have depleted fish stocks, people are always competing, but when you have a healthy fishery, that doesn't happen. It is the most valuable inshore fishery now in New Zealand.' As a result, the lobster fishery in the sounds is now in excellent shape.

'It's been a huge success,' Mark says. 'It shows what good management does with fisheries — getting the right management style and people, right amount of effort into resources and that's what you get out of it: a very healthy fishery.'

Al is about to see for himself. Mark has set a cray pot in advance, just inside the habitat line and Al tosses the grappling hook out and hauls the catch aboard. The orange-red of the creatures ripples in the wire cage long before it reaches the surface, and there they are, eight large crustaceans, a mass of waving antennae and grumpy, threatening claws. Al's bowled over. 'Oh my lord, look at the size of them!' he says.

Mark estimates that they may be as old as 20 years. Al carefully takes two, grasping them around the thorax, behind their pincers. 'They're the biggest lobsters I've ever held in my hands and in an ironic way I'm really looking forward to putting them back,' he says, holding them respectfully away from himself.

They keep a couple of the smaller ones for lunch but toss the rest back. They make a satisfying splash as they hit the water and return to their watery home.

Next page: Still evening at Snug Cove.

Doubtful Sound 147

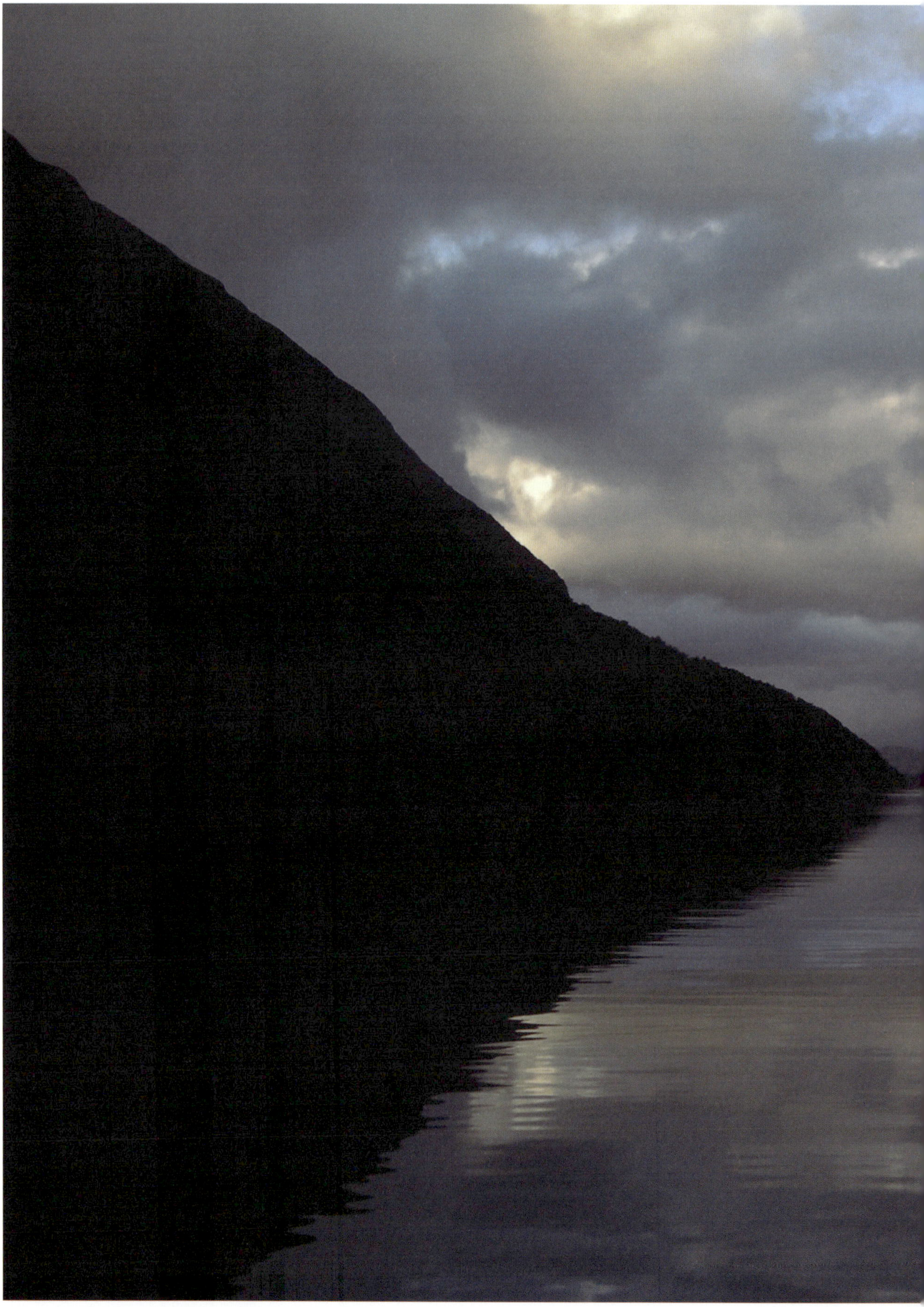

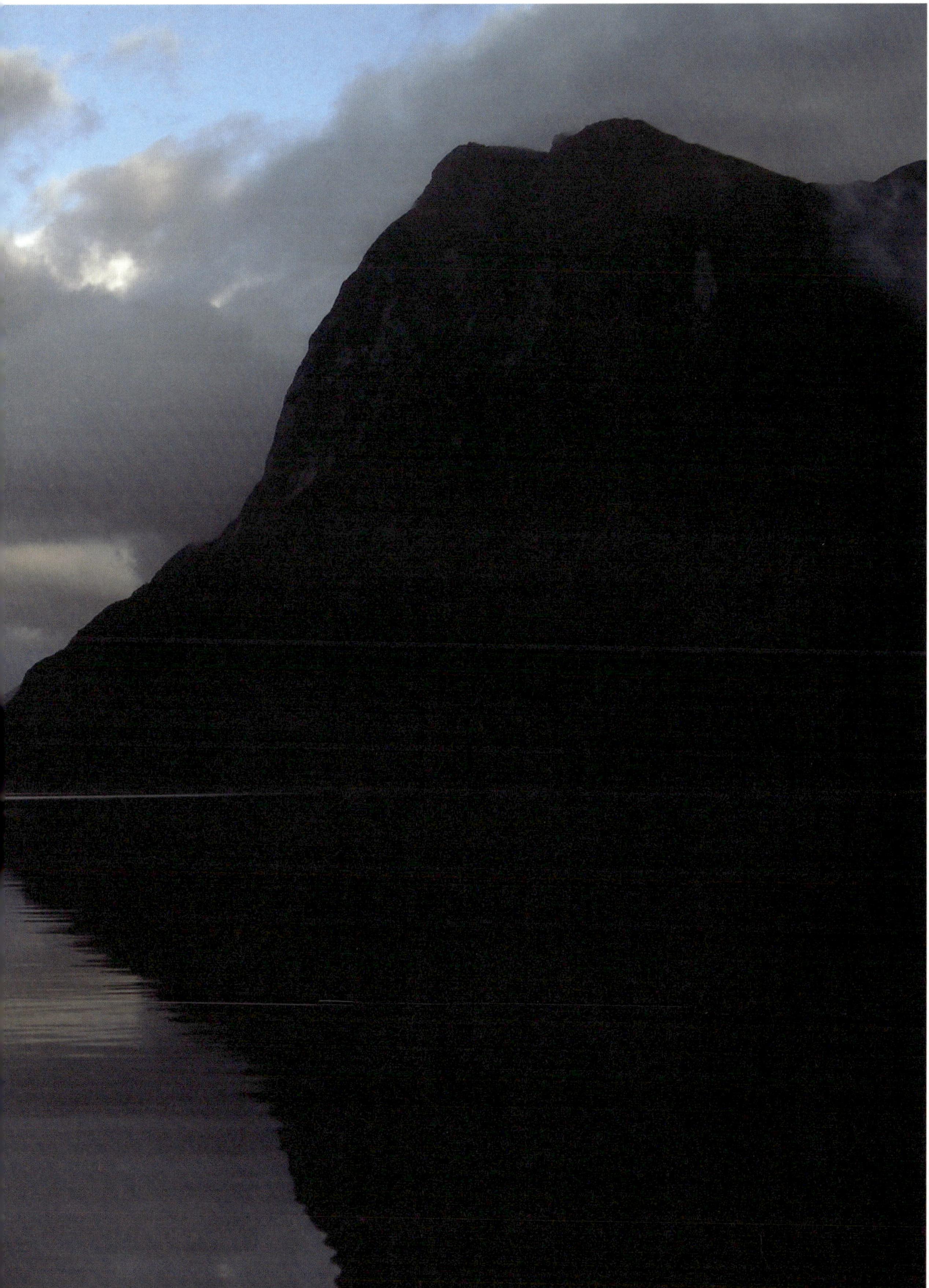

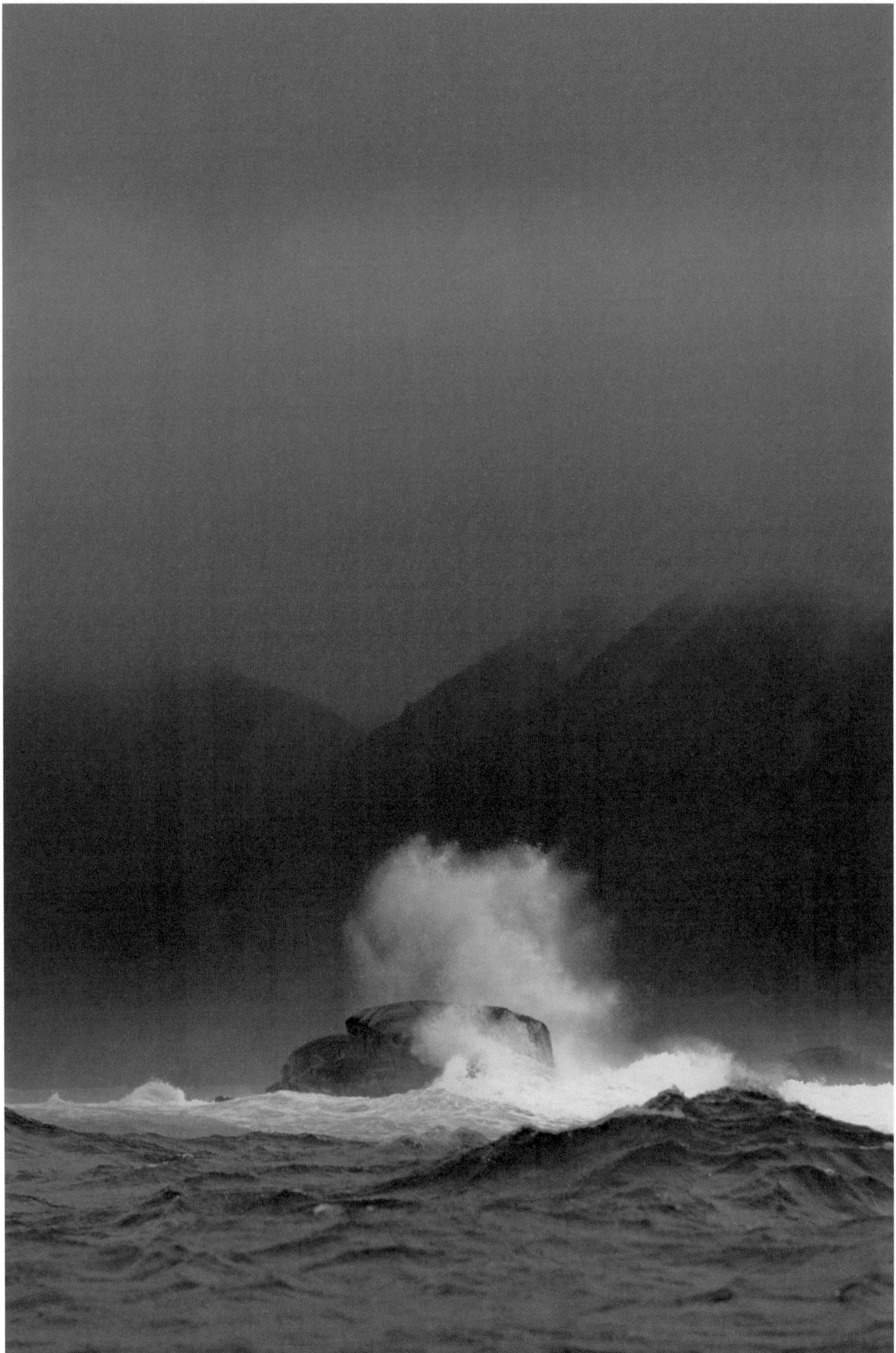

One for the birds

Al's looking forward to the crayfish but he has a stop-off to make before lunch. Mark steers *Southern Winds* across the green-black waters of the sound to Grono Bay on the south side of the 8000-hectare Secretary Island to where a lanky figure in shorts, leggings and a bright red woollen hat is waiting. It's Peter McMurtrie, a ranger with the Department of Conservation, a coaster with a long connection with Fiordland and especially this island. He heads a team that is working to rid the island of predators.

A pair of oystercatchers with a small brown chick shriek with alarm and bustle across the rocks as Al and Mark approach in the dinghy.

The story of Secretary Island is one that has echoed right around New Zealand. In the 1830s, nostalgic European run-holders went to considerable trouble to introduce rabbits to their new home, thinking perhaps of a bit of meat for the pot and a bit of sport for a weekend's hunting. A few far-sighted folk warned that what they were doing was folly, but with little appreciation of the country they had come to or the consequences of their action, they went ahead.

There were no natural predators to keep the rabbits in check and within a relatively short span of time, they ran rampant, destroying pastures and livelihoods as they hopped, nibbled and multiplied across the countryside. The uproar from farmers was impossible to ignore.

It was then suggested that the problem could be easily sorted if the rabbits' old enemies, the mustelids — stoats, weasels and ferrets — of Mother England, were introduced to keep them company. Again, there were warnings and protests but the needs of the pastoralists prevailed and from March 1882 to 1897, shipments of stoats, weasels and ferrets were imported and released in their thousands, mainly in the South Island.

It was, of course, a mistake of incalculable proportions. Not only rabbits but all living creatures, especially New Zealand's unsuspecting and defenceless birds — whether ground- or tree-top dwellers — were on the menu of the sharp-toothed, nimble, secretive immigrants. Of the three, the stoats proved to be by far the most lethal in the New Zealand environment.

'Stoats have a fascinating biology,' says Pete, who's had a long

Opposite: Wild waves near the entrance to Doubtful Sound.

Pete McMurtrie, field manager for DOC's pest eradication programme on Secretary Island, says of stoats. 'They're killing machines, scooting around looking for something to eat all the time.'

association with the stoats on Secretary. 'It's amazing how quickly they can breed and get to big numbers. They respond to high numbers of rodents — that's the way you get a large number of them on the mainland. They are very good swimmers and very agile — they can get to the smallest nests up in trees. They have to eat continuously — they're killing machines, scooting around looking for something to eat the whole time.'

TRAPPING THE KILLERS

Fortunately, there are only two introduced pests on Secretary Island — the stoats and red deer. There are no possums, wild cats or rodents, for example, making the task of restoring the island a little more straightforward than it might otherwise have been.

The deer have been in DOC's sights since 2004, with hunters systematically eradicating them, while the stoats have been targeted by a comprehensive trapping programme since 2005.

Which is where Pete comes in. The island is covered with a grid of 650 traps at 100-metre spacings, with a further 200 on the mainland nearby (to act as a buffer) and more on nearby islands. Each trap is basically a wooden box baited with hen's eggs and meat and a powerful trap that the stoat sets off as it crosses to the lure, killing it instantly. The traps are checked roughly every four months by a team of three trappers who are on the island for a week. Stoat numbers have dropped from around 100 in the first year to 15–20 annually. Sometimes, Pete says, they have the ideal round — when they catch no stoats at all.

He takes Al into the bush to show him the drill. They check trap after trap and all are empty until near the end of the round, when they find one trap with a stoat dead in its jaws. Al holds the small russet-coloured creature in his hand, its body limp, its open mouth showing two rows of tiny pointed teeth. It's hard to believe the damage it can do.

'Look at it. That's what's killing our birdsong all over the country,' he says.

The stoat control on the island has been so successful that endangered native bird species have been reintroduced: kokako, mohua (yellowhead), kakaruai (South Island robin) and rock wren among them. Pete has been in on the whole process from the beginning and has been astonished at how rapidly the birdlife has recovered, especially bellbirds and weka.

Al is impressed. 'All Kiwis should be proud that there are guys like you out here doing this, getting it back to what it was. It's pretty special. Good on ya.'

LOBSTER LUNCH

It's early afternoon by the time Pete and Al finish checking the traps. They head back down to the coast to join up with Mark on the *Southern Winds*.

Eating perched on the stern with the sun sparkling on the water and the little islands behind, in the peace and beauty of the sound. What could be better?

Going below

Close in to the cliffs on the south side of Secretary Island, not far from the ocean mouth, two people in an aluminium dinghy are wearing wetsuits, flippers, goggles and diving tanks. Kath Blakemore and Richard Kinsey, marine rangers for the Department of Conservation, are working in the shallow waters of Te Awaatu Channel (The Gut) Marine Reserve near the deepest part of the fiord, where forested

Al gets a close look at a trapped stoat — 'That's what's killing our birdsong all over the country.'

Doubtful Sound   153

Crayfish Omelettes with Tomato Coriander Salsa and Cumin Sour Cream

I don't think I will ever forget hauling up those craypots in Doubtful Sound. The size of them and the amount that were in the pots were extraordinary. It wasn't just the culinary thrill that was about to unfold, but more the sheer delight in knowing that here was a fishery in its absolute prime state, largely due to the coming together of like-minded individuals who, years previously, recognised the importance of sustainability and looking after a special resource. The recipe that follows turned out a real beauty, and as I picked all the meat away from the crayfish cavities, it reminded me how our parents used to toss us the legs of the crayfish, explaining that we wouldn't like the tails! Go figure?
Serves 6

Step 1. Cumin Sour Cream
Ingredients
1 cup sour cream
1½ tablespoons ground cumin
½ tablespoon sugar
sea salt and freshly ground black pepper

Method
Place the sour cream in a small bowl and mix in the cumin until combined. Refrigerate until required.

Method
Place all the ingredients except the salt and pepper in a bowl. Mix to combine then taste and season accordingly. Refrigerate until required.

Step 2. Tomato Coriander Salsa

Ingredients
6–8 tomatoes, diced
⅓ cup red onion, finely diced
1 clove garlic, finely diced
⅓ cup roughly chopped fresh coriander leaves
1 fresh red chilli, finely diced
½ tablespoon freshly ground cumin seeds
1 teaspoon Spanish sweet smoked paprika
juice of 1–2 limes
⅓ cup olive oil

Step 3. To Prepare the Crayfish

Ingredients
3 live crayfish

Method
Place the crayfish in an ice slurry or the freezer for 30 minutes to put them to sleep.
  Bring a large saucepan of salted water to the boil. Add the crayfish and cook for 2 minutes. Remove the crayfish from the water and cool for a couple of minutes

then remove the tails by twisting. Place the crayfish bodies back in the boiling water for another 3 minutes then remove and cool. Once the bodies are cold, remove all the flesh from the legs and cavities then roughly chop. With a sharp knife, split the tails down the centre. Reserve.

Step 4. To Cook and Serve

Ingredients
12 eggs
½ cup milk
sea salt and freshly ground black pepper
butter
12 Peppadew peppers, roughly chopped
½ bunch fresh chives, roughly chopped
½ bunch fresh coriander, roughly chopped
150g cumin gouda cheese, grated
3 limes, halved

Method
Preheat the oven to 180°C.
Place the eggs in a suitable bowl, add the milk, some sea salt and black pepper, and whisk to combine. Reserve.

Place the crayfish tails shell side down in an ovenproof dish. Smear the flesh of each with a little butter and season with sea salt and black pepper. Place in the oven for 5 minutes or so just to cook through. Remove from the oven and keep in a warm spot while you make the omelettes.

Place a small non-stick pan on medium heat, add a little butter then some of the egg mix to cover the base. Using a rubber spatula, pull the egg from the sides of the pan towards the centre, allowing the raw egg to run into the gaps, until just set. Place a line of chopped crayfish meat down the centre of the omelette, then top with some peppers, chives, coriander and a liberal amount of cheese.

Gently fold the omelette over and slide onto a warm plate. Place a half crayfish tail alongside, along with a healthy spoonful of salsa and a dollop of cumin sour cream. Garnish with a lime half then serve. Repeat the process with the remaining ingredients.

cliffs plunge vertically into green-black water. Epiphytes hang in masses above mottled rock.

Although they are not part of the national park, there are 10 marine reserves with strict 'no-take' policies inside Fiordland's boundaries. Two, Te Awaatu and Taipari Roa (Elizabeth Island), are inside Doubtful Sound. Te Awaatu (which means the channel of Tu, after the atua who hacked out the fiords) was established in 1993 and was one of the first marine reserves in Fiordland. It's also the smallest, 93 hectares, and is much shallower than the deep waters at the sound's entrance, providing a rock wall and reef habitat where corals, sea pens and lampshells thrive.

'Getting a feed of crays, are you?' Al asks, tongue-in-cheek.

Kath laughs. 'No. We're going down to look at rock lobster and fish numbers, things like that, a count-up of the main reef species down here, looking at how things change over time.'

It's that extraordinary rainfall again that creates Fiordland's curious underwater world. The huge volume of fresh water that cascades off the peaks, through the forests and into the fiords lies on the surface of the salt water in a sheet that can be as deep as several metres. Tannins are picked up as the water passes through the leaf litter, turning it amber-brown in colour. When the fresh water layer sits on top of the salt water it reduces the amount of light, so plants and animals that are normally found at depths live closer to the surface.

A stunning example of this is the red and black corals that grow on the walls and reefs. The black corals are especially important because they are only found at great depth elsewhere in the world; some of the Fiordland corals are thought to be up to 200 years old. There are also clam-like creatures called brachiopods, or lampshells, that many regard as 'living fossils' because they have changed little for over 300 million years.

This unique marine environment is fragile and vulnerable, which is why the initiative taken by the Guardians, as well as the work of researchers like Kath, is so necessary and so valuable.

> **This unique marine environment is fragile and vulnerable, which is why the initiative taken by the Guardians, as well as the work of researchers like Kath, is so necessary and so valuable.**

Al puts on his wetsuit, grabs a snorkel and joins Kath and Richard to take a look for himself.

The magic of Fiordland above sea level is reflected in the blue-green world below. A fur seal executes a graceful back-flip as it checks Al out; a troop of orange-red rock lobster line the base of the wall like a legion of armoured gladiators with weapons at the ready; a school of fish flashes past; black and red corals wave gently in the surge.

'You think it's beautiful on top of the fiord, wait till you get down there!' Al exclaims as he surfaces. 'There's kina, mussels, fish — it's extraordinary, it's beautiful! I'm having a ball!'

Like Mark and Pete, Kath and Richard are coasters who are passionate about Fiordland and keep coming back. 'I live a long way from it,' says Kath, 'but because my job solely involves the Fiordland coastline, every time we come out on one of these trips it really makes me realise how special a place it is and how much I enjoy being out there. I feel fortunate about the work that has gone on here and the special protection that they put here, and hope it goes on for future generations to enjoy as well.'

Kath Blakemore and Richard Kinsey from DOC regularly monitor the changes that occur in Fiordland's marine protected areas.

Doubtful Sound

Doubtful dolphins

Mark takes Al further up the sound to Crooked Arm, to meet his next coaster, Shaun Henderson. Shaun is doing a PhD through the Marine Science Department at the University of Otago and has recently joined the team who have been studying a very special group of residents, the population of Doubtful Sound bottlenose dolphins, for nearly 20 years. Since the age of six, Shaun's dream has been to work with marine mammals, so he's a happy man with a big smile on his face.

He and Al motor down the long, narrow channel of Crooked Arm in Shaun's speedboat in search of the pod. The dolphins are not always easy to see because they feed continuously along the walls of the sound and their grey skins blend with the greys and browns of the cliffs behind them, but Shaun and Al are in luck. The distinctive two-metre plumes of white spray from the dolphins' blowholes, like those of miniature whales, is like a beacon in the distance.

Al is ecstatic. 'There's something about dolphins! It makes you feel good, doesn't it?'

Shaun's theory is, it's the dolphins' 'natural smile'. The dolphins ride the bow-wave and a pair show off their aerobatic skills, making curving leaps out of the water.

'What a cool thing to study,' says Al.

'Yeah, it's a lot of fun!' Shaun agrees.

There are three distinct populations of bottlenose dolphin in Fiordland: in Doubtful Sound, Dusky/Breaksea Sound and a northern group ranging from Lake McKerrow to Charles Sound. They are the southernmost in the world and are unique because no other bottlenose dolphin populations live exclusively in fiords.

The Doubtful Sound group of dolphins is also very special, largely because it is practically shut off, with no interaction observed with any other populations. They live in mixed-sex schools, but in larger groups than elsewhere and appear to form extremely strong, long-lasting and stable bonds. It is thought that this tight-knit behaviour is at least in part a result of the ecology

Shaun Henderson takes Al into Crooked Arm to look for Doubtful Sound bottlenose dolphins.

'There's something about dolphins! It makes you feel good, doesn't it?'

of Doubtful Sound, where food is sparse and difficult to spot in the dark tannin-stained waters. Constantly on the move, hunting together along the fiord walls, their close knowledge of each other allows them to exchange information quickly and efficiently, and this may be a key to their survival.

Things are not looking good for them, however. When the university began the study in 1994, there were 69 dolphins in the Doubtful Sound pod, but in recent years deaths have exceeded births and the population appears to be in steep decline. There are fears that unless the downturn is reversed, these dolphins will be extinct by 2050.

No one can precisely pinpoint why this is happening and Shaun is reluctant to hazard a guess, but it's likely that rather than any single cause, a number of different factors are at

One of Doubtful Sound's bottlenose dolphins.

Taking photos of the dolphins as they surface is an important part of Shaun's research, allowing him to identify and match information about individual dolphins.

The Doubtful Sound group is also very special, largely because it is completely shut off, with no interaction with any other populations.

work together. Among a list of possibilities is the presence and intrusion of vessels — both the physical presence of the boats and the noise of them — which potentially interrupts feeding and social behaviours. Food is another issue. Since the reduction and limitation of fishing, food stocks for the dolphins are thought to have improved but the nature of the sound itself, with its layers of fresh water — including a larger-than-usual volume discharged from the Manapouri Power Station — may still be affecting the dolphins' food supply. Then there's climate change, with all the uncertainties that it may hold.

Like Kath, who is monitoring the underwater environment, Shaun's job is to keep an eye on this population, visiting three times a year for a count and comparing it with the pod in Dusky Sound in the hope that this may reveal some answers. In the meantime, dolphin protection zones have been introduced, with rules for viewing dolphins from boats within Doubtful Sound. Shaun is only too aware that even his studies, undertaken with the best of intentions, may be disturbing the pods, so he takes great care not to cause any distress.

'On any given day we try not to stay with them too long because we don't want to annoy them,' he says. 'They move continuously

160 **Coasters**

and can travel 30, 40, 50 miles on any one day. It seems like they keep doing that right through the night.

'All we do for a week is photograph to see who's still in the population,' he says. Then back on land, there's the exacting task of matching the photos to the known information about each individual dolphin. They are all known and named by distinctive characteristics such as nicks in the back or scratches on fins.

'Essentially it's a family,' Shaun says. 'The older females act as grandmothers. You'll often see SN4, for instance. She's quite old and she's been around since the very beginning. You'll often see them looking after the little ones. This year there has been a new calf so, as there weren't any that survived last year, we're really happy to see this one. We're hoping good things for it.'

It has been an amazing experience for Al. 'Fantastic, unbelievable,' he says. 'I never had any idea how big and beautiful they were. That was just one of the greatest things I've ever done in my life.'

Next page: It is thought that Doubtful's bottle nose dolphins live exclusively within the fiord.

Doubtful Sound 161

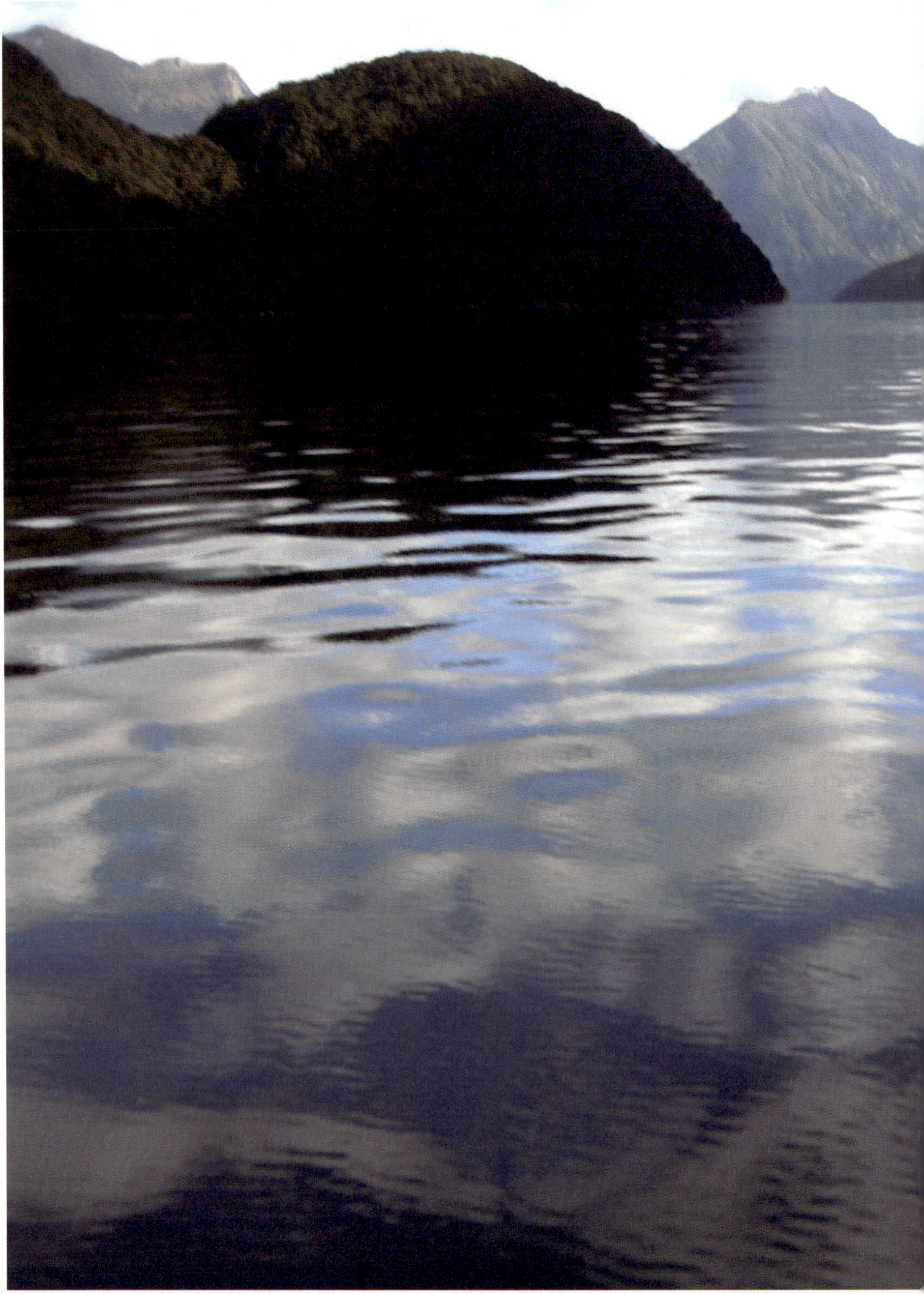

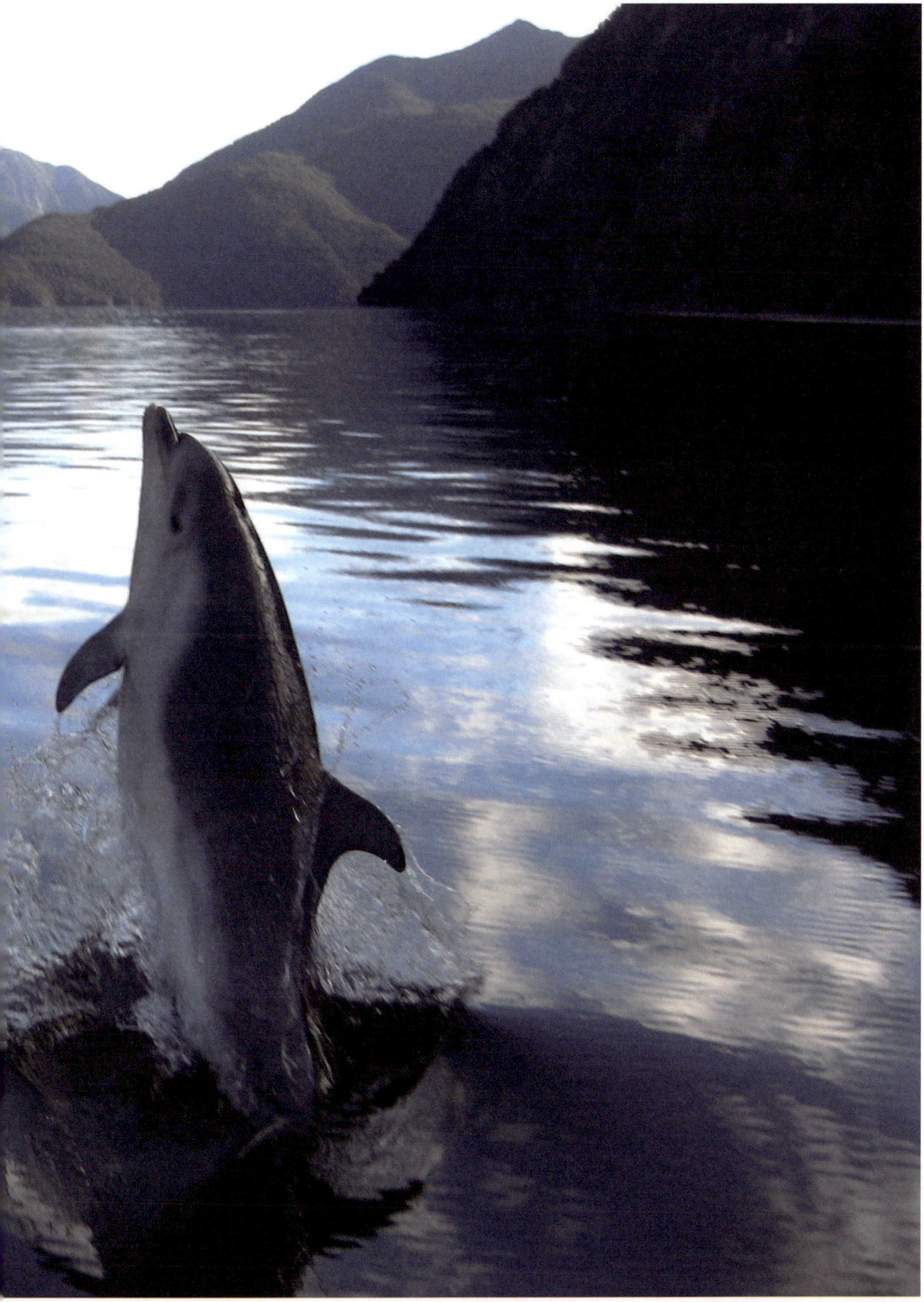

Above left: Ruth Dalley, at the helm of Breaksea Girl.

Above right: The Breaksea Girl, a 25-metre motor sail, owned and operated until recently by Ruth Dalley and Lance Shaw, takes Al deeper into Doubtful Sound.

A new page of life

Al's last Doubtful Sound adventure is on the *Breaksea Girl*, the 25-metre motor sailor owned and operated by Ruth Dalley and Lance Shaw.

Ruth, a small woman with a wide smile, and Lance, a lean, bearded man who is the essence of the seafarer in his captain's hat, black jacket and sunglasses, are committed conservationists whose great delight has been to introduce others to the beauty and treasures of Fiordland and whose absolute imperative is to teach people about its care and protection. They have run award-winning eco-tours for many years, throughout the sounds and into the Southern Ocean, visiting Auckland and Campbell Island reserves, offering penguin watching, tramping, snorkelling, diving and marine mammal viewing, all from the comfort of their elegant vessel.

Breaksea Girl is a white, single-hulled steel ketch, a workhorse, sturdy and safe, with 28 trips to the subantarctic oceans behind her. Her classic lines are utterly right in this setting; the cabin glows with the warmth of wood and it is a home away from home.

Al joins Ruth at the helm. She has many years of sailing experience both in New Zealand waters and overseas.

'What is it about Fiordland, for you?' Al asks.

'I've sailed a lot of the world,' Ruth says. 'I had my own 30-foot boat that I sailed solo but there's nowhere quite as spectacular. I think it's the merging of the shades of colours in the sounds.' As if to demonstrate, the vista before them changes moment by moment, the far peaks a faint mauve-blue, with fold after fold of mountainside, each a different tint blending into the foreground. 'It might sound corny,' she adds. 'But it's a very spiritual place.'

Al agrees. 'It's extraordinary. It's the scale that blows me away, whether it's spiritual or not — everything is like huge cathedrals all around. Everywhere you look, it's intoxicating, the beauty.'

'That's what Fiordland is about for me,' Ruth says. 'It's the grandeur, isn't it? Just looking up there, it's like opening up a new page of life. You can come here and feel like you're recharging. It's nice to go home and know this is here.'

GOD'S WINE

Water, water, everything here comes back to water. It's Lance's turn to show what makes the sound tick. He takes Al on a small side expedition into the upper reaches of the Camelot River. The Camelot flows into Bradshaw Sound, an arm to the north of Doubtful Sound. It is the source of the largest natural flow of fresh water into Doubtful and therefore a significant contributor to the layering of the waters and the ecology of the sound.

They take the small motor dinghy and are soon puttering quietly between bush-clad riverbanks. Away from the open sound,

Lance Shaw has been working to protect what he loves about Fiordland since he first visited 20 years ago.

Doubtful Sound

'It's the water that makes Fiordland.'

the perspective is much narrower: this is a world of a multitude of greens and myriad glassy reflections.

'The thing about Fiordland,' says Al, 'is there's just water everywhere, isn't there?'

'It's stunning,' agrees Lance, with the pride of a parent. 'It's the water that makes Fiordland, eh. And its isolation.'

A little further up the river, they go ashore so Al can take a closer look. Lance points out a slab of delicate moss, almost two metres long, glistening and dripping with thousands of droplets, hanging from the bank. 'It's like an overloaded sponge,' he says. 'This is the essence of Fiordland for me.'

Around the corner there's a waterfall. It's not huge but descends from the heights above with great drama, spurting in a froth of white onto black rocks and carving a deep pool stained the amber and brown of tea — or ale.

Al scoops a handful of water and drinks.

'Beautiful,' he says appreciatively. 'It's God's wine. It's straight off the mountain, it's pure, it's cold, it's soft, it's delicious.'

And there's plenty of it. Everywhere you look you see the incredible power and influence of water on this environment. Like the glaciers before, it's now the rivers and waterfalls that shape the granite faces of this extraordinary land.

LITTLE FEEDING MACHINES

Lance's next port of call is a group of small, two-legged, winged coasters — an island-based colony of 60-odd pairs of Fiordland crested penguins or tawaki. These little chaps, with their blue-black glossy feathers, pink feet and bills, and white-and-yellow eyebrows, are among the rarest of New Zealand's mainland penguins and breed only around Fiordland and Stewart Island.

'They have been pretty much wiped out on the mainland,' Lance says. 'But on the islands here, the wildlife is amazing. You've got the penguins, there was a weka there before poking around in the seaweed, there's a breeding colony of pied shags, good snorkelling, beautiful seaweed — it's an amazing place.'

Some people think it's amazing to see the penguin numbers recover and the birds return, but for Lance it's totally predictable. Once the predators are gone, especially the stoats, then all these creatures can just do what they've been doing for thousands of years, and their numbers begin to recover almost automatically.

'You're seeing this wildlife in a happy state because all these numbers are now coming back. DOC's doing tremendous work on the islands and a lot of local businesses are heavily involved, financially assisting with predator control,' he says.

They watch the penguins from the safe distance of the dinghy, and the penguins watch them back. Being on land doesn't appear easy for them. Their legs are short and stumpy and they have to jump, hop and waddle like babies in nappies from rock to rock, heading up into the cover of the bush. 'See, they go up the same little road,' Lance says fondly. 'They're just like humans. They like their routines, they walk out, disappear for a while, then come out on the left . . .'

'They look awkward on rocks but I bet that in the water they're just little feeding machines,' Al says.

The penguins' favourite food is fish and squid and there's no doubt they will be benefiting from the work of the Guardians.

Fiordland Crested Penguins, or tawaki, breed only around Fiordland and Stewart Island.

Doubtful Sound 167

'This is just such an extraordinary place,' Al says. 'People talk about the fiords but you have no idea of what they're like until you come here. They're just different from everywhere else. Around every corner there's another scene on a scale that continues to blow me away.'

LAST THOUGHTS

It's time to say goodbye, and not just for Al this time. Ruth and Lance are hanging up their skipper's hats and saying goodbye to *Breaksea Girl*. But it's not the end of their involvement in the fiords — the opposite, in fact, because even though they have loved their eco-tourism business, the additional time they gain will enable them to be even more involved in the business of conservation and

> 'The thing about the Doubtful Sound coasters is that they are some of the most passionate and caring people I've ever met. They've taken it upon themselves to be the guardians of this coastline and the beauty — well, it's everywhere.'

preservation — it's time to give something back, they say.

They take Al to Deep Cove at the head of the sound and tie up. He climbs the steps away from the shore and pauses for a moment of reflection. He has to leave but he's fallen in love with this place — the isolation and grandeur, the monumental mountains, the glistening waters and their amazing inhabitants. He's been up close to seals and dolphins; he's dived in the exquisite underwater garden of plants, corals, fish and other colourful creatures; he's admired the weka and oystercatchers picking their way along the shore and walked among the beech forests surrounding the sound; he's held a dead stoat and seen what damage it can do; said hello to a bunch of unique penguins and stood at the base of a stunningly beautiful waterfall.

And more, he's been bowled over by the people he's met — Mark, Peter, Shaun, Kath and Richard, Ruth and Lance, all of them coasters on a mission with one huge thing in common: their unwavering passion for this magnificent place and their determination to see that it remains this way for their children and theirs in turn, for as long as people can have a say in how it is.

'The thing about the Doubtful Sound coasters is that they are some of the most passionate and caring people I've ever met,' Al says. 'They've taken it upon themselves to be the guardians of this coastline and the beauty — well, it's everywhere. It just reinforces how important it is that we respect and nurture these wonderful corners of the world that we live in.'

He's off, back to the city, to streets and houses, people, noise, hustle and bustle. But something is different. He's had a taste of something grander and wilder that he will never forget. He'll be back.

Welcome to... the Coromandel

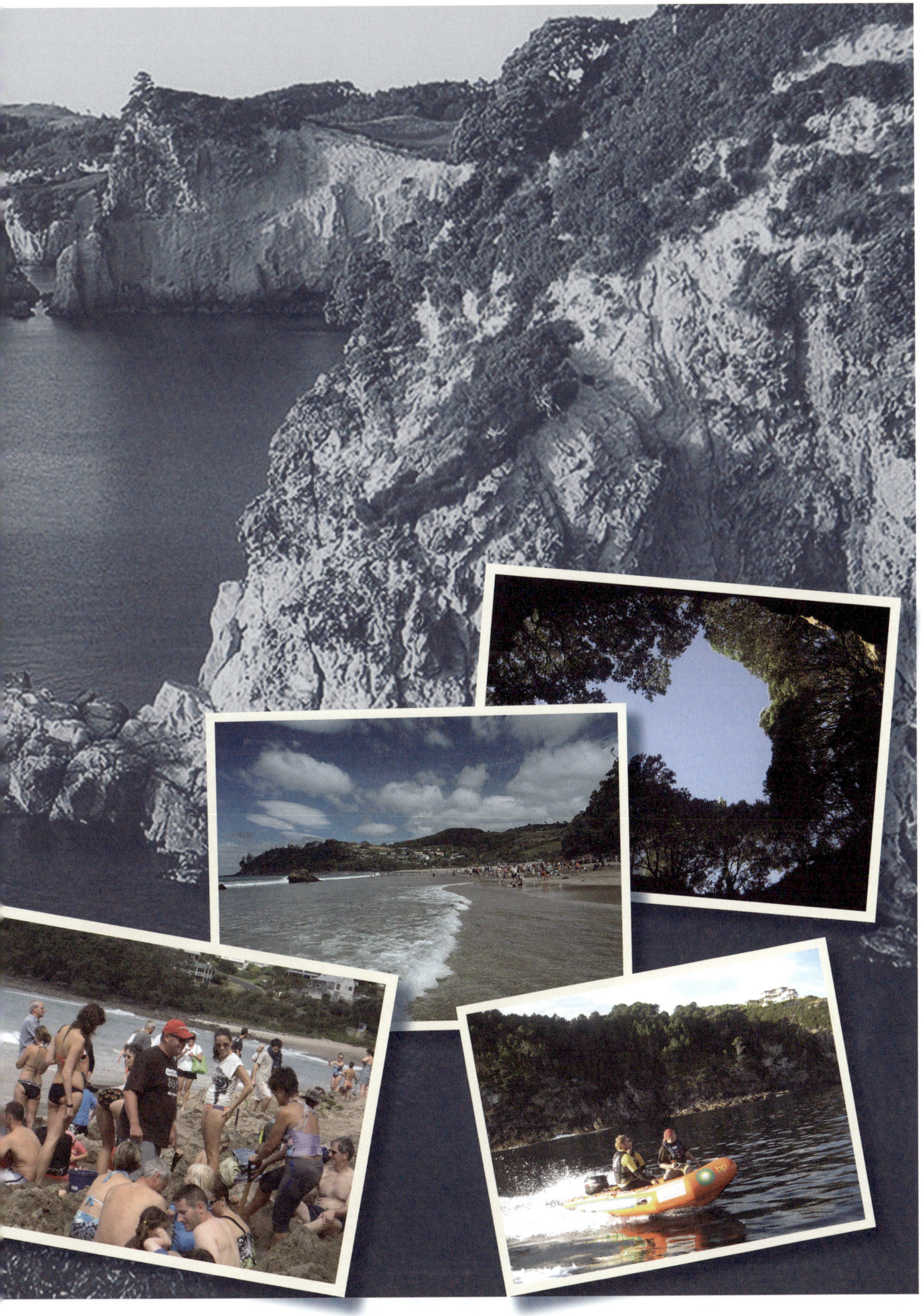

The Holiday Coast

'I'm looking forward to kicking back and having some fun on the holiday coast.' Al's standing on a knoll at the southern end of Hot Water Beach, its beautiful horseshoe bay of golden sand stretching out before him and putting a smile on his face.

His journey will take him along the ocean side of the Coromandel Peninsula, from Hot Water Beach to Ferry Landing, and will include some of the jewels in Coromandel's crown: huge coastal caves, hot pools, kayaking Cathedral Cove, and the history of Captain Cook. The peninsula is an 80-kilometre finger of land on the east coast of the upper North Island. Its western side forms the inner harbour of the Hauraki Gulf and encloses the Firth of Thames while its eastern side faces the vast Pacific Ocean. It's a stunning part of the country and because it's not far from Auckland, with ferries across the gulf to Coromandel as well as road access across the Hauraki Plains, it's always been a fairly easy place to visit. The fantastic climate, warm

Hot Water Beach to Ferry Landing

water and white sandy beaches have seen Coromandel become one of the great destinations for Kiwis wanting a bit of fun in the sun and time at the beach.

Coromandel Peninsula and Great Barrier Island to its north are the remains of over 40 ancient volcanoes. Over millions of years they have weathered and worn to form the dragon's-spine range of peaks and ridges rising as high as 900 metres, while along the coast the battering of wind and wave has left spectacular cliffs, sandy beaches, columns, caves, arches, blowholes and rocky islands.

The volcanoes have also left the region rich in minerals and it is famous for a long history of gold mining at Thames and Waihi on the base of the Peninsula. These days, the gold mines still operate while a different kind of wealth is generated from the pockets of the thousands of locals and overseas tourists who come to savour its beaches and stunning scenery and stay a while.

The Coromandel came into its own when, in the latter half of the twentieth century, camping became hugely popular — and the more laid-back the better. No matter how rich or poor, you could throw a tent in the car, pack the chillybin and the kids in the back and set

Hot Water Beach epitomises the Coromandel getaway — a sandy beach at the end of the road, backed by farmland and bush.

> Hot Water Beach is classic Coromandel: a long curve of honey-coloured sand, rimmed by the foam of waves tickling the shore and offset by intensely blue water beyond.

off for some high adventure. The invention of the caravan saw roads clogged on long weekends with these strange portable homes-away-from-home, while others opted to return year after year to the primitive cottages that northerners call 'baches' and southerners know as 'cribs'. Going to the beach became everyone's birthright.

Al's journey will take in a prime stretch of this holiday coast and we'll see what's become of this classic Kiwi pastime — hanging at the beach. And what better way to get into the swing of it than kicking back in a hot pool with a couple of hundred holidaymakers from all over the world.

A spot of Hot Water

You wouldn't know from looking at the bush-covered Coromandel range that it was once a row of active volcanoes. They stopped misbehaving millions of years ago, but even so, the hot springs that Al is headed for are a small reminder that underground, New Zealand remains massively volatile.

Hot Water Beach is classic Coromandel: a long curve of honey-coloured sand, rimmed by the foam of waves tickling the shore and offset by intensely blue water beyond. Like most New Zealand beaches, you find the usual walkers with the occasional dog, and out beyond the waves, surfers hoping for some action. Midway along the beach, however, between one and two hours either side of low tide, there's a spell of sudden activity that you won't see anywhere else. It looks a bit like a Big Dig — a treasure hunt, perhaps. Crowds of people of all ages in swimwear are making holes in the sand with spades and buckets, letting the holes fill with water and sitting and lying in them. They're the hot springs the beach is named for.

The springs are fed by a reservoir deep under the sand. Molten rock heats the water and it percolates to the surface, carrying salts such as calcium, magnesium, potassium, fluorine, bromine and silica. By the time it seeps through the sands of the beach it has cooled somewhat but can still be as hot as 64°C — enough to burn you if you aren't careful. However, if you're looking for a spa in an unconventional setting, you can dig your own and have a great soak before the incoming tide dishes out cold water to wipe the beach clean and send you packing. It's a classic New Zealand coastal tourist attraction and people come from far and wide. It's free and you don't need any fancy equipment, just something to dig your hole and a bucket to add a bit of cold now and then.

Al arrives just in time. He hires a spade for $5 from the store on the edge of the beach and joins the crowd. Each group has made its own little bath, framed by walls of sand. Hot Water Beach is firmly placed on the backpacking circuit, thanks to some very positive write-ups in guides like *Lonely Planet*, and the crowd is truly international, with a predominance of scantily clad youthful travellers. It's a remarkable scene — an empty, expansive beach punctuated by this colourful hive of activity in one spot.

'Normally I like a beach with no one on it but this is all about people from all over the world sharing a bath together — young and old — it's brilliant, beautiful and colourful,' Al says. 'I love it!'

Top: The natural hot springs that bubble through its golden sands put Hot Water Beach firmly on the tourist trail.

Above: Make room! Al joins people from all over the world for a hot soak.

The Coromandel

Gordon Pye, author, historian and local coastal character, ran the farm at Hot Water Beach and then the motor camp for over 20 years.

CAMPING THE WAY IT USED TO BE

Every morning at Hot Water Beach an elderly gentleman can be seen making his way down to the hot springs to set up the portable rescue rings. Every evening he returns to take them before heading back to the two-storeyed house on the street that bears his family name. It's Gordon Pye, who is something of a local identity and — as of relatively recently — an author, having written a book about his 82 years on the coast. It's fair to say that Gordon's seen a few changes along this stretch of the coast.

Al catches up with him and they go for a stroll. Down on the beach there's a few hundred people soaking in the springs and that's a fairly common occurrence. When Gordon was growing up, there were as few as half a dozen people per weekend.

Gordon's family have been dairy farmers in the area for over a hundred years. At first there was no vehicle access and their cows grazed right down to the beach. But in 1936 a dirt road was built and, despite its rough surface, it opened Hot Water Beach to the outside world. Slowly but surely word got out.

'It wasn't until 1941 that numbers increased,' Gordon says. People used to come from all over — mainly from the big cities: Wellington, Auckland, Hamilton.

Over the years, the beach grew organically into an informal camping ground with spaces cut in the lupins for tents and pit holes for toilets. 'People didn't mind, they thought it was rather enjoyable,' Gordon says. Everything was reasonably simple and straightforward.

'At the very beginning we didn't have any milk supplies or things like that. We'd go to the cow shed and the campers would bring their billies over and we'd fill them up. I think that was all part of the fun. It was a playground and somewhere to relax, wind down from the city life.'

As the camping spot grew, the Pyes found themselves increasingly torn away from their farming duties. So, in 1965, they formally opened a motor camp by the lagoon on the southern end of the beach. It was

> Over the years, the beach grew organically into an informal camping ground with spaces cut in the lupins for tents and pit holes for toilets. 'People didn't mind, they thought it was rather enjoyable,' Gordon says.

The motorcamp beside the lagoon at Hot Water Beach

never really something they had planned to do. 'There were motor camps springing up all over the Coromandel Peninsula, so we had to fall in line. It grew on us really... we never thought we would put up a motor camp and make money out of it,' Gordon says.

The Pyes' camping ground became hugely popular. There were 120 sites and campers returned year after year — mainly family groups, people who were happy with the laid-back atmosphere of the camp and the bay. It wasn't just the hot water that drew them, it was also the peace and quiet.

As time went on, the camping ground became more established

'It was a real family tradition those days,' Gordon says. 'During the holidays, the whole family would go to the beach. In the weekends we used to get together and share companionship with them all.'

and earned its place as a favourite amongst people who travelled from far and wide for their few weeks of summer.

'It was a real family tradition those days,' Gordon says. 'During the holidays, the whole family would go to the beach. In the weekends we used to get together and share companionship with them all. They weren't strangers — we had some campers who kept coming back for 20 years. There is a huge amount of memories for so many people around the country.'

The Pyes continued to run the camp for many years before eventually retiring and selling. It remained a campground for another 20-odd years, but at the height of the recent property boom this prime seaside land became too valuable to keep as a campground and it was closed down and turned into million-dollar sections.

Gordon and Al contemplate a bright blue sign that shouts: 'PRIVATE PROPERTY: KEEP OUT'. Beyond it is a stylish, black-clad building that's not a bach in the traditional sense of the word. However, Gordon is philosophical about it.

'Sometimes I think about what it would be like to be on our own again, but you've got to advance in time. The camp brought power into the area and good roads. We made a lot of friends and I still keep in touch with some of them. It's rather sad really but you've got to go with progress. We don't mind sharing it,' he says.

THE HUMBLE KIWI BACH

All around the perimeter of New Zealand, the story is the same. Just as once Gordon could not have imagined that one day there would be a subdivision up the hill behind him, few anticipated the changes that have occurred around the coast in the past few decades. Along with camping grounds, the Kiwi bach — which in many ways is just one step up from a tent or a caravan — has earned the dubious distinction of being placed on New Zealand's 'endangered species' list.

Almost by definition, a bach is a simple seaside structure with one — or perhaps two — bedrooms in which there are as many bunks as can decently be fitted. Derived from the word 'bachelor', it's very likely to have been built by the owner and his mates over a series of weekends or maybe years and is made from cheap or recycled materials, including lots of fibrolite. There are no floor coverings so it's easy to sweep out the sand and the furniture is old and battered. There's a smallish corrugated-iron water tank and a long-drop loo that you fear to visit at night. The shower might be inside or it might be under a kerosene tin with holes in the bottom, also out the back. There is no garden, just lawn, and maybe an outside table, maybe a barbecue. Insect screens cover windows and fly-strips hang from the door. It's affordable, it's comfortable, it's relaxed, it's casual. For many years, it was unquestionably the place to be at Christmas and on long weekends.

There are, in fact, still a lot of them about, but as time passes

Above: Once a thriving motor camp, the land has now been sold and subdivided.

Next page: The quiet side of Hot Water Beach.

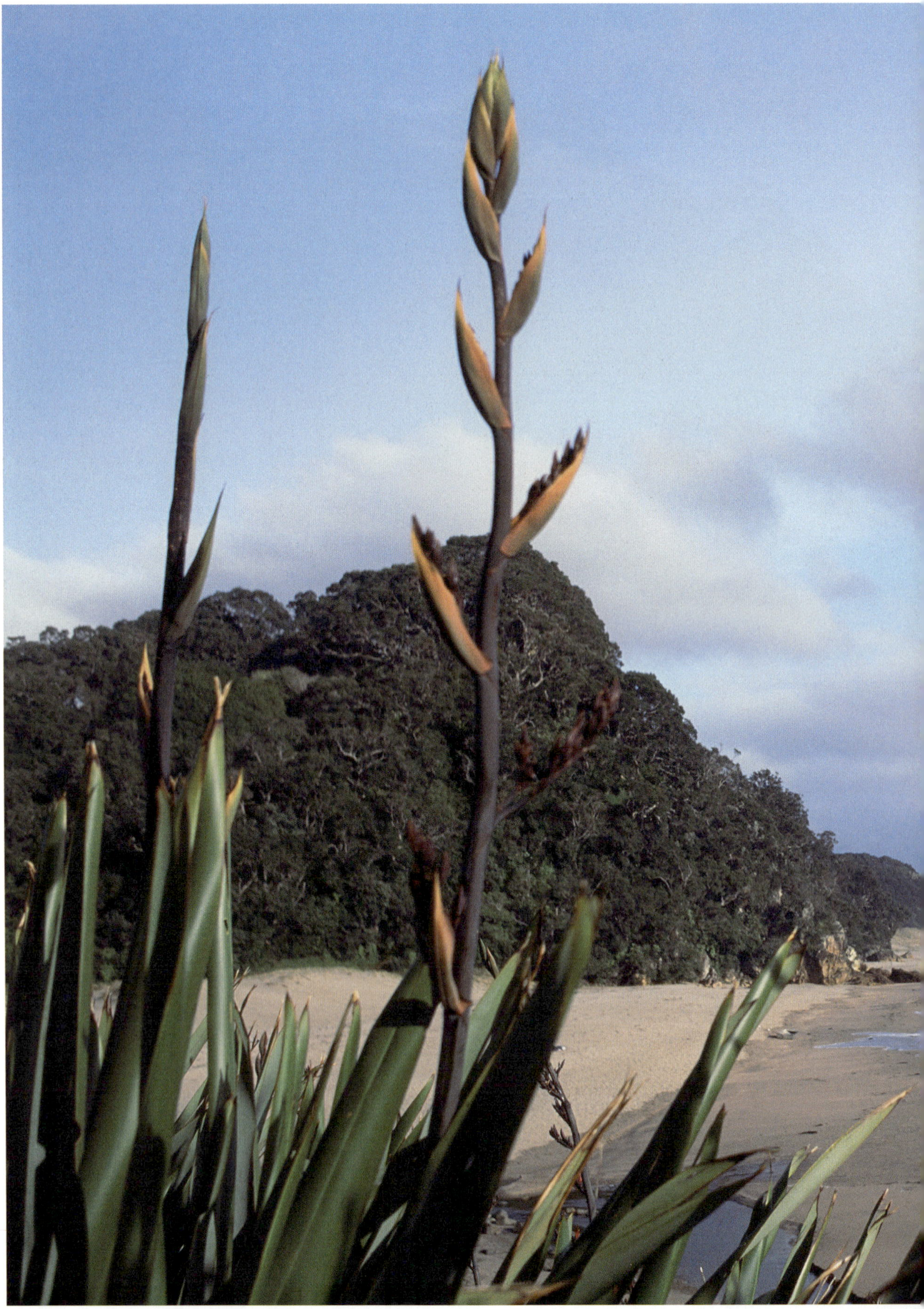

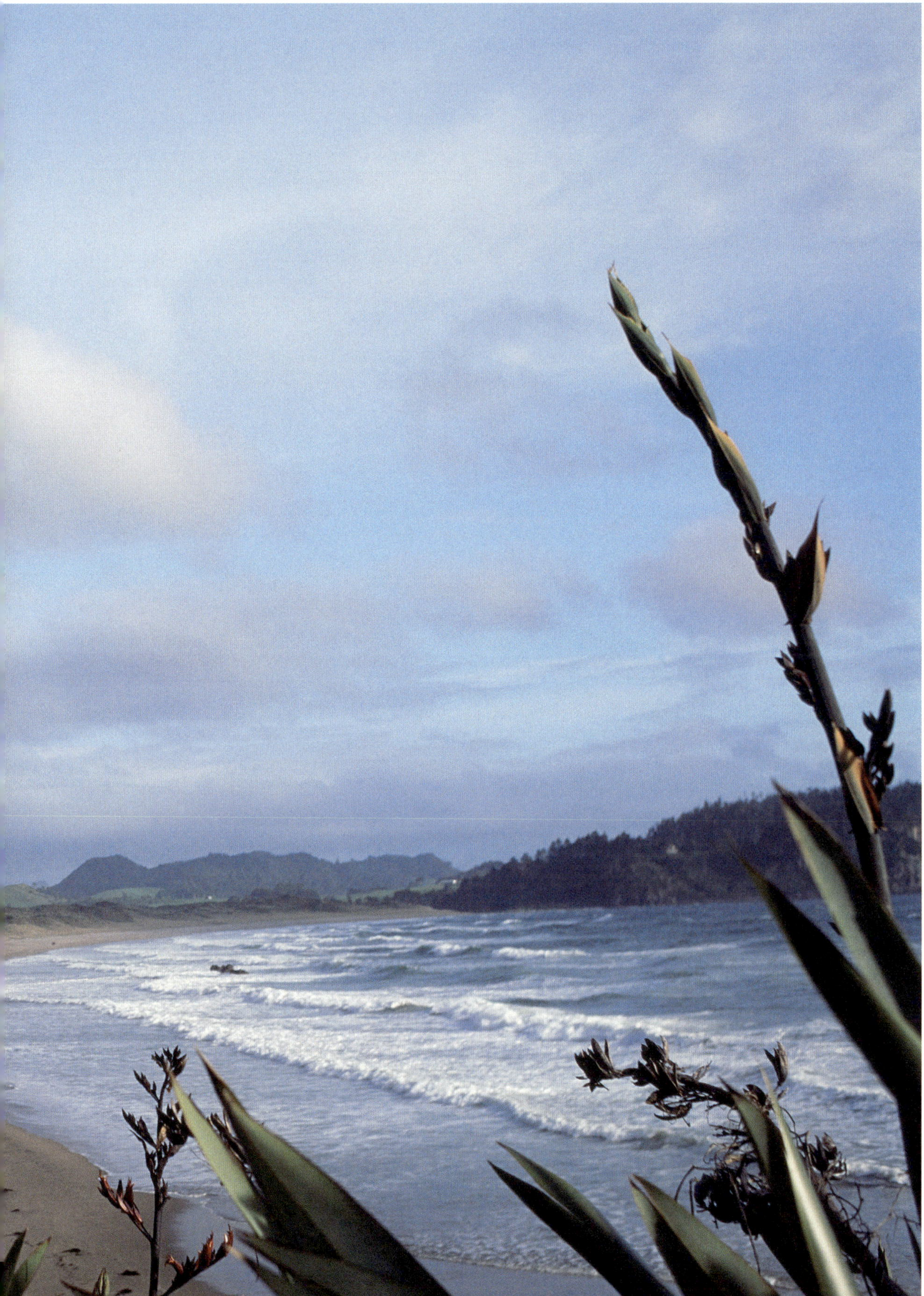

they are increasingly being replaced. Modest baches morph into headland-view-waterfront-gobbling houses while swathes of previously 'undeveloped' coastal farmland turn into canal developments, gated subdivisions, high-rise apartment blocks, reclamations, retirement villages, marinas, hotels, mini shopping centres, vineyards and restaurants. The price of coastal property has gone through the roof.

For the many of us with memories forged by long, hot and fun-filled summers, these changes are deeply concerning. It's not just the alterations and intrusions in the visual and physical landscape but also — and especially — the loss of access that comes with them. The blue sign outside property at Hot Water Beach speaks volumes: you are not welcome here. And that's a loss for everyone.

KEEPING OUT OF HOT WATER

Back down at the beach, the tide is coming in and the crowd at the homemade hot baths is packing up. Some are eyeing the green-blue waves; they fancy a quick dip after the heat of their pool, or are drawn to join the body-surfers a little further down the beach. Whatever the reason, they need to be wary because out in the water is a hidden killer that Al's next coaster knows only too well — the rip.

Local farmer Gary Hinds is president of the Hot Water Beach Lifesaving Club and he and his team of volunteers are kept busy monitoring the beach's ever-changing rips. A good summer's day will see thousands on the beach and there's a good chance that a majority are from overseas; some have never seen the ocean before and many don't know how to swim.

'So far this year we've done 55 rescues and about 11,000 preventative actions,' Gary says. 'We just go down and talk to people, let them know why they can't go swimming there.'

When Al catches up with Gary he and his fellow club members are in the distinctive yellow and orange strip outside their boatshed and HQ, an old tin shed just up from the beach. Gary and the other senior members of the club march the nippers (young members) down to the beach where their portable tower and tent is erected, providing them with a vantage point to scan the beach for any signs of trouble. This is where you'll find them every weekend and public holiday from December through to Easter, as well as every day of the summer school holidays. They mostly do it voluntarily — for them

Gary Hinds, president of the Hot Water Beach Lifesaving Club, a busy group of coasters putting it in for the community.

it's just part of being a member of a community.

Gary's one of the service's key men, exactly the sort of bloke you want looking out for you if you've suddenly found yourself in deep water. He's strong, calm and competent with a huge smile to make you feel better about being washed out to sea. The double drawcard of hot water springs and a very popular surfing beach makes running the club a busy job but as Smitty, another club stalwart, says, 'The motto goes, you're in it for life.' He and the other clubbies claim to have salt water in their veins.

Gary is not only the head lifeguard at Hot Water Beach Lifesaving Club, he's also heavily involved in training new surf lifesavers, including his own kids, Peter and Taimania, and the many foster children he and his wife Sandi have cared for over the years. Surf Lifesaving Bay of Plenty named him volunteer of the year for the 2008-2009 season and his hard work led to the doubling of the number of guards at Hot Water Beach last summer. For him, watching young people coming through training and development is the biggest buzz and possibly gave

Gary's exactly the sort of bloke you want looking out for you if you get into trouble.

Keeping an eye on the action and always wary of rips — Mike Smith, Deputy Principal of Mercury Bay Area School and volunteer lifeguard. 'The motto goes, you're in it for life.'

rise to his being named the 'Pied Piper of Hot Water Beach' by the local paper.

'The way they change and develop, the way they grow, is fantastic. You're watching our young ones coming through, from being 14-year-old lifeguards when they come in, to seeing how they mature and start dealing with people. Going down there and telling people not to swim because it's dangerous is a big thing.'

Al watches him take the youngsters through their paces. They range from barely toddlers to teenagers, all kitted out in blue lifesaving togs or wetsuits, topped off by navy and white caps. They're on the sand, raring to go: they line up in age groups to race to the water, there's lots of laughter and shouting, they grab boards and run flat out into the waves. There's a serious side to it, of course, but it's also about the joy of getting amongst the salt water, and there's not a sad face in sight.

Al joins the kids for a dash into the surf and some duck-diving. 'I can't believe it, this is so Kiwi,' he says, back on shore. 'It's just a hive of activity with all the kids down here — no Xbox, no PlayStation. They're out here learning to save lives and having fun. It's just fantastic, look at them all.'

Being a lifeguard is not all rips and rescues — it has its lighter moments as well. Gary has stories about tourists who ask when the hot water is going to be turned off for the day, and about the visitors from the Mediterranean who hung their towels over the DO NOT SWIM sign but then had to be rescued not long after. And when low tide is at night, Gary says there are some pretty riotous parties in the hot-water pools, especially when the visitors arrive by the busload ready for a good time.

The little nippers are put through their paces and Al is impressed. 'No Xbox, no PlayStation. They're out here learning to save lives and having fun.'

Above: Al hitches a lift up the coast with Gary Hinds and Logan Carter.

Below: The view looking up towards the roof of the blow hole.

Caves and cathedrals

It's time to move on and Al's found the perfect way to head up the coast — the club's IRB or inflatable rescue boat. The following morning dawns crisp and clear. Al helps Gary and fellow lifeguard Logan Carter launch the Zodiac and in no time they're skimming over a smooth, calm ocean. The first rays of sun are tinting the clouds with pink and the headland to their north casts a long blue shadow. It's cool now but there's a hot summer's day ahead.

They pass rocky headlands, jagged islets and craggy, folded, creased and fractured cliffs, all flanked by the blue of the sea and the white of breaking waves. 'Each bay is just beautiful,' Al says. 'It's got its own character.'

They round a headland and turn towards the cliff. The rock here has the texture of an aged and twisted tree, where a lava flow has solidified to create an extraordinary fingerprint-like whorl. At its base there's a tide-filled arch and a cavern beyond. Logan slows the motor and they cruise into the gloom.

They pass through a tunnel of fawn-pink walls with the cave gradually opening to the giant marine tomo known by locals as the blow hole. Sheer walls of volcanic rock rise from dark waters to a massive tree-fringed circular opening in the roof with the bright blue of the sky beyond. Their reflections ripple and twist beneath them. Al is awe-struck. 'That must be 50 metres high — this is magical, just magical!'

Out on the open water once more, they round a protruding headland before heading back in towards Hahei Beach. Logan opens the throttle to give the boat a final push in to shore and Al makes a dramatic touchdown, being impelled at speed from the rubber craft onto the sand as it bumps ashore. The sand is soft and he recovers his feet with an impressive roll and hearty chuckle. He waves them off.

'Thanks a lot, Logan,' cheers Gary. 'Go save some lives!'

KAURI FOR THE TAKING

Hahei is a small settlement nestled behind a long, brilliantly white sandy beach that faces north-east into the Pacific Ocean. The Maori name for the area, Te Whanganui a Hei, is after Hei, the master of *Te Arawa* waka, which reached the area around 1350. He and his people, Ngati Hei, lived throughout the area and occupied two pa

The stunning coastal cliffs between Hot Water Beach and Hahei are best viewed by boat.

on the southern headland of the beach, Hereheretaua and Hahei, now both part of Te Pare Historic Reserve.

In the 1840s, an Irishman named Robert Wigmore settled at Hahei with his family. Wigmore was an eccentric chap, fond of a drink but also known for his skill as a builder and cabinetmaker and for his great height — he was reputedly over two metres or 6 foot 8½ inches tall. When he constructed his homestead, now called 'Sunnyside' and still standing, opposite the general store, it was proportioned to match, with a 2.5-metre bed made by Wigmore himself — and cut down to size by a later owner.

It was kauri that first drew Wigmore to the Whitianga district. The ranges of the Coromandel Peninsula were clothed in this mighty tree and it was Wigmore's task to assess its quantity and value on behalf of a group of Scottish investors. Kauri was valued by Maori, who used its trunk for the making of waka, its timber for the shaping of tools and containers and its gum for making dye, but it was an even greater resource for European settlers, who harvested logs for their ships and built whole towns from its lumber — fences, house frames, walls, roofs, finials and even the furniture for the front parlour. And after the timber, there was the equally important, rich golden gum that was used to make varnish. Both provided the basis of the local economy, with a substantial milling operation at Ferry Landing in Mercury Bay from 1838 exporting an estimated 500 million-plus feet of wood. The mill finally shut up shop in 1922, by which time the forests were little more than a distant memory.

Wigmore and his family were quite a team. They milked cows, made cheese and butter, kept pigs, made bacon and grew their own vegetables. There was no road but that didn't slow them down — they loaded the rowboat with produce and, with Wigmore's

> Kauri was valued by Maori, who used its trunk for the making of waka, its timber for the shaping of tools and containers and its gum for making dye, but it was an even greater resource for European settlers, who harvested logs for their ships and built whole towns from its lumber.

daughters on the oars, made the 80-kilometre round trip up the coast to sell it to bush and gum camps.

In 1915 the farm was sold to the Harsant brothers, Horace and Walter, and for the next 45 years continued to produce food to sell up the coast. In 1960, a descendant, Vaughan Harsant, developed a camping ground and, in the 1970s, a subdivision. A small bach community sprouted, dedicated to the great Kiwi holiday. Today, it's a mix of a seaside getaway and a small but vibrant tourist town.

ABSOLUTE PARADISE

Mike Grogan didn't set out to run a kayaking business — it just turned out that way. He originally took a two-week placement at Hahei with Cathedral Cove Sea Kayaks while he was studying for a Diploma in Outdoor Recreation. He fell in love with the job and this part of the coast, and eventually, with a degree in sport and

Above: Hahei, a town dedicated to the great Kiwi getaway, and gateway to Cathedral Cove.

Next page: The jewel in the Coromandel crown, Cathedral Cove.

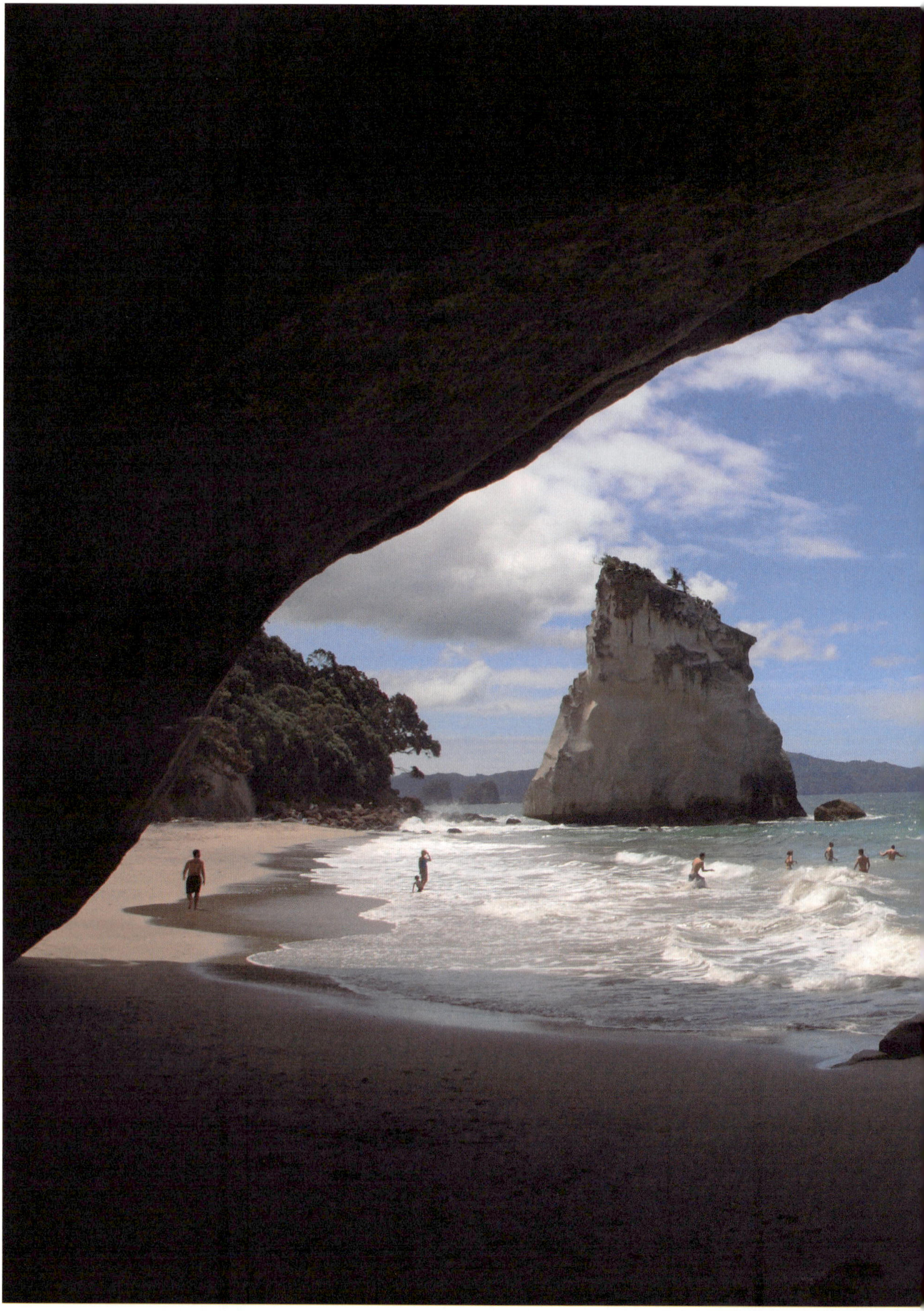

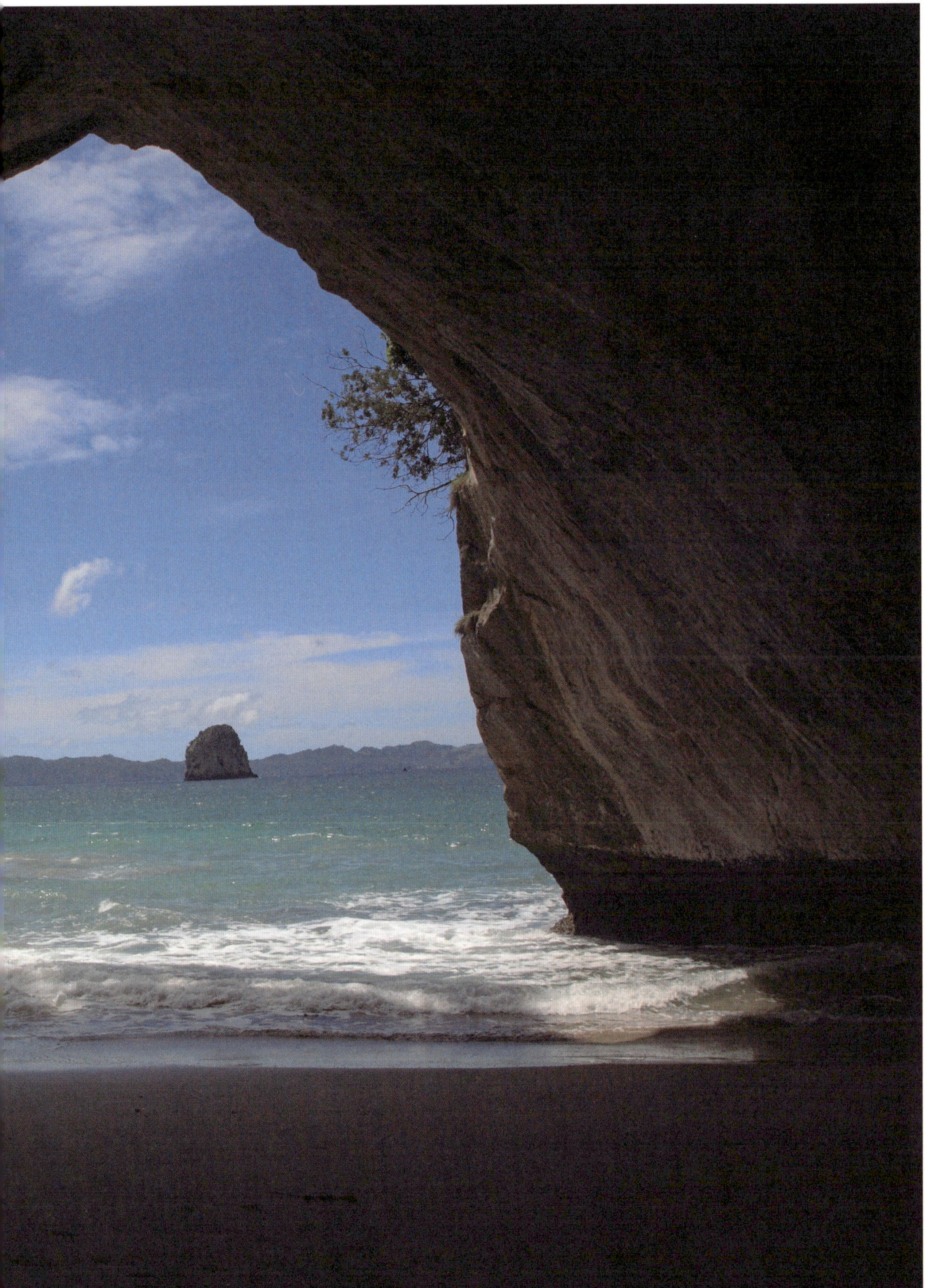

Above: Al gets a helping hand from Mike.

Below: Mike Grogan of Cathedral Kayaks didn't set out to run a kayak business — it just turned out that way.

recreation, returned to work for the business. A few years later, when it came on the market, he jumped at the opportunity to buy it. Today, it's flourishing with seven full-time tour guides on the payroll, who, during the peak season, work from sunrise to sunset. Like many operators in Hahei, Mike's main business is centred around people heading to Cathedral Cove, the stunning beach just north of the village.

There are basically two ways to get to the cove. You can go by foot on the 45-minute walking track that takes you along the top of bush-lined cliffs from Hahei Beach, or you can go by sea with Mike. Al joins him on the beach at Hahei and after a short lesson in the dos and don'ts of kayaking, they paddle up the coast, past a succession of small coves: Gemstone Bay, Stingray Bay and Mare's Leg Cove (the Mare's Leg, a rock formation, has been eroded away but the name still stands). White cliffs are crowned with dark green pohutukawa trees.

It's easy to chat out on the water, with only the sound of the wind, the soft splash of the paddles and the calls of seabirds.

'One of the things I love about the business,' Mike says, 'is that it's low impact. You have a few kayaks, you push them out, there's no noise, no smell — just the sound of the waves. It's a beautiful way to do it.'

He meets a huge range of people of different nationalities, many of whom have never seen or been in a kayak before. 'It's just a treat, a real privilege to be able to share this with them.'

Almost from the moment they leave the beach, they are paddling through the waters of Te Whanganui a Hei Marine Reserve. It is one of New Zealand's earlier marine sanctuaries, created in 1992, and has nine square kilometres of protected ocean stretching along the coast from just north-east of Hahei to Cook Bluff and then out to sea, to Mahurangi and Motukorure islands.

There is a huge diversity of environments — underwater reefs, caves, rocky platforms, arches and soft sandy areas, each with unique

Te Whanganui-a-Hei Marine Reserve creates a nursery ground for snapper and other fish.

and complex plant, crustacean, mollusc and fish communities. There are seaweed forests, sponges, anemones, corals, crayfish and starfish and a huge variety of fish including snapper, marblefish, butterfish, red moki and black angelfish. All this can be seen on a snorkelling trail that's been created with buoys to mark the different habitats.

After a short paddle, Al and Mike draw their canoes up at Cathedral Cove, a crescent of white sand that is famous for a dramatic natural rock arch formed from eroded rock in the cliffs. The cliffs take their colouring from volcanic rock, ignimbrite or 'fire-rock' — extremely hot particles of ash that have become welded together during an eruption. Although ignimbrites may be a range of colours, these ones are white. As well as the arch, dramatic columns and stacks of this rock rise from the sea.

Al is bowled over. 'What a spot. What a trip to get here! Until you actually visit these places, until you see the scale and raw beauty of it, you just don't realise how gorgeous they are. And it's free — anyone can spend time here. I bet tourists can't believe it.'

'Mate,' Mike says, 'they've got a smile like yours — from ear to ear.'

They walk through the cave. It's a photographer's dream, a spectacular frame for the scene beyond. Up to five or six couples a year make their wedding vows in this amazing place. Other people, coming down from the walking track, are also exploring the beach. The colours are intense: green-blue sea, vivid blue sky, white-grey cliffs, the contrasting green of pohutukawa, white-gold sands and a rim of white tide nibbling their feet.

'Sometimes I ask myself, "what could make this picture better?",' Mike says, and then answers himself, 'Nothing. It's all here'.

In Cook's footprints

After Cathedral Cove there's another run of bluffs before the coastline swings inland, marking the beginning of Mercury Bay, a large natural cove with plenty of the white sandy bays, beaches and harbours that the Coromandel's famous for.

Cooks Beach lies in the south-eastern corner of Mercury Bay. Here, the bluffs flatten to a lower profile and there's a long, sandy, north-facing beach with the slow-flowing tidal Purangi River at its eastern end, spreading, braiding and ambling across a small mangrove-fringed estuary. There's a neat criss-cross pattern of streets, houses and baches on the relatively level land behind the beach.

'Welcome to the Purangi,' says Sue Grierson, crossing the sand to greet Al. She and partner Rod McLaren live on the eastern bank of the river, not far from where it meets the sea. Their home is a modest cottage in the Stella Evered Memorial Park, one of the most idyllic spots in Mercury Bay.

The story goes that the park's namesake, Stella, and her husband Eric Evered, were picnicking here many moons ago when the farmer who owned the land told them to clear off. Eric was a purposeful chap and by the end of the afternoon, he had purchased the property. He and Stella built a house and, over the years, established a park-like garden with native and introduced trees.

Rod and Sue arrived on the scene about 30 years ago when Rod came to work on the farm while Susan, with a degree in horticulture, came to assist the elderly Stella. Rod met Sue and that was the end of the story — or the beginning. When Stella died, her garden was left in trust to the public so that all might enjoy it, with Sue and Rod staying on to run it.

Sue Grierson, caretaker of Stella Evered Memorial Park, lives above the slow flowing tidal Purangi River.

Sue shows Al where Cook's men were believed to have filled their water kegs.

All around this landscape, Captain James Cook left his fingerprints. He and his men, including the astronomer Charles Green, botanist Joseph Banks and a number of other scientists and artists, arrived in the bay on 3 November 1769. They had departed from England in August 1768 with two tasks ahead of them. They had accomplished their first, the observation of the passing of Venus across the face of the sun in Tahiti in June 1769, and were midway through their second: finding out if there really was — as it was thought there might be — a great Southern Continent. When Cook arrived here, he was looking for a sheltered spot where he could stock up on food, water, wood and general supplies.

Sue takes Al a small distance up the river, to show him where Cook and his men reputedly came ashore, replenished their water supplies, helped themselves to oysters and found greens to combat vitamin-C deficiency. They called the Purangi the 'oyster river' because of the shellfish they gathered there.

'Imagine living on salt crackers for months — oysters would have been pretty good after that!' Al says.

Sue shows him a small stony stream where clear water trickles from pool to pool.

'This is the spot,' she says, and for an instant, over 220 years melt away and Al can feel the presence of Cook and his men, standing under the trees, looking about, feeling the land beneath their feet and marvelling at the place they had come to.

'They would have ridden in on the longboat with some barrels,' she says. 'There are some bigger holes that they probably used to get

> **'This is the spot,' she says, and for an instant, over 220 years melt away and Al can feel the presence of Cook and his men, standing under the trees, looking about, feeling the land beneath their feet and marvelling at the place they had come to.**

the water out because there is obviously not much happening at the moment, but in winter it's so loud you can hear it coming down, and it does look beautiful, water splashing down over the rocks.'

There's a waterfall upstream that Cook's men may have visited. Pohutukawa along the riverbank that are old and magnificent today would have been just youngsters in Cook's time. The explorer noted in his diary that his crew carved initials into a tree along this part of the coast but any traces have long since disappeared beneath layers of twisted, corky bark.

The trees come into their own at Christmas time. 'The flowers are absolutely stunning,' Sue says. 'Unfortunately, they last such a brief time and even though you live here and see them every year, each time you stand there and go WOW!'

COCKLES ON THIS SIDE, PIPIS ON THE OTHER

Between the bounty from the sea and the mild growing climate, Sue and Rod can have a relatively self-sufficient lifestyle. They're both keen fishers and the results of their last foray is in the fridge in the form of a healthy-looking snapper. 'That gets me thinking,' Al says. 'Estuary . . . cockles . . .' With snapper and cockle stuffing on the menu it was simply a matter of gathering the missing ingredients.

Rod and Al head down to the Purangi with a bucket. There's a dozen or so people on the far side, heads down, bums up, with the same idea. 'Cockles on this side and pipis on the other side,' Rod says. They flush out enough shellfish for a feed and on their return trip Al picks a green bouquet from Sue's vegetable patch.

Rod and Al gather cockles just outside the front gate.

Oven-Roasted Snapper Fillets with Clam Stuffing Crust

I am sure we can all relate to times where we have promised visiting friends and family a feed of fresh fish from our 'go to' secret spot in the bay, only to return slightly embarrassed with a limited catch from a tough afternoon's fishing. It is the nature of the sport and is part of the reason we love to fish, as it's the anticipation and the unknown that drives us out onto the water time and time again. I have got smarter over the years and generally have a plan 'B' for those frustrating days when you're convinced there's no fish left in the ocean! An example is the following recipe. With only one snapper caught it was a matter of stretching the meal somehow, and as is so often the case, there will be shellfish on offer at low tide somewhere nearby. Tuatua, pipis, clams, mussels and cockles are in abundance along most of our coast. All these wonderful-tasting shellfish are a great way to bulk out a meal of fresh kaimoana when the fin fish are scarce. Cooked on the side with a little white wine, garlic and fresh herbs, or as a stuffing as I have done here, it's a great way to let everyone know how it wasn't that you're not a great fisherman, but more to the point, that you celebrate all the seafood on offer, and sustainability is always front of mind!
Serves 6

Step 1. To steam the clams

Ingredients
120 clams or cockles
1 cup white wine

Method
Scrub the clams to remove any sand or grit from shells then place in a large saucepan and pour the wine over.

Place a lid on the saucepan and cook the clams over high heat. After 4 or 5 minutes give the saucepan a shake-up. Place back on the heat for a couple more minutes. Remove the clams as they open and discard any that do not open.

Remove the clam meat from the shells, chop roughly and discard the shells. Strain the cooking liquid through a fine sieve and reserve.

Step 2. Clam Stuffing Crust

Ingredients
100g butter
3 cups finely diced leeks
½ cup finely diced celery
1½ tablespoons finely chopped garlic
1 tablespoon finely grated lemon zest
1 tablespoon finely chopped fresh thyme leaves
1 tablespoon finely chopped fresh tarragon leaves

½ cup cream
2 tablespoons lemon juice
2 cups roughly chopped stale bread
¾ cup breadcrumbs
sea salt and freshly ground black pepper
½ cup finely chopped parsley

Method
Put the butter in a medium to large saucepan and place on medium-low heat. Once melted, add the leeks, celery, garlic, lemon zest, thyme and tarragon. Sweat for 30 minutes until the vegetables are soft and cooked through.

Add 1 cup of the reserved clam cooking liquid, the cream and lemon juice. Simmer to reduce for a couple of minutes before folding in the clam meat, stale bread and breadcrumbs. Mix thoroughly, taste and season with sea salt and black pepper.

The stuffing should be moist but not too wet. You can adjust by adding more breadcrumbs or, if too dry, add a little more of the clam cooking liquid.

Fold in the parsley. Use this stuffing immediately or refrigerate until required.

Step 3. To cook and serve
1kg skinned snapper fillets (or similar white fish)
sea salt and freshly ground black pepper
cooking oil
3 lemons, halved

Method
Preheat the oven to 180°C.

Season the snapper fillets with a little sea salt and black pepper and place in an oiled ovenproof dish. Top each fillet with a liberal amount of the stuffing.

Place in the oven for 8–10 minutes until the snapper is just cooked through and the stuffing is crusty, golden and slightly crunchy. Serve on warm plates with a half lemon and a green salad on the side.

Sue, Al and Rod dig in.

Above: Crossing the Purangi River to Cooks Beach.

Below: Toby Morcom shows Al the cutting-edge technology of Cook's time, the sextant.

'I've got serious garden envy here, Susan,' Al says. 'That's gorgeous. It's so simple, so New Zealand.'

While Al prepares the meal on the table outside, they chat about the coast over a glass of wine. 'This is the Coromandel as it used to be,' Sue says. As land is subdivided and some of the old feeling of the holiday coast is lost, she and Rod, working through the trust, are doing their bit to retain that old charm. They've added a lot of young plants to the old trees already in the park. 'We've put walnut and chestnut trees in so that locals who haven't got room on their sections can come here. I think it's really important, especially with all the development that's happening, that there is a place that people can come,' she adds.

After they eat, Rod takes Al back down to the river, past the classic rope swing hanging from the old pohutukawa tree where, in summer, kids from Cooks Beach, having swum the tidal river, leap into the water. The tide is on its way in and Rod rows Al to the other side. On the lawn behind them, they see Sue waving goodbye with her blue hat.

Cook and the transit of Mercury

On the other side of the Purangi an empty Cooks Beach stretches out before them. It's a long, curving, creamy sand beach with a low grass-covered dune at its back. Al wanders along from the river mouth and not far up the beach meets his last coaster, Toby Morcom. Toby is a retired sheep farmer, an amateur historian, president of the Mercury Bay Historical Society and a mine of information about Cook and his doings. Toby has lived in the Cooks Beach area for almost 60 years. His wife Diana is a concert pianist.

Al first meets Toby on the beach. 'So this is where Captain Cook landed?' he asks. Toby points out a spot on the serene blue waters, about 150 metres west of the river mouth. 'Over there.'

By the time Cook arrived in Toby's neck of the woods, he had been down the east coast of the North Island, as far as Cape Turnagain, and back. He was seeking a safe harbour to replenish supplies but he had an even greater need: to be on land under a cloudless sky in order to observe the transit of Mercury across the sun, an event that would help him and the ship's astronomer, Charles Green, establish the *Endeavour*'s precise longitude — as Al says, 'a big deal when you're mapping an unknown coastline'.

Toby pulls a sextant out of its carry case and peers through the eyepiece in search of the horizon. In Cook's day this was one of the measuring instruments that everything depended on. 'The exercise needed quality telescopes, an accurate clock and cutting-edge technology of the time — a sextant,' Toby says. Using the sextant, the navigators would line up the horizon with the position of the sun. At that moment the reading was taken that determined longitude or distance from Greenwich, England. 'But the timing had to be absolutely precise,' says Toby. 'A few seconds out would translate to an error of two or three miles.'

Al is impressed. 'I can just imagine Cook pulling that out and all the crew thinking this would have been the Apple Mac of the time!'

Above: Lonely Bay and Cooks Beach from Shakespeare Cliffs.

Next page: Al takes time out at Flaxmill Bay.

The Coromandel 201

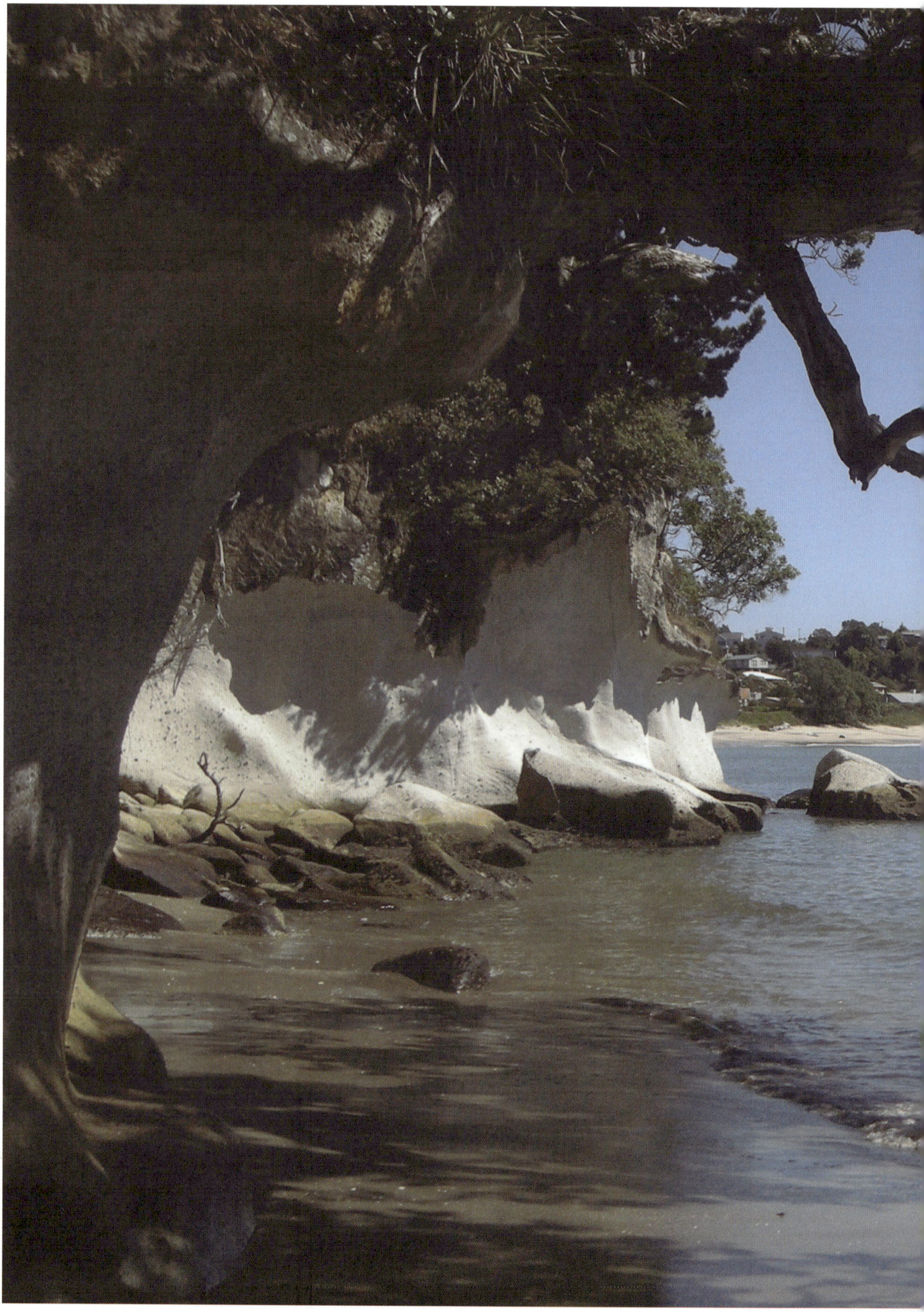

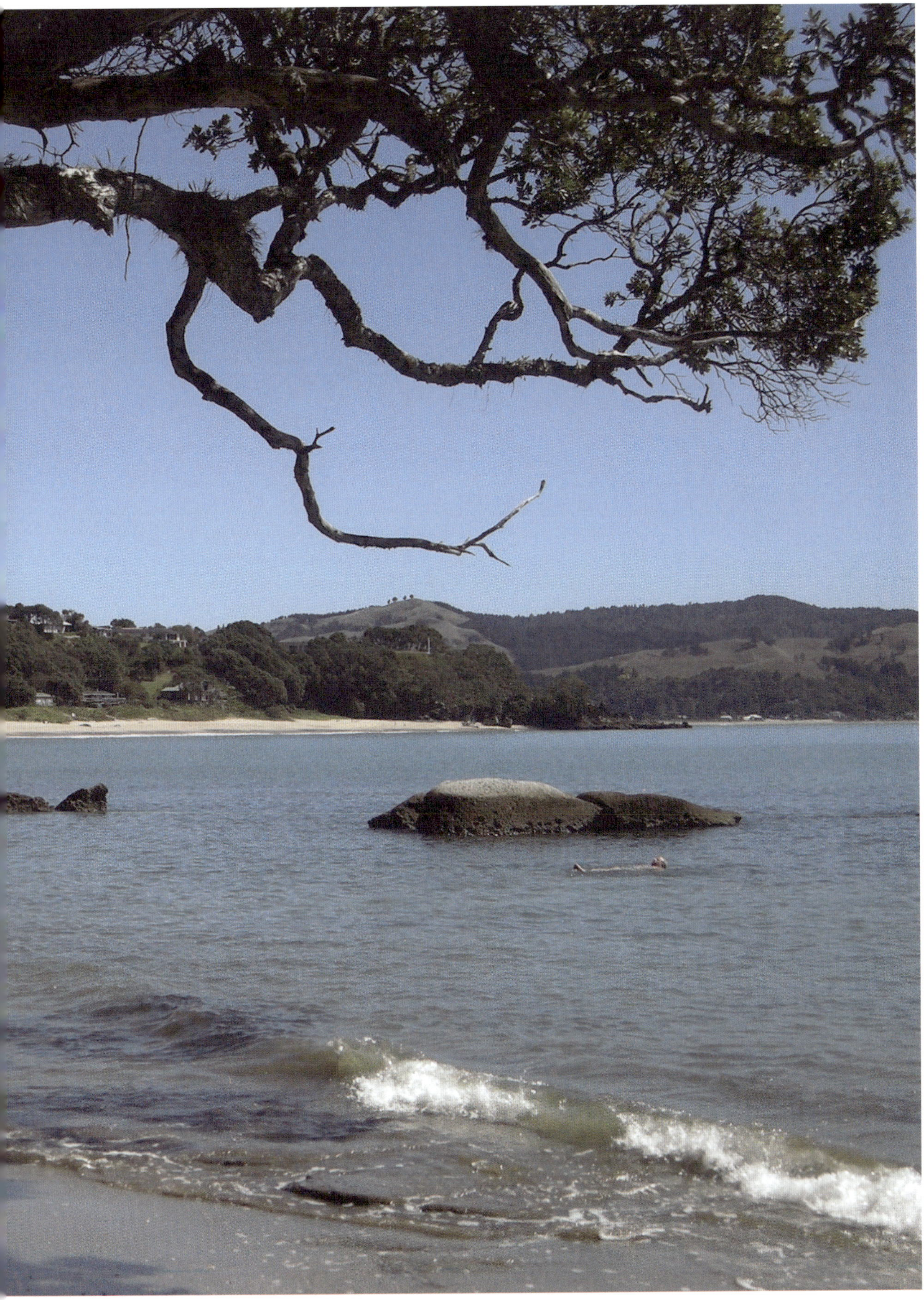

he says. 'He was working out where everything was — it's an amazing piece of equipment.'

It all went according to plan for Cook and Green: the skies over Mercury Bay were clear and the sun and horizon were both visible. A successful sighting was made and the bay was carefully charted before the *Endeavour* moved on. They had been in the bay for 11 days.

Today a plaque placed on a cairn on the beach by the Historic Places Trust announces the spot where the reading was made. 'Mercury Bay. Near this spot on 10 November 1769 James Cook and Charles Green observed the transit of Mercury to determine the longitude of the bay.'

CLASSIC AND FUNCTIONAL

Al and Toby continue north along the beach. With its safe swimming, settled weather, walking tracks, good fishing and boating from the ramp in the Purangi River estuary, Cooks Beach has been a popular destination ever since Kiwis started to discover the charms of the Coromandel. The first wave of baches went up around the same time that Gordon and Lois Pye opened their camping ground at Hot Water Beach. Many are still here but as they pass from hand to hand they are being modernised and often replaced. And behind them more farmland is being zoned into residential areas almost every year. It's changed a lot in Toby's time.

'The beach had three baches on it and all the hills were bare. I planted a lot of those trees up there on the skyline. This part of it had been surveyed and opened up and for quite a few years they were building baches. There was one little wooden bridge over the back there and people came over that and drove across the beach in one direct line until the road was formed.'

Amongst the line of older baches Al picks his favourite, a small white-painted cottage with an enclosed verandah running across the front. 'It's just classic and functional and I bet it's full of great coastal memories,' he says. 'What I love about these places is that the baches are all different shapes and sizes. I can just imagine them filled with families who come back time and time again, sharing this piece of paradise and creating memories year after year. Even if the architecture changes, you can't change that.'

The story of the bach is the story of the Coromandel, really. Simple and uncluttered, under pressure from the march of progress, but still standing. The holiday coast clings to that great Kiwi tradition. It's still a place to get away to, where memories of long, hot summers are made and, like the bays and beaches, stretch on and on forever.

BACK TO THE BEATEN TRACK

It's time to leave this lovely piece of coastline. Across the hills east of Cooks Beach, past Shakespeare Cliff Scenic and Historic Reserve, where there are more walkways, views across Mercury Bay, and a track to the beautiful Lonely Bay; past Flaxmill Bay where a mill on the stream was still being used until 1907, the road ends at Ferry Landing — the oldest stone jetty still used for its original purpose in Australasia and built in 1840. They're on the eastern head of the Whitianga harbour, looking across the water at the town.

The two-minute ferry ride to Whitianga from here will save you the 45 minutes driving around the head of the harbour. For Al it's a perfect end to his journey and while he waits for the boat he reflects on what he's seen. The holiday coast has lived up to its reputation. These days it's not just New Zealanders enjoying this classic beach holiday, it's people from all over the world, sharing what has become an important part of Kiwi culture — the ability to unwind, relax and spend precious time with friends and family.

Al heads back to the beaten track on the ferry to Whitianga.

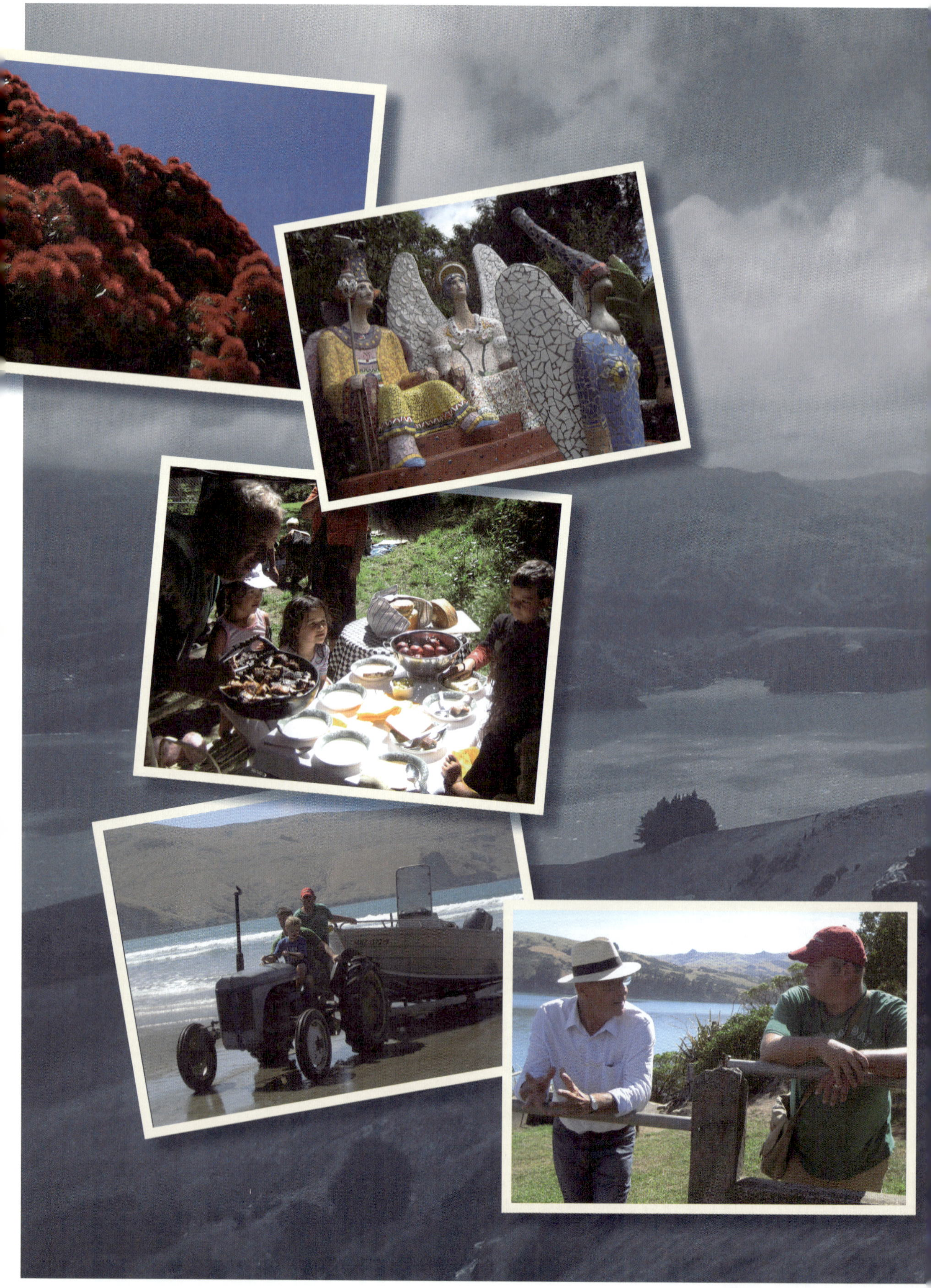

Welcome to...

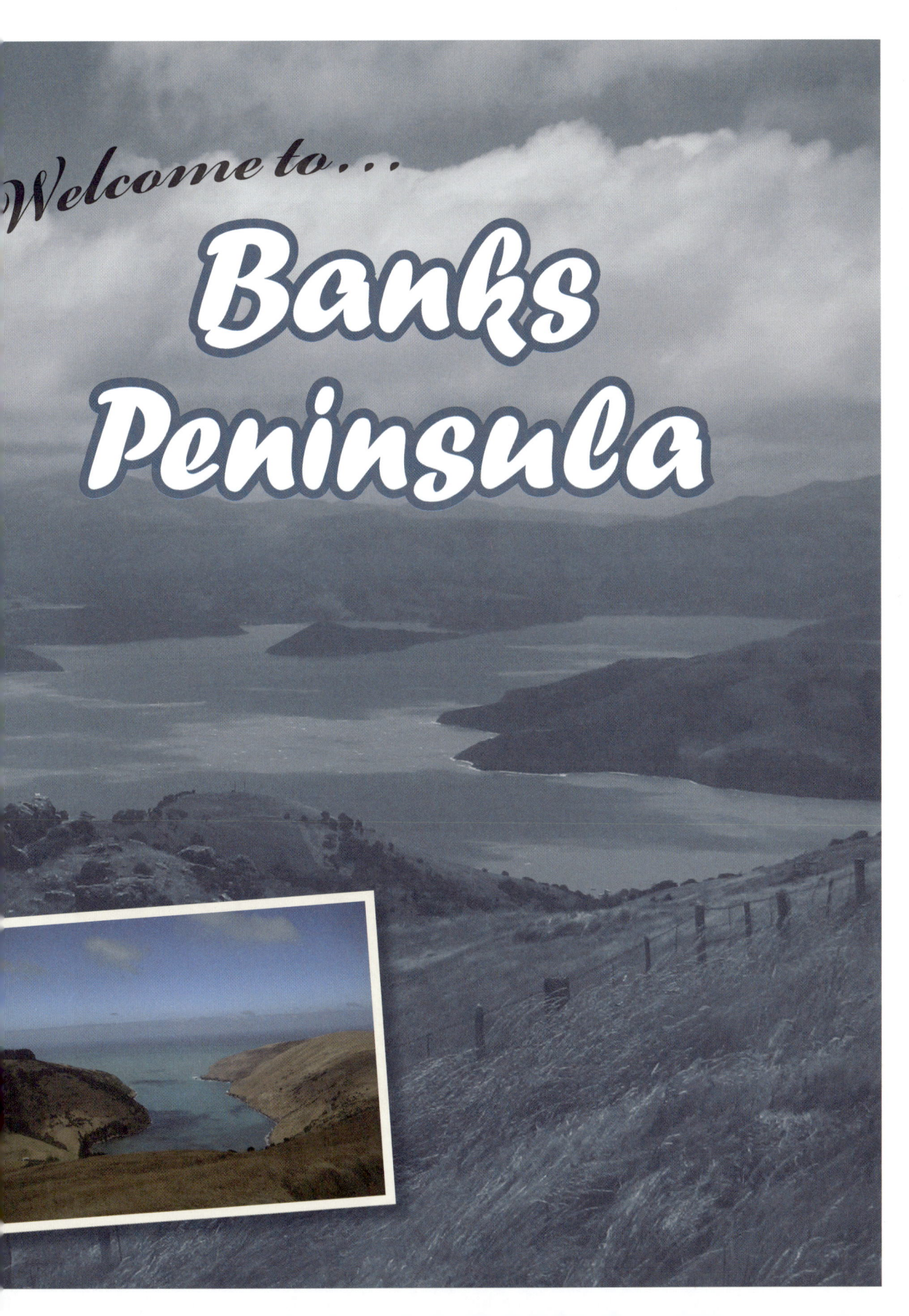

Banks Peninsula

The Wild Side

The southern coast is known to residents of Banks Peninsula as 'the wild side' because it bears the brunt of the powerful storms that stalk up the east coast of the South Island from the Southern Ocean.

It can be quite calm on the northern side — the waters of Pigeon Bay with barely a ripple, and Diamond Harbour living up to its name — while on the wild side, great breakers are piling onto the rocks and the wind is 'muscling up a bay', as local writer Fiona Farrell puts it in a poem, 'tossing birds over its shoulders'. So that's where we're

Above: The south coast of Banks Peninsula from Birdlings Flat.

Previous page: Akaroa harbour.

Birdlings Flat to Le Bons Bay

208 Coasters

heading: from Te Roto o Wairewa (Lake Forsyth) at the northern end of Kaitorete Spit where the local iwi is doing great things in restoring the traditional food resources, over and across to Akaroa, with its unique past and its status as one of the tantalising what-ifs of New Zealand history; up and over again to Flea Bay, where a wildlife sanctuary preserves the habitat for a number of marine species, to Stony Bay, where a little museum commemorates the way of life of the European settlers; on to Otanerito, from where Al is picked up by boat for the final run of the journey around the eastern reaches of the Peninsula to Le Bons Bay, with the chance to pick up a cray or two and perhaps a blue cod along the way.

Te Kaio, Tumbledown Bay on the wild south side of Banks Peninsula.

Al and Robin Wybrow looking out over Kaitorete Spit at the end of Te Roto o Wairewa (Lake Forsyth).

And of course, as we go, we'll have an eye out for the people who live along this wild coast. What you notice is that Banks Peninsula has the power to draw people back, and to make them stay. So many of those you meet living along there seem to have fallen in love with it at first sight. And as much as the grandeur of the land- and seascape, it's the history of the place. If anything distinguishes the coasters of Banks Peninsula, it's a consciousness of their part in the pageant of history, and their obligations to it. You don't hear much talk of ownership as you make your way along here. You get more of a sense of stewardship.

A highway for Ngai Tahu

Al's approach to Banks Peninsula is along Kaitorete Spit, the 28-kilometre shingle spit that separates Te Waihora (Lake Ellesmere) and Te Roto o Wairewa (Lake Forsyth) from the sea. It's a magic walk: the Pacific sucks and heaves at the seaward side, rattling stones smoothed by the ages to and fro in a hypnotic rhythm. You can pick up semiprecious stones here. You can also spot lizards of various kinds, and katipo spiders, if you know where to look, and the area is the haunt of a rare, flightless moth. Kaitorete has the last large natural remnants in Canterbury of the low-growing coastal sedge pingao, prized by Ngai Tahu weavers for its bright orange foliage. The spit is a favourite surfcasting spot for Christchurch and Banks Peninsula anglers, who'll usually get amongst the kahawai and gurnard on their day.

When you walk Kaitorete, you're also treading what was the main highway to Banks Peninsula for the Ngai Tahu people, as Al's first coaster, Robin Wybrow, explains.

Rob is chairman of the Wairewa Runanga, and has a wealth of knowledge and a strong spiritual connection to the area. He tells Al that the Waitaha lit the first fires of occupation on Te Wai Pounamu — the South Island — arriving in the mighty waka Uruao, and led by Rakaihautu who was so taken by the beauty of Banks Peninsula that he decided to stay. In his honour and in recognition of the abundance of food resources the people named the peninsula Te Pataka o Rakaihautu — the great storehouse of Rakaihautu.

Moa were plentiful here in the early days of human habitation, and the forests that blanketed the steep slopes were rich in birdlife; fur seals bred on the rocky margins, and there were seabirds, fish and shellfish aplenty, too.

Perhaps the single most important resource was the tuna (eel) fishery provided by the pair of lakes at the base of the peninsula, Te Waihora and Te Wairewa. The tuna fishery was important, because it was seasonal, predictable and manageable, permitting those who knew how to exploit it to settle in the area rather than pursue the hunting-gathering lifestyle of the moa-hunters.

Robin Wybrow, chairman of the Wairewa Runanga, who have a vision for the future of their lake, Te Roto o Wairewa.

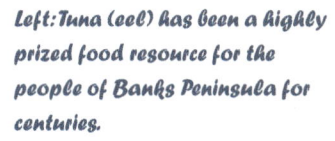

Left: Tuna (eel) has been a highly prized food resource for the people of Banks Peninsula for centuries.

Next page: Lake Forsyth at dawn looking over Birdlings Flat and Kaitorete Spit.

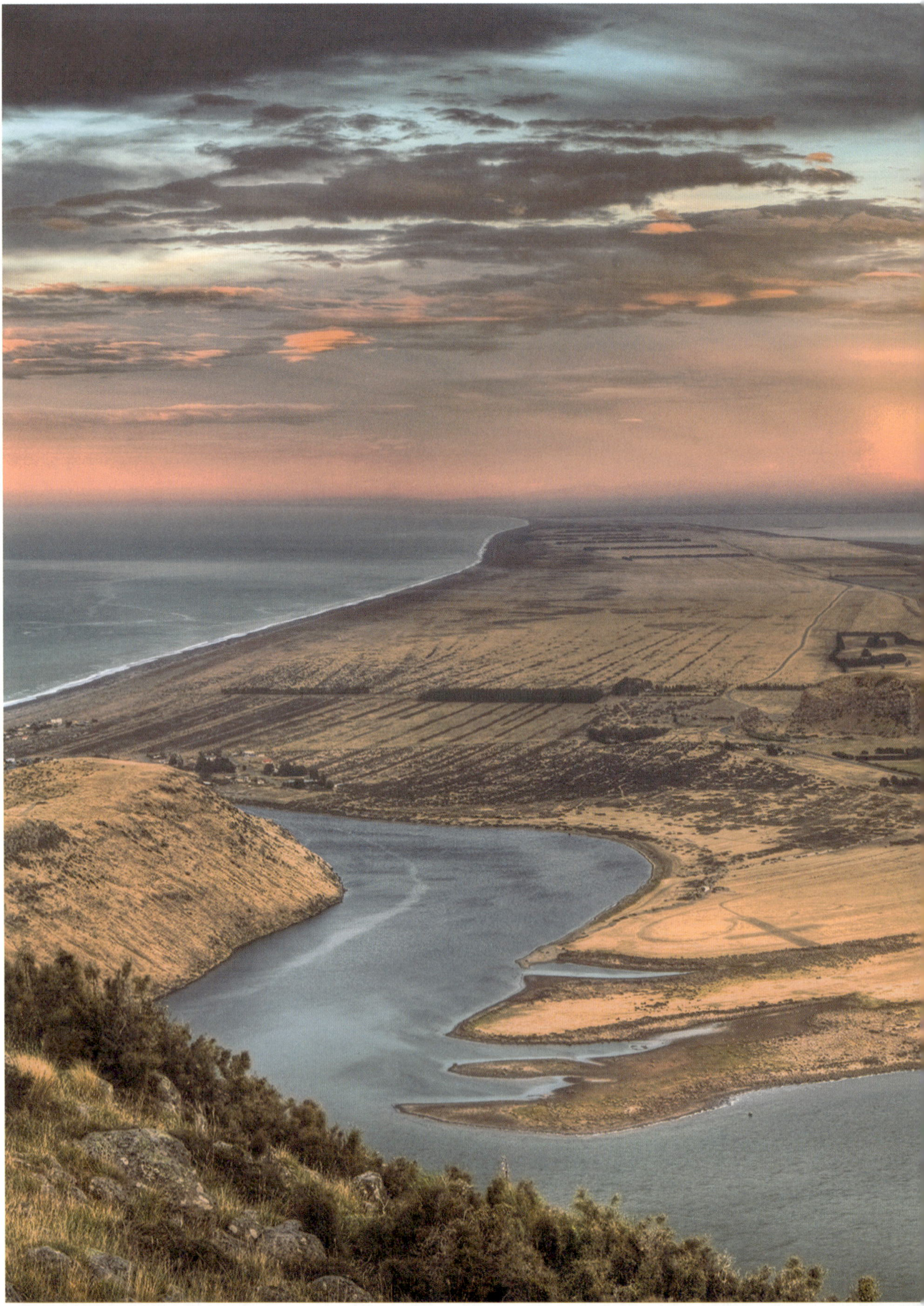

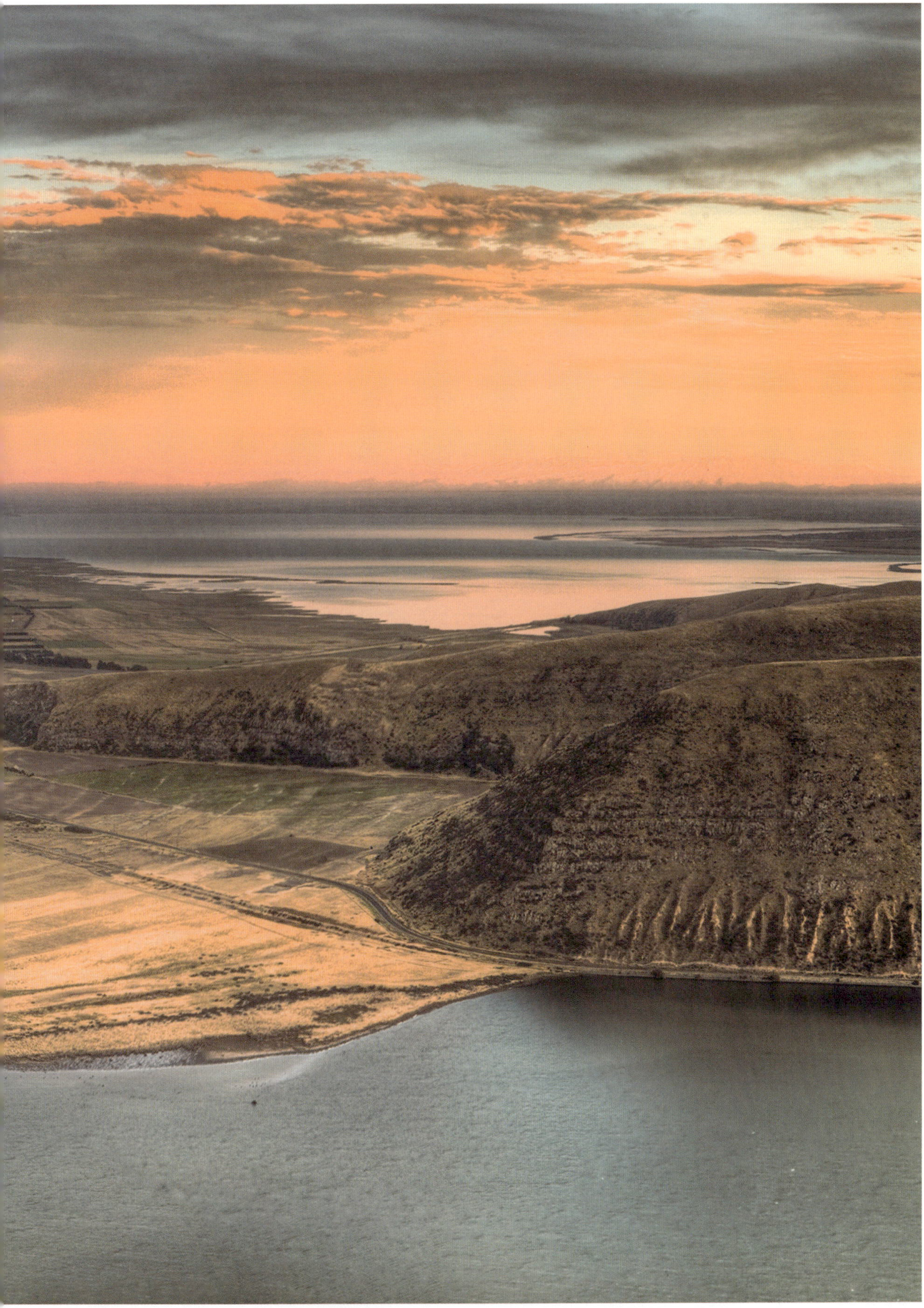

'If you think of the lake as the heartbeat or the takiwa of the area, the tuna were the life-force of the area, the lifeblood,' Rob tells Al.

The bounty of the lakes were gifts of the atua, and, since the ancient times of the Waitaha tribe's occupation of the vicinity, the gathering of food has been accompanied by elaborate and highly sacred rituals intended to keep the atua sweet — this is the concept of mahinga kai (literally, 'working the food'), which interweaves the cultural and technical aspects of food gathering with the resource itself.

REFLECTED IN THE WATERS

Within Rob Wybrow's turangawaewae (place of standing) is Matahapuka, close to the present-day settlement of Poranui or Birdlings Flat, which was named after William Birdling, the first European to farm in the area. If you stand at Birdlings Flat on a

Sowing grass seed. After the trees were felled, or burned, farming became the mainstay of the economy.

calm day, the high hills of Banks Peninsula are reflected in the still waters of Te Roto o Wairewa. The hills are pretty bare these days, green in the winter and spring, and sere and brown in the hotter months, although that wasn't always so. They were heavily covered with podocarp forest — predominantly matai, rimu, totara and kahikatea — but with the arrival of the Europeans, the clear felling began. A sawmill settlement was established at Little River, a short distance up the valley, to carry timber back to the growing town of Christchurch. Most of the Garden City's gracious colonial homes were built with Banks Peninsula's native timber. Where the trees were too inaccessible or where the difficulties in transporting them to the mills were simply too great, the forest was burned to make way for pasture and farming became the mainstay of the economy.

For a spell, starting in the late 1800s there was a boom in 'cocksfooting' — growing and harvesting the seed from a perennial pasture grass named cocksfoot. By 1905, 85 per cent of the pasture grown in the North Island was sourced from Banks Peninsula. The hillsides were rippling with seedheads until a virus in the 1930s put an end to it. By this time another boom was underway. The first refrigerated cargo shipment to the United Kingdom in 1881 opened up the world market for dairy products, and at one time no fewer than nine cheese factories operated across the Peninsula, producing both cheese and butter for export. One by one, these closed as transport difficulties on the Peninsula's steep country made them uneconomic. Until then few sheep were run on the Peninsula, but with the 'scientific' improvement of pasture and addition of superphosphate and other artificial fertilisers from the 1920s, sheep farming finally found its place.

All of these changes were reflected in the waters of Te Roto o Wairewa, and not just on the surface. First, the erosion of the hillsides newly cleared of forest brought a massive influx of silt to the lake — a metre and a half, according to core sample studies of the lake bed commissioned by Wairewa. 'Originally the lake was a hapua, a lagoon or an estuary open to the sea. But that changed when the build-up of alluvial gravel closed off the lake,' explains Rob.

Wairewa can be translated as rising waters, its name a direct reference to the tides swelling the estuary levels twice a day. In pre-European times, it had been possible to paddle a waka from the sea, along the channel through the shingle bank at Birdlings Flat and right into the lake. After the first impact of deforestation, this link with

Harvesting cocksfoot on Banks Peninsula in 1910.

Rob shows Al how the spit has closed Te Roto o Wairewa off from the sea.

the sea rapidly became choked. The removal of forests throughout the region meant more gravel than usual entered the river systems through erosion and was transported up the coast and deposited where the estuary was open to the sea. As a result, Kaitorete Spit was no longer a spit but became a barrier beach, and the lake sediment could no longer escape.

The silt alone would have been enough to alter the ecological balance of Wairewa's waters. But the intensification of farming since the 1920s, and the nitrogen-rich run-off from fertiliser use and the dung and urine of livestock, have had a catastrophic effect. 'Eutrophication' — literally, the 'creation of perfect conditions' — has occurred, and while this sounds like a good thing, it's only good if you're a member of a certain group of algae. The nutrient-enriched waters sustain explosive population growth — algal blooms — that consume much of the oxygen otherwise available to other organisms, so that little besides the algae can survive, pulling the rug out from under the entire foodchain. And once the algae die, the lake is all but void of life. In recent times, Wairewa, like the neighbouring Lake Waihora and numerous other New Zealand inland waterways, has been pushed to the brink.

EVERY ACTION HAS A REACTION

Each autumn, when the king tides wash on the seaward side, some of the tuna of Te Roto o Wairewa make their way across Kaitorete to the sea, where they migrate thousands of kilometres to breeding grounds that are believed to be in the vicinity of Tonga.

After spawning, the larvae float on ocean currents and eventually some find their way back to maintain the lake population. But since the formation of a beach barrier at Kaitorete, the population cannot be fully replenished, and it has sharply declined. Nor, once the beach barrier had closed over, could inanga (whitebait), formerly plentiful in their season, make their annual run into the lake and its tributary streams, and with their numbers severely depleted, birdlife has also suffered. Rakaihautu's storehouse has been all but bare of late.

In pre-European times the lake's outlet used to be a two-way street, with the nutrients that naturally flowed from the lake creating a fertile zone in the Canterbury Bight. These waters were exploited by southern right whales, and humpback whales making their migration from feeding grounds in Antarctic waters to their breeding grounds in the north. It's no coincidence that some of the country's earliest whaling stations were established along Banks Peninsula's southern coast.

'Every action has a reaction,' Rob explains.

The slow and steady demise of the foodchain, coupled with algal blooms and their virulent toxins, has seen the annual tuna heke — the harvest — and traditional practices of capture, preservation and manaaki, now in danger of being lost forever.

'So nothing's been done about all this for nearly 200 years?' Al asks.

'Well, no constructive solution's been put forward since it all started in the 1880s,' nods Rob. 'Until now.'

WHITEBAIT TO WHALES

Under the shadow of the cliffs at the eastern end of Kaitorete, Rob points to the groyne that has recently been constructed in an effort to open a channel between the ocean and Wairewa in the hope that the natural action of the tides will help the lake to 'breathe'. The groyne and canal are, he explains, a 'bioengineering' solution to the lake's present-day troubles and, he hopes, the salvation of the tuna fishery and a plank in the restoration of the wider ecology, too.

Ngai Tahu, Rob's people, have been managing the tuna fishery of Wairewa and Waihora since before the arrival of Europeans. They

Above: Tuna (eel) has always been an important food source for the people of Lake Forsyth.

Below: The constructed canal linking Te Roto o Wairewa to the sea.

have sole rights to it. Tuna were harvested annually by carving channels in the shingle of Kaitorete that led to shallow pools, from which they could be gaffed. Once cleaned and gutted, the tuna were hung on a wooden rack called a whata, dried, and smoked, so that they could either be stored against the lean, hungry months of winter, or traded up and down the coast for other kai and commodities. The heke still happens, but the fishery is only just hanging on. These days Te Roto o Wairewa is so severely degraded that a couple of years ago experts estimated the tuna fishery here had only 10 years left to live, making remedial action on the state of the lake essential.

The effort to restore Wairewa and to renovate the tuna fishery is all part of an initiative to revitalise mahinga kai in the area, largely driven by the Wairewa Runanga but involving other organisations, such as the Ministry of Agriculture and Fisheries, the Department of Conservation, the Canterbury Regional Council, and various consultants. The first step of the project — the construction of the half-kilometre-long canal and groyne — was completed in 2009 but it is a work in progress. The next stage will be the building of a longer canal linking Te Wairewa to the much larger Te Waihora, in the hope that the combined flows will have the energy to sweep away gravel build-up at the end of Kaitorete Spit, creating permanent pathways for whitebait, eels, flounder, sea trout and other fish to migrate to and from the ocean. It's hoped the permanent lake opening will also allow nutrient-rich waters from the lakes to flow back to the sea and

The homestead that was gifted to the Wairewa Runanga in 2006 by James Winston Wright. Rob says, 'It was a magnificent gesture and one we'll never forget.'

Sharing the kai: home-grown potatoes, freshly baked bread and tuna from the lake.

nourish the fauna that live there, restoring the traditional fisheries.

The groyne project is termed 'Whitebait to Whales', in recognition of the importance of the link between Wairewa and the sea to the wider regional foodchain, and of the regional foodchain to the wellbeing of the people, too.

'When those whales return,' Rob says, pointing out to sea, 'we'll know that we've succeeded.'

SHARING THE KAI

Rob and his family live on a hill overlooking Te Roto o Wairewa, Matahapuka and Kaitorete, bending into the misty distance to the south. It's a view his people have commanded since Ngai Tahu settled the area in the fifteenth century.

The restoration of Te Roto o Wairewa is part of a larger programme Rob's Runanga has underway, intended to transform the lake and their land into a Mahinga Kai Cultural Park. The Runanga controls 1100 acres (450 hectares) of land between Magnet and Tumbledown bays, thanks to the bequest of Pakeha farmer James Winston Wright, who gifted his farm to Wairewa Rununga in 2006.

'It was a magnificent gesture, and one we'll never forget,' Rob says. 'He really liked what we were trying to do with the lake, plus the fact he could understand our spiritual connection. He had a very strong spiritual connection to the land himself, and he decided that we would be a good bet.'

As you stand at the homestead looking down to the rugged coast, you can't help but be aware that the land is priceless, with a value immeasurably beyond what it might yield when drenched in superphosphate and stocked to the max. Set amongst lush organic gardens of heirloom kumara, corn and potatoes, along with fruit trees, today the old farmhouse is now the Wairewa Project's base.

Cooling off at Tumbledown Bay.

Rob's wife, Ngaire, explains that the land is being used to experiment with the cultivation of traditional crops — Banks Peninsula is at the southern limit of the range of kumara, and its cultivation here is only really possible because of the area's benign microclimate.

'These are the ancient kumara that haven't been planted here for around 4–500 years,' Ngaire tells Al. There are also some of the early varieties of potato that would have been a Ngai Tahu staple. The land is also being used to plant the seed in the consciousness of young people, both from Ngai Tahu and from outside, providing hands-on education in both traditional and organic farming techniques.

'It's about manaaki — manaaki being nurturing and caring of,' says Maatakiwi Wakefield, who is weeding amongst the flourishing root crops with a group of youngsters. 'If we manaaki Papatuanuku, she gives us sustenance for our body, which enables us to manaaki

'In everybody's busy lives it's great to hang out under the tree, great kai, good laughs and you can go back to your job and whatever it is you do and know that you could always come back.'

our manuhiri, manaaki our tamariki, manaaki our kaumatua and of course manaaki ourselves.'

Rob and Ngaire's vision of the Mahinga Kai Cultural Park is to create a place that attracts the young people back to the land. 'In everybody's busy lives it's great to hang out under the tree, great kai, good laughs and you can go back to your job and whatever it is you do and know that you could always come back,' says Ngaire as she kneads the bread for lunch. 'Ultimately this land will never be sold. The Runanga and their members have a duty to the kaitiaki; there's no ownership, it belongs to the people.'

Al is invited to share a traditional meal of tuna and potatoes. It's easy to sense the pride that Rob, Ngaire and their whanau feel as they walk and work the land, overlooking the rugged coastline — the wild side — below. Sit in the shade of a tree with the cicadas droning overhead and taste locally grown and gathered kai — riches from the Pataka of Rakaihautu — and there's a sense of balance and continuity.

Al with Ngaire and Maatakiwi at Tumbledown Bay.

'We have a saying within Ngai Tahu,' Maatakiwi says, 'which is: "Mō tātou, ā, mō kā uri ā muri ake nei. For us more importantly for the generations to follow. For us, more importantly, for the generations to follow." That's what we'd like to think we're concerned with here.'

After lunch Al ventures down to the beach with Rob's whanau. Te Kaio (Tumbledown Bay), beneath the homestead, is just one of the many gorgeous, sandy bays nestled between the ridges of the ancient lava flows that Banks Peninsula thrusts into the Pacific.

Heaped up high

The great James Cook made few cartographical errors in his voyages of exploration in New Zealand waters. He overlooked Wellington harbour (surprisingly easy to do), he depicted Stewart Island as a peninsula of the South Island, and he mistook what we now know as Banks Peninsula for an island. He named it on 17 February 1770, in honour of Joseph Banks, an aristocrat who had joined Cook's first voyage as a botanist.

Had he only sailed by a couple of million years earlier, Cook would have got it right, as Banks Peninsula began life as an island. The result of numerous basalt-charged volcanic eruptions from about 12 million to eight million years ago, two large, overlapping

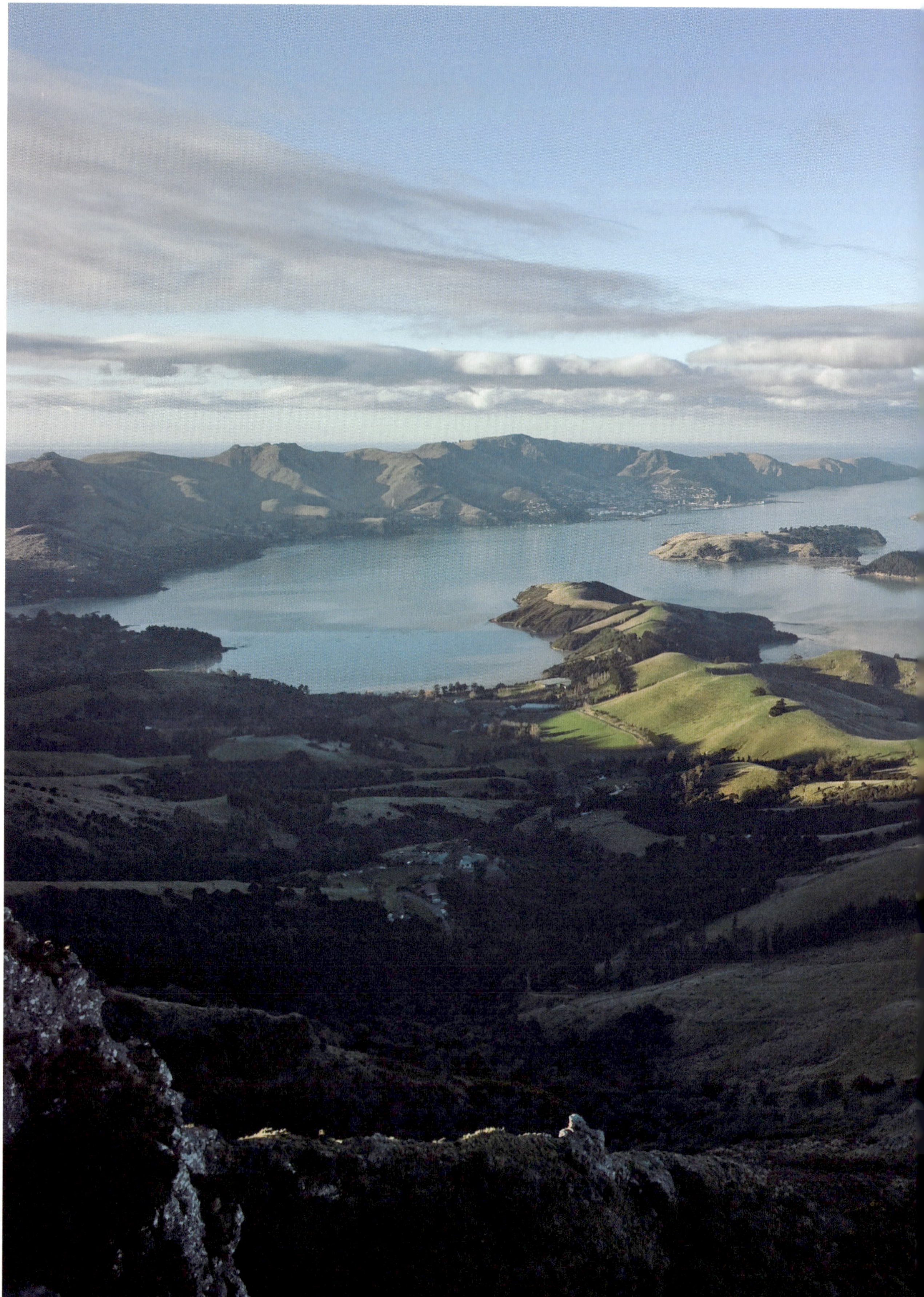

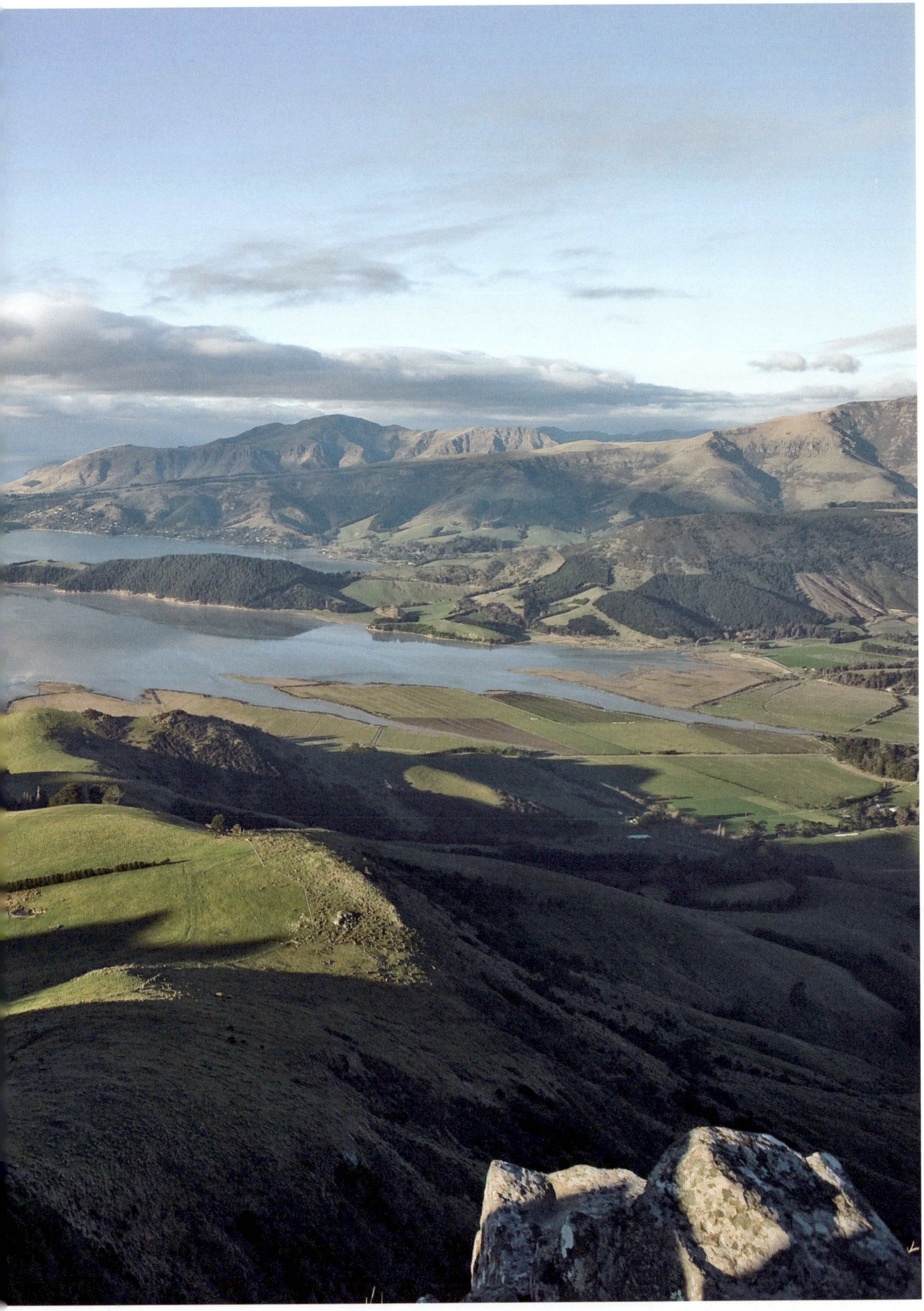

volcanoes rose from the sea about 50 kilometres to the east of the coast of what became mainland Canterbury. The main calderas — the volcanic craters — were centred on Lyttelton and Akaroa harbours respectively. Sea level rises since the last ice age drowned them, and a combination of the erosion of the volcanic cones and of the Southern Alps bridged the gap between the vast, alluvial Canterbury plains and the volcanic outliers. So low is the adjoining land that when you view Banks Peninsula from a few kilometres out to sea, particularly on a blustery or hazy day, its hard, high contours seem both distant and distinct from the mainland. It certainly fooled the canny Cook.

That's the geologist's version of the origins. There are at least a couple of slightly more poetic Maori accounts. The prevailing one is that Banks Peninsula was created by the legendary Rakaihautu at the end of his labours digging the great lakes of the South Island with his ko, or digging stick. The last two lakes he gouged from the earth were Waihora and Wairewa. Finished with his work, he jabbed his ko into the ground and left it there. This became the peak known as Tuhiraki, which translates as 'heaped up high', the summit of the ridge above Akaroa Harbour also known as Mount Bossu.

A LONG HARBOUR

From Tuhiraki/Mount Bossu, Akaroa harbour unfurls like a flag. The name means 'long harbour', and that's what it is, all right: a long, lovely incursion of turquoise sea into the high, surrounding land.

Standing at Greens Point overlooking the township, former Akaroa Museum director Steve Lowndes sweeps his arm around at the vista with obvious pride. Akaroa is known as the jewel of Banks Peninsula, he says, and it's hard to argue. You can readily see why a couple of French whalers, Jean-François Langlois and Etienne François Le Lièvre, looked at this bit of landscape back in 1838 and liked the cut of its gib. Langlois bought up 30,000 acres centred around Akaroa harbour from a group of Maori who solemnly declared they had the sole right to sell it, and then happily returned to France. He and Le Lièvre established the Nanto-Bordaleise Immigration Company, with the stated aim of annexing the South Island of New Zealand for France and settling Akaroa (which was renamed Port Louis-Philippe after the French king, who had given his blessing to the enterprise).

Previous page: Looking out to the entrance from the head of Akaroa harbour.

Above: The township of Akaroa.

The company's ship, the *Comte de Paris*, sailed on 20 March 1840 with 57 settlers aboard. A month prior the *Aube*, a French naval corvette, was dispatched to smooth the way for the colonists under the command of Captain Charles Lavaud.

The *Aube* reached New Zealand in July, and when he called on the British governor in the Bay of Islands, Lavaud learned that the British had already laid claim to both islands of mainland New Zealand. To make it absolutely clear that any French presence established in the South Island couldn't amount to an annexation, Governor William Hobson dispatched two magistrates aboard the HMS *Britomart* to Akaroa.

'Captain Stanley came down from the Bay of Islands and planted that flagpole,' Steve points, 'and raised the Union Jack and declared a court. It didn't matter if there was nobody to appear before it. It was a matter of "O yea, o yea, this court is now in session." In terms of international law, that put the question of sovereignty beyond doubt.

Above: Local historian Steve Lowndes says of Akaroa, 'you've got to keep the French influence in perspective'.

Banks Peninsula

On the French seeing the Union Jack: 'The penny must have dropped well and truly that the idea of establishing a French colony in the South Island was doomed'.

And a few days later when the French arrived, they saw the Union Jack flying. The penny must have dropped well and truly that the idea of establishing a French colony in the South Island was doomed.'

When you're standing under the flagstaff on Greens Point above the town of Akaroa, Steve says, you're standing on the precise spot where Hobson's magistrates convened the first court session in the South Island under the auspices of the new colonial administration. This ritual was an act of sovereignty charged with significance under international law, and served to underscore the existing British claim.

When Charles Lavaud arrived five days later, one of the first things that caught his eye would have been the gay red, white and blue of the British flag, a splash of colour against the greens of the hills. Its significance would have been all too obvious to him.

The land remained under British rule but the French settlers were permitted to take up their allotment, upon proof of purchase. Those were the terms upon which the French settled at Akaroa. The details of their claim to the full 30,000 acres were fiendishly difficult to determine and it turned out there were plenty of other people who also believed they'd bought the same tract of land. Still, Lavaud, who was nominally in charge of the French settlers, and C. B. Richardson, the magistrate chosen to represent the British Crown in Akaroa, hit it off, and whatever ancient antipathy exists between the French and the English, it wasn't allowed to strain relations in this remote outpost of both nations.

C'EST LA VIE

Today, many of the local businesses, especially cafés, restaurants and boutique hotels, flaunt the Frenchness of Akaroa for all it's worth, but the flavour is largely artificial.

'Is there any French influence obvious in the architecture?' Al asks Steve.

'You've got to keep the French influence in context. What you've got to realise is that it wasn't too long before you couldn't call it a French colony any more. There were 57 French settlers who arrived here in 1840, and by 1850 they were outnumbered by British and other settlers, so it isn't a French village, it's a colonial village and boasts the best collection of colonial architecture in New Zealand.'

You have to look hard to distinguish anything distinctively French about the old houses and commercial buildings or anything else beyond a few street names — Rue Lavaud, Rue Jolie, Rue Balguerie, for example — that commemorate those first settlers.

Still, the house that Langlois himself built and occupied —

Steve shows Al 'the best collection of colonial architecture in New Zealand.'

> 'There were 57 French settlers who arrived here in 1840, and by 1850 they were outnumbered by British and other settlers, so it isn't a French village, it's a colonial village.'

one of the oldest buildings in the South Island — survives, and accommodates a museum.

Akaroa manages to carry itself off as a little slice of Bordeaux in the Antipodes simply because it's possible to do things here with real Gallic panache. Surrounded by high hills and by sea, the town has its own highly congenial microclimate, and while those southerly busters can keep everyone indoors in winter, the summers are long and sultry. Dining al fresco at any one of a number of top-class waterfront restaurants, on dishes prepared from local produce, washed down with a glass of a little something from Crater Rim . . . *c'est la vie!* These days Akaroa's main industry is tourism. The town's fascinating history is part of the attraction. Its own natural charm accounts for the rest.

ONE COLOURFUL COASTER

That natural charm has drawn artists and writers to Akaroa, too. Wander just up the hill from the waterfront, and you'll see the imposing house built in 1880 for the manager of Akaroa's first bank — the cocksfooting boom was in full swing back then, and the district was awash with money.

'The story goes,' artist Josie Martin tells Al, 'that the local children were pretty impressed by the house and thought giants must live there. That name has stuck.'

Josie dresses and does her hair with the same eye for vibrant colour as she brings to her art: today, she's wearing a yellow and magenta fabric flower in her blue hair, a lime green tunic, and daffodil-yellow shoes. She used to come here with her family on holidays and for day trips from Christchurch, and like Langlois 150-odd years before her and countless others since, she was drawn back. She took on the house and slowly renovated it, doing much of the work herself. When it was the garden's turn, she found herself digging up old, broken china in the rich soil where she was planting her roses. She had the idea of resurfacing the front step with mosaic

Artist Josie Martin started renovations at her home in Akaroa by building a mosaic front doorstep and hasn't been able to stop.

made of the fragments, since she couldn't afford tiles.

'That's where it all began, really,' she says, gazing about the wonderland that her garden has become as though she, too, can hardly believe it. 'It just happened, really, piece by piece.'

'It looks perfect,' says Al.

'Oh, it's not finished. It's never finished.'

She's populated the whole property with sculptural figures finished in mosaic — angels, a king and queen, Adam and Eve, dancers, swimmers around a fountain, and (her current project) a jazz band. It's a work of art on an immense scale, all curves and sweeps and colour, all the more impressive when you consider that the figures are created over a frame of reinforcing steel, formed with wire mesh and plaster, applied by Josie's own hand, before the painstaking work of applying the mosaic can even begin. Al asks her how much concrete has gone

The 'Giant's House' was originally built in 1880 for the bank manager. Since moving in Josie Martin has made the odd alteration

Banks Peninsula 229

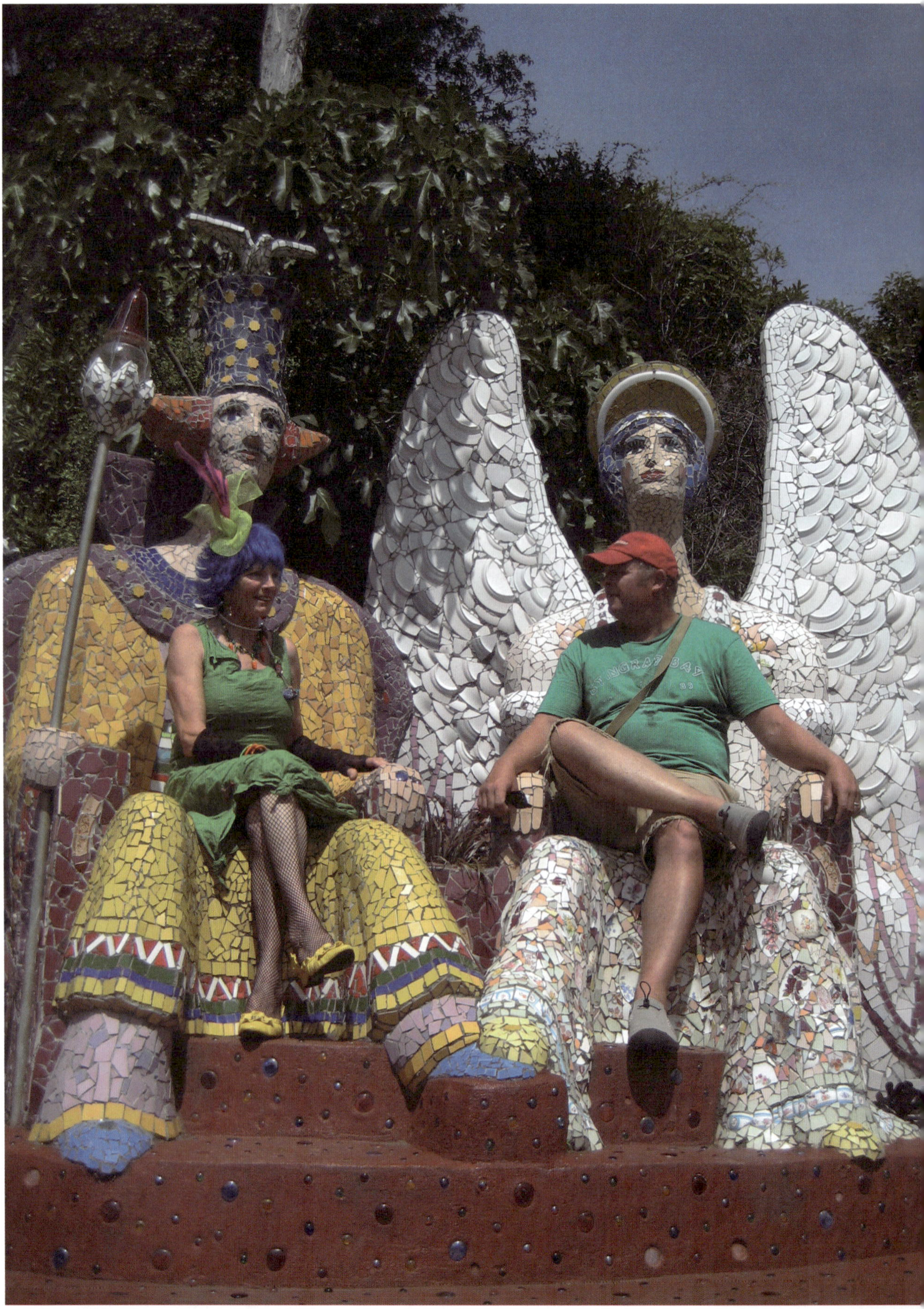

into the whole thing and Josie just groans.

The Giant's House attracts dozens of visitors a day. Josie offers bed and breakfast accommodation for up to six guests, and she has recently opened a gallery of modern art and a café in the garden. For her own part, she lives and works at The Giant's House in the summer months, and then migrates for the winter, taking up artist's residencies overseas. She has an international reputation as a painter, and is much in demand. This year, she is travelling to France to take up a residency outside Paris. Coming from Akaroa, this coaster will feel right at home there.

Roaming the Outer Bays

Beyond Akaroa, Banks Peninsula comprises a number of high ridges and plunging valleys, each terminating at the coast in a secluded beach. These are known locally as 'the Outer Bays', and as their name suggests, they're pretty isolated. You can get there by road, although some of them are fairly hairy, dropping as they do from the high ridge down the steep valley walls to sea level.

If you do drive, you'll appreciate why it took so long for wheeled traffic to make it out here in the first place. The early settlers, and even some of the later ones, mostly got in and out by boat. The peninsula may as well have been an island for all the use that land-based transport was to you back then.

Left and above: One of many colourful corners in Josie Martin's garden, a 'must-see' in Akaroa.

Opposite: Josie and Al take a seat in the garden. The angel wings are made from broken saucers.

Below: Onuku Church, on the way to the Outer Bays.

Banks Peninsula 231

These days there's another way, and that's the way Al's going. At Onuku, just out of Akaroa he swaps his jandals for a pair of walking shoes, and sets out along the Banks Peninsula Track. Opened just over 20 years ago, this 36-kilometre walk was established by a handful of cash-strapped, conservation-minded farmers looking for ways to diversify their income. It's New Zealand's first private walking track.

A bus gets you to the end of the road at Onuku, and after that you're on your own. Al climbs the ridge, and gets a breathtaking view of the pleated coastline.

'Man, serious walk,' Al gasps. 'But the view you're taking in here. Extraordinary. Banks Peninsula at its best: beautiful day, sea as flat as a pancake. I'm loving it.'

FLIPPERS ON THE BEACH

Al follows the track down the valley to another of those gorgeous inlets, Pohatu, or Flea Bay. The cool blue of the water is like the offer of a cold drink to a parched mouth. Al takes the opportunity to have a refreshing dip before he meets Francis and Shireen Helps, who are lucky enough to live and farm here.

Francis and Shireen first came to Flea Bay in the late 1960s, and Francis still remembers their first night.

'Couldn't sleep,' he says. 'Couldn't sleep for the noise.'

Penguins are surprisingly noisy birds.

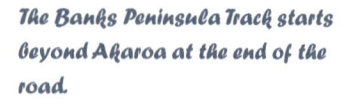

The Banks Peninsula Track starts beyond Akaroa at the end of the road.

Above: The view of Pohatu, Flea Bay, as you walk down the valley to the coast

Francis and Shireen had both been brought up on Banks Peninsula and were well aware of the value of what they had at Pohatu: pods of Hector's dolphins regularly visit the bay, seals haul out on the rocks, a few breeding pairs of hoiho, the endangered yellow-eyed penguin, frequent the area. It also happens that Pohatu is one of the last refuges of the koraro, or white-flippered penguin, a subspecies of the Australasian little blue penguin, found only on the Canterbury coast — even in happier, predator-free times. But pressure from people and the constellation of critters they brought — cats, rats, mice, stoats and weasels — has dramatically reduced their numbers and the sites where they could safely breed.

For a while, Flea Bay was one of those sanctuaries.

'But we started finding feet and flippers on the beach,' Francis says. 'Feral cats, stoats. We were seeing predation here, too.'

For over 20 years, the Helps have been nurturing the koraro breeding colony, getting rid of predators and maintaining a network of 300 nesting boxes in the bush adjacent to the foreshore. They were also instrumental in establishing the Pohatu Marine Reserve. Proclaimed in 1999, it was the first on Banks Peninsula.

Below: Shireen hand rears orphaned chicks until they learn to swim and can fend for themselves.

Banks Peninsula 233

Shireen and Francis have provided the penguins at Pohatu with a range of accomodation 'They'll nest anywhere,' says Shireen.

Koraro come ashore to breed between August and January and, during this period, the bay resounds with their eerie, honking calls. At the most recent count, according to Shireen, there were 1063 breeding pairs in Flea Bay.

'They'll nest anywhere,' Shireen says as she shows Al some of the nesting boxes they've constructed. 'So we just give them a helping hand. The nesting boxes take the heat out of the fights. Otherwise they'll be fighting over the burrows.'

Al lifts the lid on a nesting box and there's a chick in there with tufts of brown down clinging in patches to the slicker, blue feathers.

The chick is fledging, and its new feathers not yet waterproof, the Helps explain. It's still totally dependent on its parents, and it's vulnerable to predation. At this stage, especially late in the season, Francis and Shireen keep a close eye on the chicks because if one or both parents abandon them — perhaps because they've got the urge to moult, or because they've come to grief at sea — that's the end of the chick, too, unless the Helps intervene to feed them.

'They eat a surprising amount of fish. It costs a lot to keep them fed,' says Shireen.

234 Coasters

Cliffs on Banks Peninsula Track.

They funded the work they did with the penguins from their own back pocket for the first 15 years. But lately they've received more and more assistance, with government agencies such as the Department of Conservation supporting them, and a charitable trust helping with the costs.

Besides the accommodation that the Helps provide walkers on the coastal track, they offer guided tours of the bay, or sea kayaking excursions for those keen to observe the other beneficiaries of the marine reserve — seals, seabirds and fishlife galore.

And their latest project is the construction of a predator-proof perimeter around the penguin colony.

'You must get a heck of a buzz out of this,' Al says.

'I do,' says Shireen, and Frank nods. 'You see a beautiful, lovely, fat penguin going to sea. It might be one more that's going to return.'

AN EYE FOR AN OPPORTUNITY

From Flea Bay the track skirts the clifftops, offering some of the most spectacular coastal views found around the Peninsula and, for that matter, the entire country.

'They're just mindblowing,' says Al, stopping for a breather. 'They're so big and powerful and they just keep going and going and going.'

He follows them for another couple of hours before the track winds down into Stony Bay, where the collection of buildings nestled amongst the trees offers a warm welcome.

Mark and Sonia Armstrong run the farm at Stony Bay, living in the house that Mark himself was raised in. They offer accommodation for the walkers — a mix of cottages and outbuildings that over the years have organically grown with the ingenuity and inventiveness

Sonia Armstrong and her husband Mark from Stony Bay Farm share their piece of paradise with people from all over the world.

Banks Peninsula

Al about to make his descent into Stony Bay.

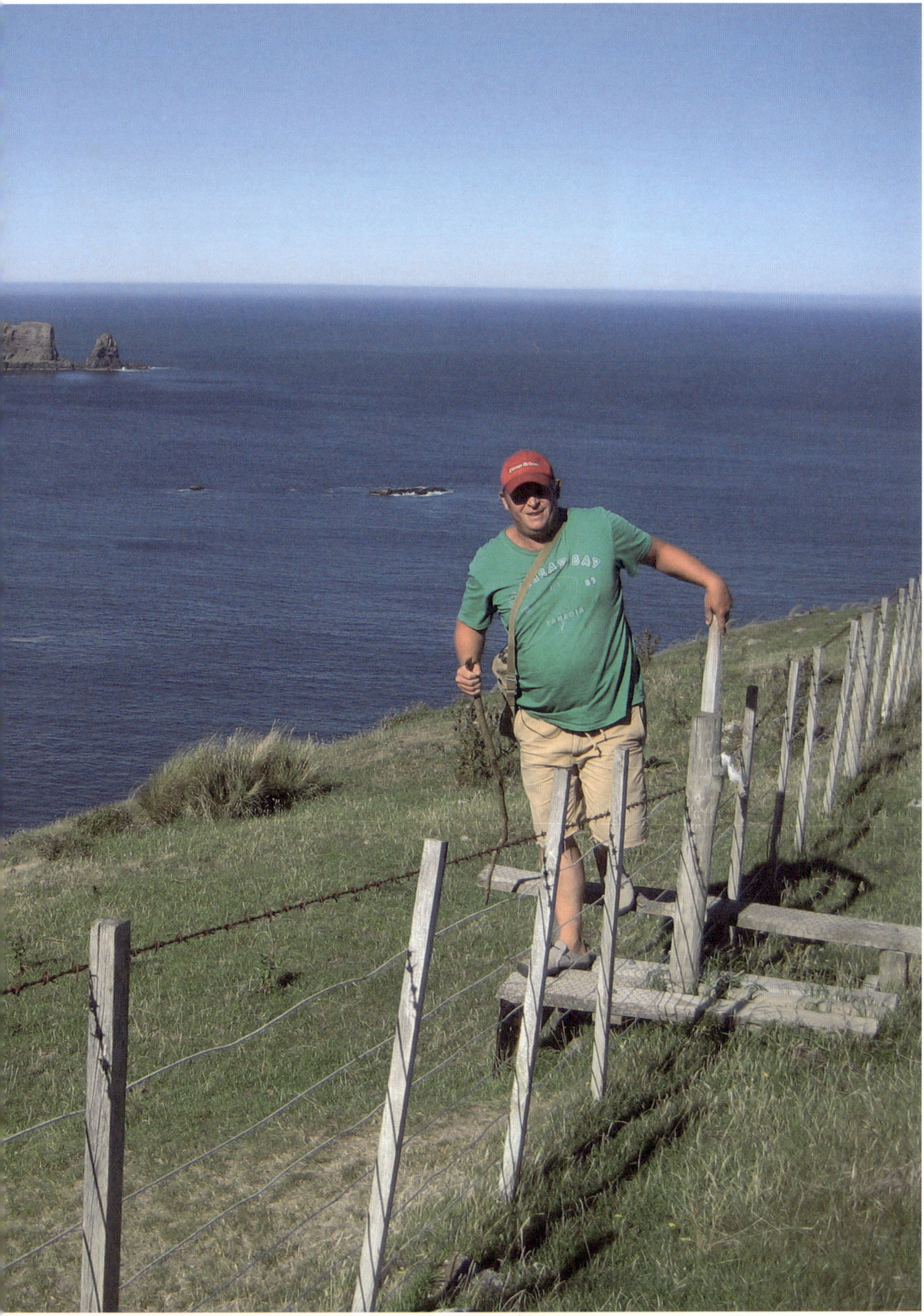

The walls inside this small family museum tell an intimate story of isolation on the coast.

that living at the end of an isolated road requires. Whether it's the paint-tin pockets on the homemade pool table or the spoked plough wheels providing ventilation for the shower, there's plenty of evidence that these coasters have an eye for an opportunity, which is how the track started in the first place.

Mark leads Al to an old corrugated iron shed at the end of the garden. It's his family's museum and tells a story of isolation and determination that echoes that of the many other coastal families in the area. It was Mark's father who originally bought this farm at Stony Bay, doing so in the hope that it would convince his sweetheart he was a man of substance and that she should marry him. It worked, and that's why Mark is around today.

Mark points to a photograph on the museum wall, the newlyweds bringing in their worldly possessions on a sledge behind a carthorse. One or both of them would ride out — a long and often hazardous trek on horseback — every two weeks to get supplies. Come shearing time, and the wool bales would be manhandled over the rocks and down to the beach, where they would be taken out to waiting vessels in a rowboat. It was an unimaginably hard way of life.

Another reminder of those pioneering days without electricity was a petrol-powered clothes iron Mark's mum used. 'Flames used to fly out of it sometimes,' says Mark. 'She used to iron with the window open and if it played up she would just throw it out the window into the garden.'

That's the way things have always been done in this part of the world: no nonsense, just get on with it.

Like Josie Martin, Mark and Sonia have turned up heaps of old crockery in the soil surrounding the homestead, and the next museum piece Mark shows Al is a billyful of broken china.

'Your mum must have had the dinner set outside when she chucked the iron out the window,' Al says, and Mark grins.

It's interesting to look at the fragments of the china and ponder the place it once had in the tough lives of the people who lived here — starting out as something fancy, a wedding gift, perhaps, dragged in here on a sledge, and brought out only on special occasions. But with wear and tear, it went down in the world, finally finding its way into the midden.

The isolation at Stony Bay was somewhat broken down by the arrival of the telephone in 1914. This remained a single, fragile line that the residents at Stony Bay had to maintain themselves until much later. Mark remembers helping his dad isolate faults on it when he was a boy.

'He'd send you out to the point where the wires joined, and get you to hold onto the wires while he wound the hell out of the crank. If you got a shock, he knew the fault was further on, so you'd go to the next junction and do it again.'

Sonia's garden is an oasis for weary walkers.

Above: Al and Fiona Farrell at Otanerito.

Opposite: Otanerito beach, Long Bay, on the Banks Peninsula Track.

Mark and Sonia eventually took over the farm, and made a go of it, although isolation made it hard for them, too. Like other coasters in the Outer Bays of Banks Peninsula, they weathered the downturn in farming in the 1980s — just — but began casting around for another string to their bow. The best prospect was the coast itself. All of them living in this magic part of the world knew that what they have is too good to keep all to themselves: it was suggested they pool their resources and open up their bit of paradise to tourists. The coastal walkway was born and 20 years down the track the results speak for themselves, a summer fully booked with walkers coming from all over the world.

A PLACE WHERE THE WEATHER WINS

From Stony Bay, the track climbs through regenerating bush and meanders along the awe-inspiring sea cliffs again: in summer, the buzz of the insects and the sweet, drowsy hay smell are the perfect appetiser for your descent into Sleepy Bay, where there's a bushy gully complete with waterfall and perfect solitude.

Up and down again, and you get your first look at Otanerito, or Long Bay, with Pompeys Pillar at the end of the northern headland.

Al picks his way down the well-used farm track and is greeted by Otanerito's resident wordsmith, Fiona Farrell.

Fiona first came here in 1992. At the time she was writer-in-residence at Canterbury University, and had met Doug Hood at a poetry reading she was giving. He offered to bring her out for a weekend at Otanerito, where he was working on the Hinewai Reserve, a reforestation project in the valley that includes Otanerito. She agreed, and hopped on a shuttle to Akaroa, but wondered whether she had done the right thing as Doug, whom she had known for three hours, drove them along increasingly narrow, winding gravel roads in the black of night with fewer and fewer signs of life visible through the windows. The road tilted downwards, and after a long, slow trip, they arrived in a clearing in the bush.

They walked through some long, wet grass to a little building. Doug opened the door, and all Fiona's doubts disappeared. A fire was burning in the grate, the aroma of dinner reached her from the stove, music was playing and the interior was a haven of light in an impossibly black night. It was, says Fiona, like the picture of the interior of Ratty's house in *Wind in the Willows*.

That Christmas, Doug and Fiona had the opportunity to buy the

Weather

*I like a place where
the weather wins.
I like a place where
it rains till the road
slips and the mail
can't get through.
I like a place
where rivers rise
and the ferry's
cancelled and trees
go whoopsydaisy.
I like a place where
snow says watch my
hands hoopla and the
road's gone.*

*I like a place where
the wind muscles
up the bay
tossing birds over
its shoulder.
I like flash and
boom behind swags
of dense cloud
and the raging of
a headstrong gale.
I like to be released
to run, arms spread
before the storm,
my tiny routine
ripped to shreds.*

Fiona Farrell

Above: Garry Brittenden, lifelong Le Bons Bay coaster.

Below: On the boat journey to Le Bons Bay Garry and Al find the makings of a seafood banquet while taking in the sights.

Opposite: New Zealand's largest population of Hector's dolphins lives in the water around Banks Peninsula.

house and three acres of the land around it. Behind their home they provide accommodation for the final night on the track. Doug runs that and Fiona has a hut up the hill in which she works. She's one of New Zealand's foremost novelists, with a number of awards to her credit. She's also an acclaimed poet and playwright.

A theme in Fiona's writing that seems to derive from the place she lives is the way in which nature trips up all humanity's grand pretensions. It's a brief meeting with Al but before she bids him farewell, on the bank overlooking the beautiful Long Bay, Fiona shares one of her Banks Peninsula poems.

Al listens, and nods. A southerly at Otanerito will do that every time.

Out to sea

From Otanerito the Banks Peninsula coastal walk heads inland, up the valley and over the hill to Akaroa. But Al's journey takes him out to sea, with a coaster who knows the Eastern Bays intimately. Garry Brittenden pulls up at Long Bay in his tinny and whisks Al away for the final leg of his journey, by boat to Le Bons Bay.

'This is the way to appreciate the Peninsula, isn't it?' Al yells over the sound of the outboard as they pass the sheer sea cliffs.

Garry points to the hills of the crater rim, rising some distance beyond. 'The volcano was about the height of Mount Cook,' he says. Those cliffs would have stretched a couple of kilometres more out to sea, but the sea's just knocked them back.'

It's the view from the water that gives you a feel for the volcanic origins of Banks Peninsula. On a good day, you can nose into caves that were once vents of the Akaroa volcano. You can read the story of the successive eruptions in the layers of red rock, as clearly as if they were written down in a book. The reddish tint of iron oxide and white streaks of guano stain the rugged sentinels off the headlands where several species of shag roost. Seals lounge on the rocks, too, or surface with their heads at an interrogative angle as the boat idles past.

'The seal population's really bouncing back,' says Garry. 'In the last 20 years, the numbers have picked up. You saw the odd female coming ashore, then the odd pup. That's when you know they're really breeding here again.'

Setting baited pots out here will generally get you a feed and

Coasters

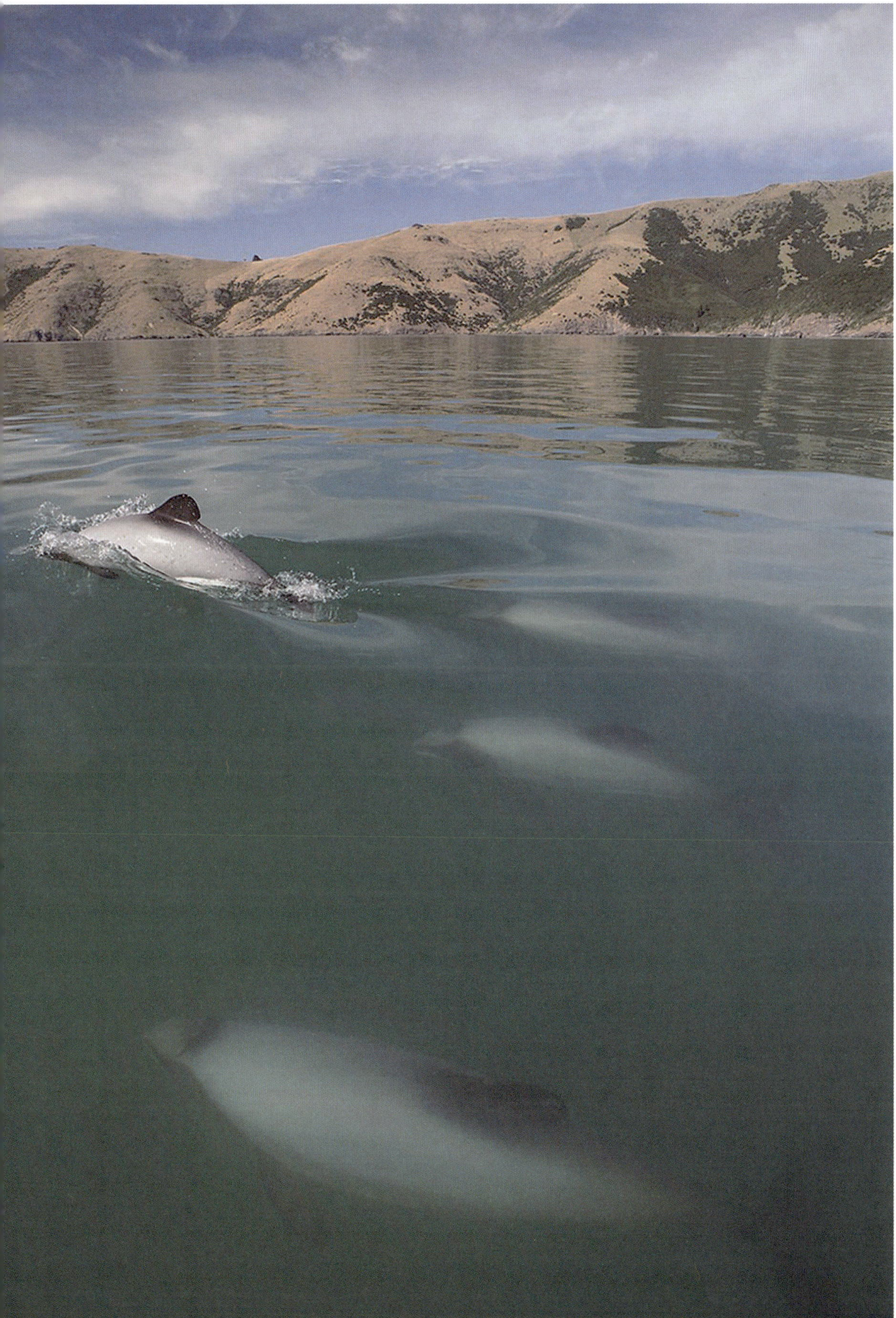

Garry's son Finn helps bring in the tinny.

Al's hoping for a good one to complete his Banks Peninsula journey. Making their way around to Le Bons Bay, they stop off at half a dozen pots that Garry set earlier. Pulling them up from the depths by hand gives Al an appreciation of the old timers that did it for a living, and it was well worth the effort. Slowly but surely their Banks Peninsula feed turns into a banquet — blue cod, crayfish and paddle crabs.

'What's your favourite thing about the Coast, Garry?' Al asks as they head for home. 'The variety,' says Garry without hesitation. 'Each headland you pass there's a new vista: sheltered bays, bush, waterfalls . . .'

The view along the coast is one of headland receding behind headland, and as Al and Garry pass the easternmost point on the Peninsula, a small pod of Hector's dolphins distracts them from the journey home. With only an estimated 7500 in total, and all of them living in South Island waters (if you ignore the extremely rare North Island subspecies, the Maui dolphin), the large proportion of Hector's dolphins live around Banks Peninsula.

At 1.5 metres when fully grown, it's the world's smallest marine dolphin and is instantly recognisable by its rounded 'mickey mouse ear' dorsal fin. In the last 30 or 40 years their numbers have plummeted and

> 'The title wasn't issued until 1955, so I suppose the farmer could have claimed it back,' Garry says. 'I suppose a handshake was enough back then.'

in 1988, New Zealand's first Marine Mammal Sanctuary was declared in the waters around the Peninsula, primarily to protect them from becoming by-catch in set nets. Such are the ongoing threats to these diminutive dolphins, however, that the sanctuary was significantly extended 20 years later in 2008 in an effort to halt their decline.

Garry steers into Le Bons Bay, a large bay just to the north of the very tip of Banks Peninsula. Just before he beaches the boat, there's one last pot for two pairs of tired arms to pull, and it comes up trumps with a windfall of paddle crabs, which turns their Banks Peninsula feed into a feast.

The catch on board, Garry trailers the boat and with his tractor drives up the sandy track and home — not a bad commute.

Garry's family crib. The land was bought for £4 in 1932.

COMPLETELY HOOKED

Garry has a long family connection with Le Bons: his great-grandfather worked at the Le Bons Bay sawmill in the 1870s, and though his grandfather worked in Christchurch, he bought a plot of land at Le Bons from a farmer for £4 back in 1932, the deal sealed with a handshake.

'The title wasn't issued until 1955, so I suppose the farmer could have claimed it back,' Garry says. 'I suppose a handshake was enough back then.'

His grandfather built a crib on the land with materials sourced from his own demolition business.

Garry grew up in Christchurch, but the Bay was calling. He just loved getting out there, and when he got his first boat at age 12, he was completely hooked. He bought his own house at the Bay in 1972 for just $300. It was advertised as 'a poor quality hay barn', but he saw it for what it was: a small cottage of pit-sawn totara built in 1875 by Danish settlers. His great-grandad probably knew the building and the builders.

Garry was one of the two schoolteachers at Le Bons Bay during the 1980s, when there had been a bit of a trend for people to move out from the city to their holiday homes and sort of 'live off the land' —

the school roll was booming. He managed to fit a fair bit of overseas travel in, too, but the Bay kept calling him back. From 1991 to 2009, he and his wife Heidi ran a backpackers' hostel in the restored cottage. They've only just shut up shop, as Garry has a job as a schoolteacher again, teaching history, appropriately enough, at Akaroa Area School.

These days, Le Bons Bay has a population of about 100, and because the original plots of land sold there were between 10 and 100 acres, no large landowners have come to dominate as they have elsewhere in coastal New Zealand, and elsewhere on the Peninsula. It's always had a bit of a bohemian feel to it — artists, craftspeople and writers are drawn to it — and it retains a strong sense of community.

With the cod on the barbecue and the cray simmering in a sauce that Al puts together, he, Garry and Garry's wife and kids sit and watch the Peninsula's shadow lengthening over the sea.

THE WILD SIDE

Most stretches of New Zealand coastline are rich in history, but the Wild Side — the southern coast of Banks Peninsula — seems richer than most. The people you meet along here seem particularly conscious of what a privilege to have inherited this place: from Matahapuka, where the tangata whenua are seeking to restore the traditions of mahinga kai; through the bays — Akaroa, and all its associations with that quirk of history that nearly saw it named Port Louis-Philippe; Pohatu, where the Helps are helping to preserve the ecosystem of the bay and foreshore; Stony and Le Bons bays, where the Armstrongs and the Brittendens are but the latest in their family line to cherish the land — there's a consciousness of stewardship, of kaitiakitanga. And time and again, listening to people's stories, a theme recurs, where people are washed up along here by chance and then return or remain by design — from the tipuna of the Waitaha, Rakaihautu, through Jean-François Langlois, to poet Fiona Farrell and artist Josie Martin: the story is one of a kind of deeply felt affinity, a spiritual connection made in the way that seaborne seeds will tumble onto a beach and, sensing the right conditions, set down roots and flourish.

And talking to the coasters of the Wild Side, both the tangata whenua and those who have come since, you become acutely aware of the give-and-take arrangement that exists when people live in the proper relation to a place: look after the land and its treasures, and they will look after you.

Plating up al fresco. Al shares lunch with Josh, Finn, Heidi, Rosey and Garry Brittenden.

Crayfish, Crab and Tuatua Spaghetti with Arrabiata Sauce

I am often asked what is my favourite seafood to eat. It's the sort of question that annoys me as I find it near impossible to answer. I garner as much pleasure from the humble tuatua and paddle crab in this following dish as I do from the decadent crayfish. I have said it many times and will continue to do so: we are incredibly lucky to be surrounded with such prolific waters teeming with a truly world-class array of delicious seafood. There is something wonderful about cooking more than one species at a time for a dinner, as it celebrates how fortunate we are and how bountiful our New Zealand coast is. If you have no crayfish or paddle crab, make the dish just with the tuatua — it will be just as satisfying.
Serves 6.

Step 1. Arrabiata Sauce

Ingredients
⅓ cup olive oil
2 tablespoons minced garlic
½ teaspoon chilli flakes
½ cup port
½ cup red wine
2 x 400g tins whole peeled tomatoes, blitzed to a purée
2 tablespoons tomato paste
1 tablespoon sugar
25g butter
sea salt and freshly ground black pepper

Method
Place the oil in a medium-sized heavy-based saucepan on moderate heat. Add the garlic and chilli flakes, and stir continuously with a wooden spoon, watching the garlic start to change colour. Once the garlic takes on a nice dark golden colour, immediately add the port and red wine. Be mindful that as you add the alcohol it will spit and bubble for a few seconds.

Simmer the wine for 5 minutes, then add the tomatoes, tomato paste and sugar. Reduce the heat and simmer for another 15–20 minutes until nice and thick. Remove from the heat, whisk in the butter, then taste and season accordingly. Cool to room temperature, then refrigerate until required.

Step 2. Preparing the Crayfish and Crabs

Ingredients
1 live crayfish (about 1kg)
18 live paddle crabs

Method
Place the crayfish in an ice slurry or the freezer for 30 minutes to put it to sleep. Bring a large saucepan of salted water to the boil. Add the crayfish and cook for 5–7 minutes. Remove and cool, then extract all the meat from the tail, cavities and legs, and roughly chop. Set aside.

For the crabs, pull the shell off with your

thumb from the back towards the head. This kills the crab instantly. Snap the body in half down the centre. Get rid of any obvious guts and remove the feather-like gills. Take a pair of scissors and cut the outer joint off each leg and discard. Plunge the crab halves into the boiling water and cook for about 3 minutes. Remove and cool slightly then roll a rolling pin over each piece to extract the meat. Pick out any small pieces of shell. Reserve.

Step 3. To Cook and Serve

Ingredients
1 packet spaghetti
olive oil
60 tuatua
1 bunch fresh basil
knob of butter
freshly grated parmesan

Method
Bring a large saucepan of salted water to the boil. Add the spaghetti and a shot of olive oil, stir for 1–2 minutes then leave to cook.

Place 20 or so of the tuatua in a dry skillet or on the flat top of the barbecue and set on high heat. As the tuatua open, remove and place in a bowl. Repeat with the remainder.

Heat the arrabiata sauce to a simmer.

Once the pasta is cooked, drain and place in a large mixing bowl. Pour the hot arrabiata sauce over then fold through the crayfish, crab meat, tuatua, fresh basil and a knob of butter.

Spoon into warm bowls, top with a little parmesan, hit each plate with a splash of olive oil and devour with abandon.

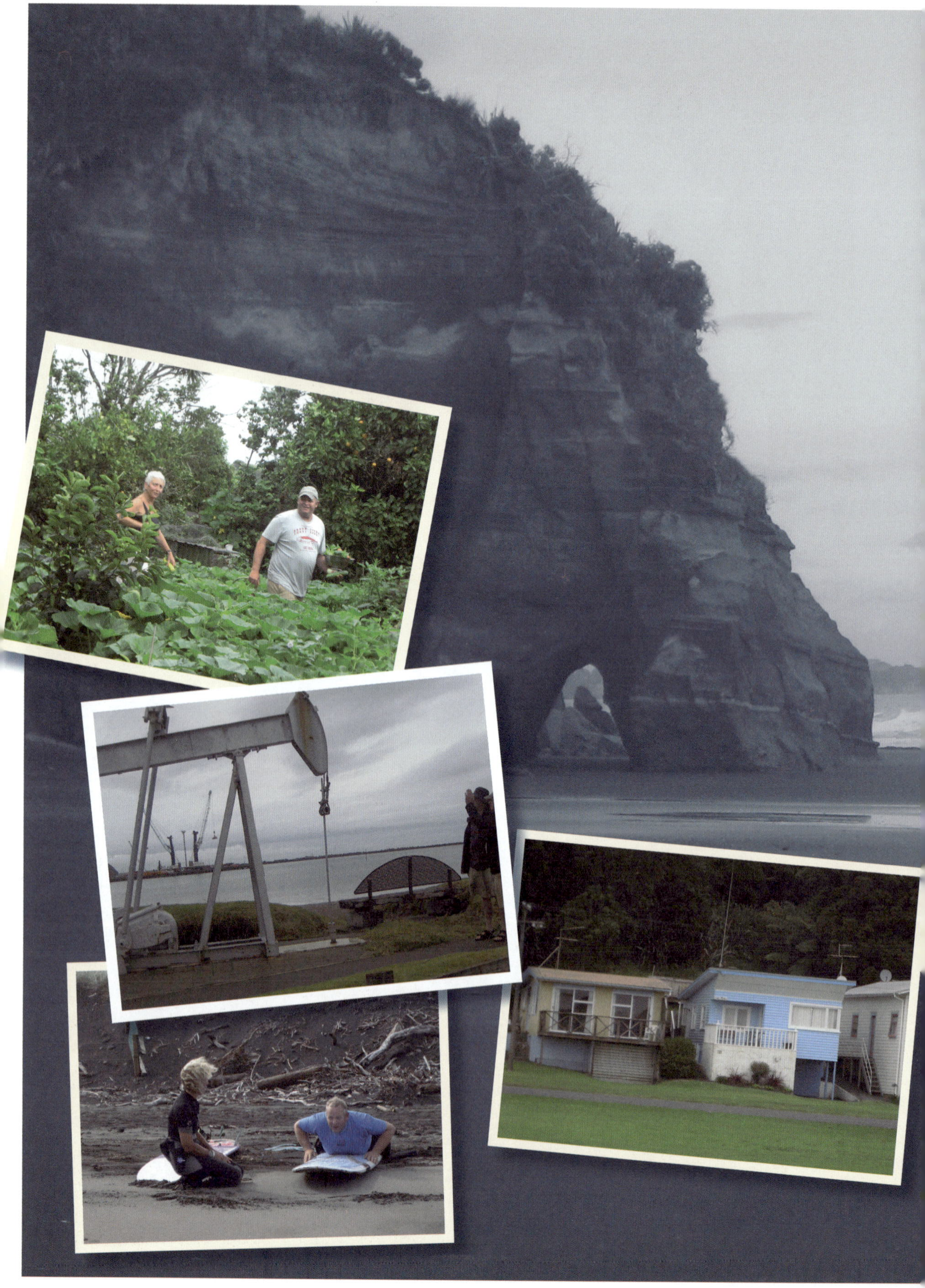

Welcome to... Taranaki

The Energy Coast

From the tip of its beautiful and majestic, though once very energetic and outright explosive mountain to the waves thundering along its shores, and the oil and gas beneath its rocks, Taranaki's all go!

It's the combination of mighty forces: the upthrusting, ever-moving land beneath your feet; the explosive volcanoes that have risen, eroded, collapsed and risen again, shaping the enormous circle of the Taranaki plain; and that supreme coast-shaper, the Tasman Sea, the source of the waves that surfers dream about and the provider of seafood to warm the cockles of your heart.

The coasters Al meets all share the vitality and energy of the region. There's a geologist who loves this coast so much that he returns time and again; there's the farmer who would rather be fishing, diving or just hanging out beside the ocean; an artist who is inspired by the coast; surfers who draw the energy of the waves into

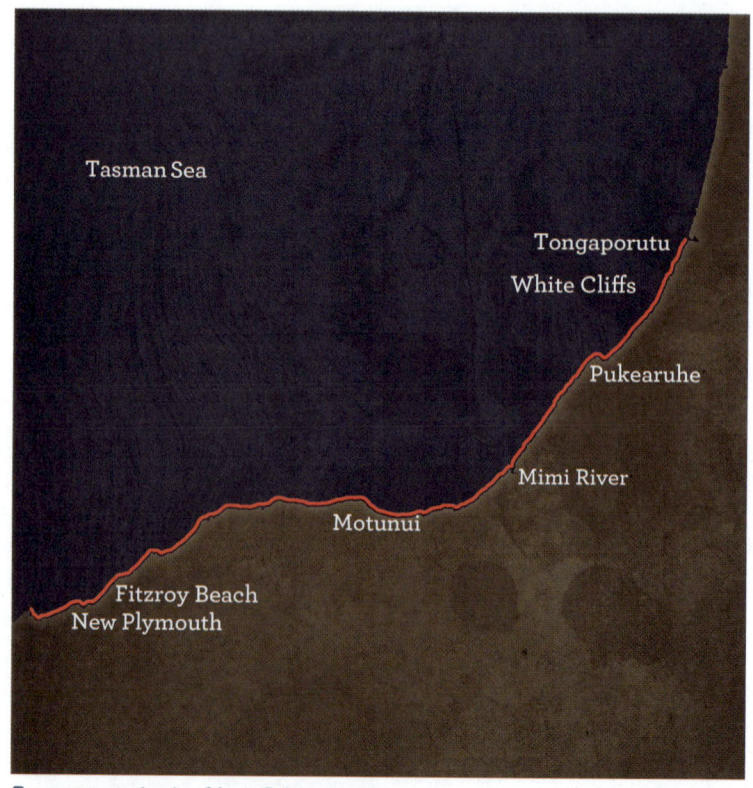

Tongaporutu to New Plymouth

their souls; and an engineer whose magic puts into motion the work of famed New Zealand artist, Len Lye.

White Cliffs Beach at low tide with Mount Taranaki behind.

THE SISTERS

Al's adventure begins in north Taranaki, where the slow-moving Tongaporutu River eases its way to the sea, collides with ocean rollers and backs up to form a wide estuary. Low tide reveals stretches of black, iron-laden sand forming elegant curvilinear patterns along the waterline. The folk who inhabit the colourful baches that cling to the river's south edge venture out to fish, take a stroll to the river mouth or beachcomb among driftwood and pools on the high tide line.

Above: This photo of the iconic rock stacks The Three Sisters was taken before they were reduced to two in a 2003 storm.

Below: Professor Vince Neall has a passion for the north Taranaki coastline.

This coastline is never still, never the same. From tide to tide, from day to day, it speaks of the might and force of the Tasman Sea as sun, wind and wave create a blasted, ever-eroding, rock-tumbled landscape of pools, caves, cliffs and columns.

Shoes in hand, Al heads off to explore the ocean's edge at the south side of the river. This is where you find the 25-metre-high rock stacks known as 'the sisters'. Craggy and striped like enormous chunks of layer cake, they are evolving landmarks, much-loved by tourists and photographers. They make particularly fine subjects at dawn and dusk when they cast reflections in pools and on the smooth, wet sands, creating dramatic silhouettes against the pinks, golds and blues of the sky. There were four of these rocky siblings at the turn of the twentieth century, but first one crumbled under the pounding of the waves, and then, in 2003, a further sister was reduced to a toothy stump.

But while the ocean removes, it also replaces — recently a new stack has emerged from the cliffs. 'Like Mother Nature's art gallery,' Al muses as he pauses in admiration and looks up at the towering forms. 'Full of individual sculptures, really — like they've all just been carved out.'

To Al's right, waves sweep in ceaseless rows, high and dangerous, the spume flicking off their tops; while to his left and ahead lie the sheer mudstone walls of the Parininihi or White Cliffs. Standing up to 245 metres high at the northern end, they are named after their limestone counterparts on the coast of Dover in Britain. The 'white' of these cliffs is more a pale blue-grey, from the mudstone known by its Maori name of 'papa'. Interleaved with the papa, like a giant gateau, are bands of more coarse yellow-orange sandstone and, sometimes, layers of stones and boulders. Early European travellers reported that nodules of brilliant blue clay found in the papa, called 'pukepoto', were prized by Maori as a pigment.

The cliffs are soft and erode easily, the result of ash-fall and avalanches over hundreds of thousands of years, all directly or indirectly from the volcanoes that were ancestors of today's Mount Taranaki, a summer-blue triangle seen snoozing peacefully on the distant skyline.

Rocking on

'G'day, you lost? What are you doing out here?' Al laughs as he greets a lone figure primed for the elements in a striped rugby shirt, floppy hat, large sunglasses and spade, who pops out from behind one of the sisters. It's Vince Neall, passionate geologist and Massey University professor in earth science. If anyone knows about the world below the earth's crust in Taranaki, it's Vince, a coaster who has long been fascinated by the volcanology of the area. He's here to fill Al in about the rocks and to explain why Taranaki is known as the 'energy province'. Using his spade as a pen and the black sand as his canvas, Vince sketches a picture.

Like most of New Zealand, Taranaki has had its share of volcanic action. The region's distinctly rounded coastline has been built by eruptions — first Ngamotu on the coast, then, moving in a south-east

Vince tells Al the story of the Taranaki oil — cooked in hydrocarbon kitchens kilometres below the sea.

Taranaki 255

256 *Coasters*

*'Like Mother Nature's art gallery.'
Al walks beneath Elephant
Rock, near the mouth of the
Tongaporutu River.*

Taranaki 257

> The first hints of this energy-rich subterranean world came very early when Maori and Europeans noticed the black stuff seeping through the sands of New Plymouth's Ngamotu Beach further along the coast.

direction over a long span of time, a succession of eruptions: Kaitake, Pouakai and, finally, Mount Taranaki, which was active as recently as 1755. Each volcano in turn was weathered to a shadow of its former self and ultimately replaced by a later one, all the while adding ash and debris to the Taranaki plain. It is thought that Kaitake, now only 680 metres high, was once as high as Taranaki — which is 2518 metres. That's a lot of debris and a great deal of it has been washed out to sea.

Over a period of 80 to 100 million years this process formed a vast sedimentary basin up to seven kilometres deep under the sea to the west of where Al and Vince are standing. Peat bogs and forests from a long-ago coastline were buried and trapped beneath porous siltstones and harder, impermeable mudstones. They slowly decayed and over immense periods of time were pressure-cooked into hydrocarbons — crude oil, natural gas and condensates. The hydrocarbons filled reservoirs of the porous rock but were unable to escape because of the layers of harder rock above. To further compound the situation, buckling and movement of the Earth's crust has caused faults that also create pockets where oil and gas may be trapped, or may provide a route for the oil and gas to rise to the surface.

The first hints of this energy-rich subterranean world came very early when Maori and Europeans noticed the black stuff seeping through the sands of New Plymouth's Ngamotu Beach further along the coast. 'That was where the first well was drilled in the British Empire,' Vince says. Just like the opening sequence from *The Beverly Hillbillies*, oil was seeping through the sand, hinting at the larger reservoirs that would be found in the 1960s and the boom exploration period of the 1970s.

The approximately 100,000-square-kilometre basin is largely offshore, although the majority of producing fields are onshore, the main exception being the Maui field which was discovered in 1969 and is now almost depleted. Out at sea the tower of the well that

Opposite: Alpha Well at Ngamotu Beach in New Plymouth. The harbourside wells began producing as early as 1865.

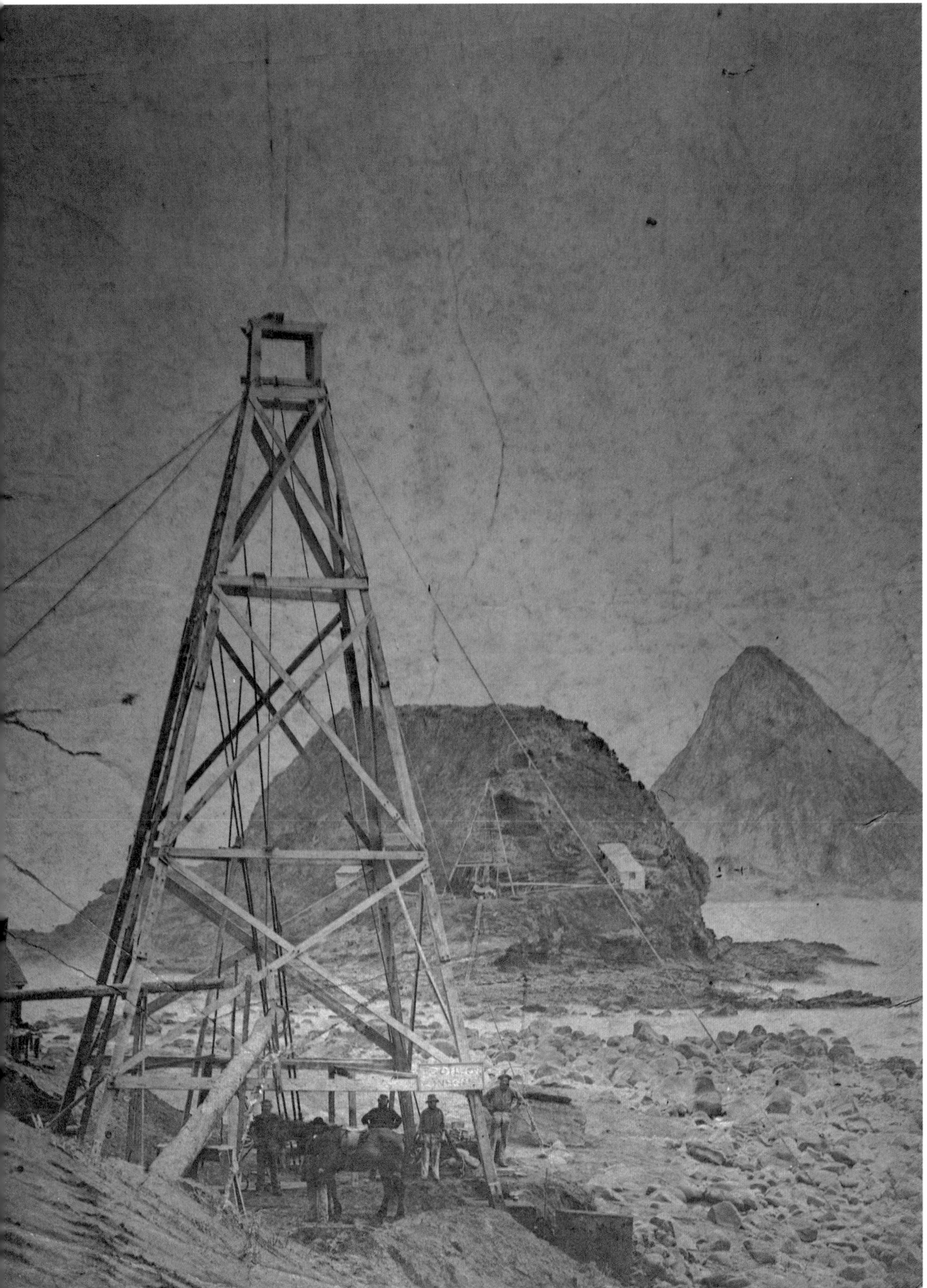

The low tide coastal trail between Tongaporutu and Pukearuhe hugs the base of the White Cliffs.

draws gas from the Pohokura field can be seen from many points along the coast, shimmering in the marine light.

It's time to move on. Vince hefts his spade and is gone, while Al continues his journey south.

Treading an older trail

Al's bare feet sink into the sand as he begins his walk. He's heading in a south-westerly direction as the coast of the North Island spreads and widens into the bulge that is the Taranaki peninsula. Behind him, the state highway loops inland from Tongaporutu but Al is, in fact, treading an older trail.

For centuries Maori used this route to move between the Waikato and Taranaki — right around New Zealand, beaches were more easily travelled than the inland alternatives, with the bonus of fish and shellfish on hand and sometimes caves for shelter. All travellers along this coast need to time their journeys carefully, as it's impassable at full tide when the sea is deep at the base of the cliffs. Even so, before roads were built inland, it was much easier to move along this low-tide route than the heavily bushed, swampy, hilly country of the interior.

The coastal route ends at Pukearuhe, approximately 14 kilometres south-west of Tongaporutu, where a headland that juts inconveniently into the sea forces travellers inland. The Maori name for the headland

The armed constabulary redoubt settlement above the cliffs at Pukearuhe as it stood in the 1870s.

is Ruataniwha, which suggests some form of sea-dwelling monsters, but it also became known as Rigby's Point after Constable John Rigby drowned while attempting to swim three horses around it in 1883. Even though the cliffs are lower at this point, early travellers still had to scramble up from the beach through a narrow gully via steps and vine ropes.

Because the coastal route was effectively the only practical north–south access, it had strategic importance for pre-European Maori — especially as it was the path taken by war parties in the ongoing struggle between Waikato and Taranaki iwi. Its southern entrance was commanded first by Pukearuhe Pa and then, during the Land Wars of the 1860s, the same site became a two-storeyed blockhouse, again because of its strategic value. The blockhouse was unexpectedly sacked and burned by Maori in 1869, resulting in the deaths of the family of Lieutenant Gascoigne, two other men and the Reverend John Whitley.

In more peaceful times Pakeha settlers also used the route, especially once they had created a better access from the beach at the south-west end. In May 1859, one William Chadwick won the tender to hack a 100-metre tunnel through the cliff. Te Horo stock tunnel, as it is now known, was not only an engineering challenge but it was also hindered by the Land Wars. Chadwick's efforts were delayed by fighting through the 1860s. Then, when construction resumed in 1888, the tunnellers from each end missed each other in the middle. However, the job was finally complete and the tunnel opened for use in 1889. It was used for the mail run north until 1909, and in later times, for moving sheep and cattle to the freezing works at Waitara. Again, they had to keep an eye on the tide or animals could drown.

John Cawley, retired farmer, surfer, diver and fisherman, loves his stretch of north Tarranaki coast.

A HIGH-ENERGY MARINE RESERVE

Hydrocarbons are not the only source of energy beneath the surface of the ocean. The Tasman Sea, off New Zealand's west coast, is so turbulent that it prevents land-derived sediments from settling and, as a result, the sea floor and the creatures that live on it are not smothered and clogged by silt from the land. That in turn allows a diverse collection of sea plants and fish to flourish, which has created a unique undersea environment.

Since 2006 the White Cliffs have formed the land edge of the Parininihi Marine Reserve, an 1800-hectare protected area that is administered jointly by the Department of Conservation, the Taranaki/Whanganui Conservation Board and Ngati Tama iwi. The reserve's most notable feature is the offshore Pariokariwa Reef where, as well as an abundance of rock lobsters and a large variety of fish species, there is a world-class underwater garden of rare and exotic sponges.

Many local fishermen were initially opposed the no-take zone for Parininihi, but a compromise was reached with an inshore area just south of the White Cliffs being excluded from the reserve. This allows surfcasters to continue to throw their lines out, even though the reserve's inner boundary, running parallel to the shore, is not far away.

THE FARMER AND HIS FACTORY

Retired farmer John Cawley knows this area well. He's an ocean-loving coaster and keen fisherman, who has lived on his farm at Pukeruhe at the southern end of the White Cliffs for 30 years. An active member of the local community, a surfer, a founding member of the Urenui Dive Club and, now that his son has taken over the running of the farm, a cabinetmaker, he lives in what was once the Whitecliffs Dairy Factory. Built in 1927 the factory had 12 suppliers in its heyday but was derelict for many years before John took it on and made it home. Basically, it's a huge shed with a bedroom, bathroom and somewhere to rustle up a bit of grub tacked on.

Al first spots Cawley, sack in hand, gathering mussels on the low tide with the waves sloshing around his gumboots. 'Pukearuhe Takeaways!' he beams, lifting his sack in the air.

Above: John's pad, the old White Cliffs dairy factory.

Opposite: 'Pukearehe Takeaway': Al and John gather Greenshell mussels just outside the marine reserve.

John Cawley doesn't mind the difficult track to his favourite fishing spot. 'That's the way I like it; it keeps the crowds away.'

'Unbelievable!' says Al. 'Who needs Pak'nSave when you got mussels right here?' He joins Cawley and gives him a hand to pick the largest and fattest from the forest of black shellfish. 'I always get so excited when I come across some resource on our coast and it's just here for the picking — locals down here grabbing a feed. It's so simple, so bloody Kiwi, I love it.'

With enough for a feed, they make a dash to collect rods from Cawley's shed and head off to what he describes as the 'back of the farm' for something to go with the mussels. To Al's delight, this means fishing from a ledge on the cliffs. You need to have a good head for heights for this little escapade because there's a sheer drop to the blue-green water and the white skirt of waves slapping against them at the bottom. They have to descend along a narrow track through flax with only a rope to hold on to. 'Looking pretty extreme, mate!' says Al. 'Are there OSH issues here?'

'That's the way I like it,' Cawley says. 'It keeps the crowds away.' They laugh.

For all that, Al notices that Cawley carries a coil of rope. In case anyone goes over, Cawley says.

'Yeah, everyone brings a rope here. I saw one guy fishing here and he jumped off the ledge over there.' He points to the stark edge with nothing beyond.

'I went around wondering what was going on. He'd got a 20-pound snapper, never had a basket, jumped over, put the rope through its gills and climbed back up the rope. Yeah!'

The ledge is a narrow strip above a 30-metre vertical drop to the blue-green tide. 'It's nerve-wracking being up here, but it's extraordinarily beautiful!' Al declares.

While they wait for bites, Cawley fills Al in on the neighbourhood. 'It's a mixture of farmers, engineers, guys who work on the oil rig in town, a lot of lifestyle blocks,' he says. 'People are prepared to travel for the enjoyment of being in this situation. There are a lot of family farms — been here for generations. It hasn't changed a lot in 30 years, maybe more lifestyle blocks, the odd section sold off. A lot of people don't come for the sea, they go pig hunting in the back bush, up in the rough country.'

'A diverse sort of community,' Al observes.

'Yeah,' Cawley agrees. 'And tight, it's brilliant.'

They cast a few lines but only catch a small snapper and kahawai that are returned to the sea, so they head south down the coast, to the

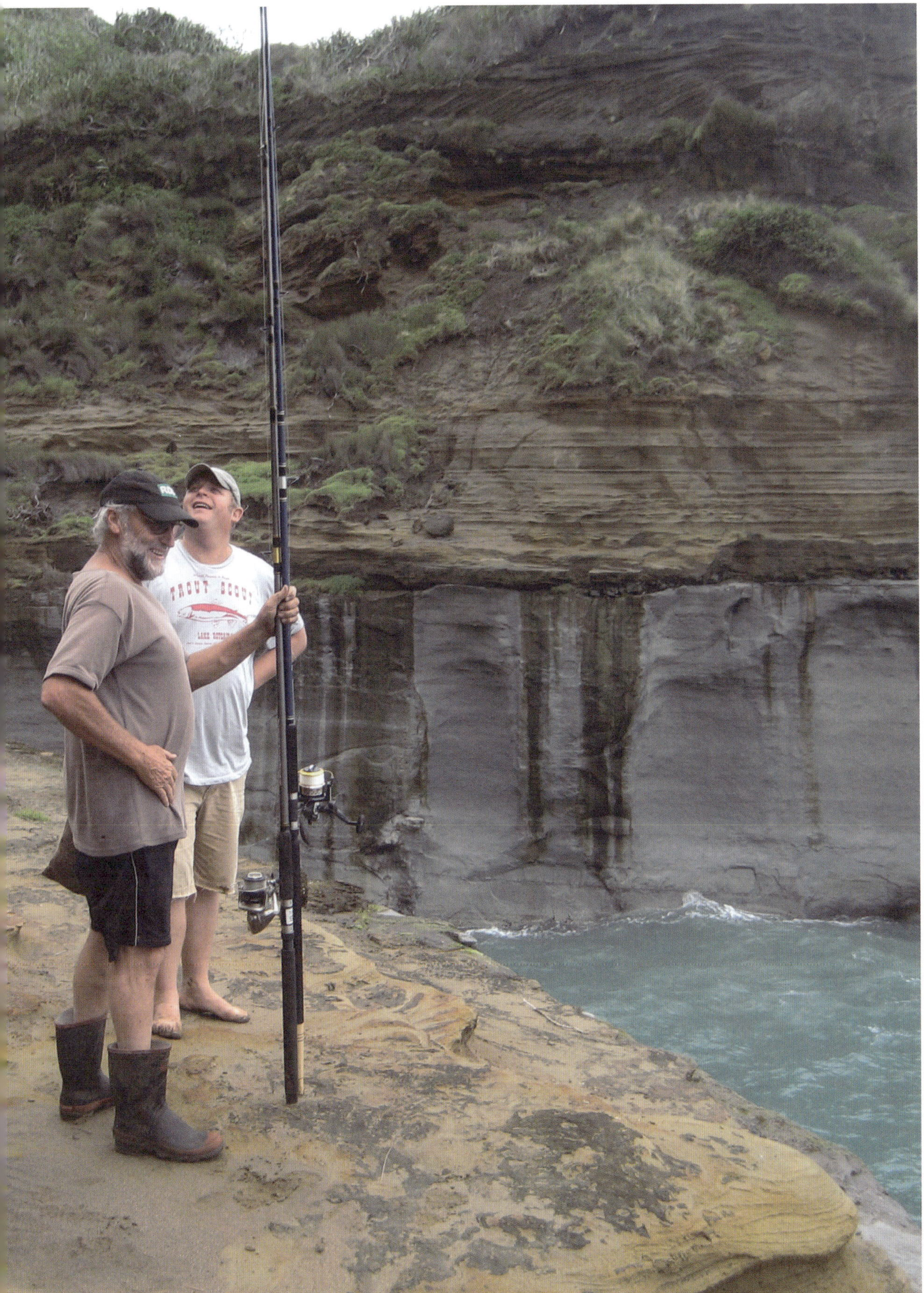
TROUT SCOUT

Taranaki artist John McLean is inspired by the dramatic northern Taranaki coastline.

Mimi River mouth. Here the cliffs give way to a tumble of wave-worn rocks, the open river mouth, expanses of blue-black sand and the possibility of flounder.

THE PAINTER OF THE SEA

Not far from the mouth of the Mimi River, with the sound of the surf at their doorstep, live a couple of Cawley's mates, artist John McLean and his wife Chris. Like Cawley, they are coasters through and through. They built their house 28 years ago on a slope overlooking the river and the sea. While McLean paints and sculpts, Chris gardens. Their lives are a response to the beauty of their environment, lived in rhythm with the seasons. That they are passionate about this stretch of coast, their home, their paradise on earth, is clear from McLean's paintings. They are so utterly about the sea, the shore and the strip of land behind it that they could not have been set in any other place in the world.

McLean's work is full of larger than life characters inhabiting a dream-like Taranaki coastline. Primarily a landscape painter, he has moved in recent years to explore the world below the surface — to seek for deeper layers of meaning, the undercurrents, rips and tows beneath the sunny exterior of coastal life.

On the day Al calls, McLean is putting finishing touches to the last of 19 large, colourful paintings that together form two interconnected sequences, *The Farmer's Wife* (2008) and *The Farmer* (2009–10). The tattooed McLean has a roomy, well-lit downstairs studio where he paints. His large table is busy with sketches and watercolour studies, gaping drawers spill oil paints, jars bristle with brushes and there are protective coverings on the floor. Beyond, through the windows, he can see and hear the coast and the ocean. He knows he is a lucky man.

The 7 paintings in *The Farmer's Wife* tell of a woman who is lured away from her life with her dairy farmer husband by a stranger on a white horse. Through her journey with the handsome stranger she finds freedom and learns to make her own way in the world. The next 12 paintings trace the journey of the farmer as he slowly moves

> **McLean's work is full of larger than life characters inhabiting a dream-like Taranaki coastline.**

John paints **Housekeeper's Daughter Showing Farmer Beneath the Surface** *(2010).*

from misery to joy through a series of events that take him finally to the edge of the land. 'He took to the sea, which, in the terms of this allegory, means he is changing his element. He is getting off the firm footing and going onto the water, which is unfamiliar. He's taking himself into this other zone. He has arrived with people who have found joy, and that's the coastal people.'

McLean's painting are filled with images of the oddly muscular, cat-eyed people, the pasture-clad, spiny hills of inland Taranaki, the native forests, the iconic white and yellow cliffs, but most of all, of the blue-green rivers and oceans. McLean is a master at transparency, from the rocky pools of the inland streams and waterfalls, to the floating gossamer dresses of the wife and to the underwater gardens of the seashore, and his paintings are unsettling and memorable.

'The paintings would be recognisable as Taranaki anywhere in the world,' Al says later as they take a late afternoon stroll along the coast. 'Walking down here and seeing this, and coming from your studio, starts to make sense to me.'

'It's like a good relationship,' McLean says. 'Familiarity doesn't breed contempt, it breeds deeper love. The more I know the place, the more I feel like I've been taken in by it. I can't possibly imagine leaving here. You don't find places like this twice in your life.'

John McLean walks daily along the coast: 'The more I know the place, the more I feel like I've been taken in by it.'

A MEAL FOR THE FISHER KINGS

It's time for a feed and since Al and John Cawley didn't get much more than a few mussels from their efforts up the coast, they and John McLean take the net down to the Mimi River mouth for a spot of flounder fishing.

Cawley takes one end of the net, McLean takes the other, Al holds up the middle and the dog supervises from the bank. The trio are soon chest-deep in the incoming tide. 'We've got to get a feed,' Al says, but it's not their day as he pulls only one small flounder from the mesh.

'Looks like a day for loaves and fishes,' McLean says dryly. They laugh.

'Looks like we're going to need a good salad!' Al says.

Back up the hill at the McLeans', Chris takes him through the garden. It's her pride and joy, filled with vegetables, fruit, the resident rooster and McLean's sculptures.

'It's a fantastic climate and amazing soil,' Chris says as she and Al harvest rocket, lettuces, tomatoes, onions and herbs. 'We're living the dream here.'

Al is in his element. The catch may have been light, but the mussels they gathered earlier will make it go a lot further. Mussel fritters au Brownie, pan-fried flounder and the fresh salad make a meal for the fisher kings — bon appétit!

The lagoon and organic vege garden provide the makings of lunch: pan-fried flounder, mussel fritters and fresh salad.

Mussel Fritters with Sautéed Whole Flounder and Herb Butter Sauce

I think if there was to be a New Zealand holiday signature seafood dish it would quite possibly be a 'fritter' of some sort. Everyone seems to have a recipe passed down from generations, often covered in oil and flour stains, pinned to the wall of the bach, referred to year after year. Usually made from shellfish, it often involves a traditional outing for the whole family or whanau at low tide, as young and old leisurely stroll down the beach complete with bucket and onion sack in hand to their favourite spot. Kids adore fossicking for shellfish as it's like digging for treasures (which it is), and it is also a terrific opportunity to teach them about where food comes from and the importance of only taking enough for a feed. It connects our children to our coasts and forms some of their first iconic memories of gathering for the pot. Serves 6

Step 1. For the batter

Ingredients
4 eggs
1 cup flour
1 teaspoon baking powder
2 tablespoons milk
salt and freshly ground black pepper

Method
In a blender with a whisk attachment or similar, whisk the eggs to combine then add the flour, baking powder and milk. Whisk to a smooth batter. Add a little salt and pepper to season. Refrigerate until required.

Step 2. Mussel Fritters Mix

Ingredients
100g bacon, rind removed
oil for frying
450g cooked mussel meat (from about 2.5kg live mussels in the shell)
2 cups fresh corn kernels
⅓ cup finely diced red onion
¼ cup finely diced Peppadew peppers
finely chopped zest of 1 lemon
1½ tablespoons lemon juice
¼ cup roughly chopped basil leaves
¼ cup roughly chopped parsley
1 teaspoon sugar
sea salt and freshly ground black pepper
2 egg whites

Method
Place a frying pan on medium heat and fry the bacon in a little oil until slightly crisp. Remove from the pan, chop into small dice and place in a mixing bowl.

Place half the mussel meat in a food processor. Process until quite finely minced, then add to the bowl. Chop the rest of the mussel meat into fine dice and add to the bowl along with the corn, onion, peppers, lemon zest and juice, basil, parsley and sugar. Season with sea salt and black pepper.

Mix all together then fold through 1 cup of the fritter batter. Whisk the egg whites until stiff then fold into the batter to lighten the mix. Cook a little of the fritter mix and check the consistency and seasoning.

Step 3. To Cook and Serve

Ingredients
canola oil for frying
6 flounder, gutted, and skin removed from the top fillet
sea salt and freshly ground black pepper
1½ cups flour
200g butter
¼ cup extra virgin olive oil
½ cup finely chopped shallots
1-2 fresh red chillies, finely chopped
1 tablespoon finely chopped garlic
⅓ cup capers, roughly chopped
grated zest and juice of 2 lemons
1 tablespoon finely chopped fresh tarragon leaves
⅓ cup finely chopped fresh parsley
⅓ cup finely chopped fresh basil
lemon wedges for serving

Method
Preheat the oven to 100°C.

Place a skillet or sauté pan on medium heat. Add a little canola oil then drop in spoonfuls of the fritter batter. Cook for 1–2 minutes on each side until golden and cooked through. Place the fritters in an ovenproof dish in the oven while you cook the remaining batter in batches.

Season the flounder with sea salt and black pepper and dredge with flour, then cook in batches in a frying pan over medium-low heat with a little canola oil or butter. Once golden and cooked through, remove from the pan and keep warm in the oven while cooking the remaining flounder.

For the sauce, wipe out the pan and place back on low heat. Add the butter, olive oil, shallots, chilli, garlic, capers, and lemon zest and juice. Cook on low for 5 minutes then add the herbs, and season with a little sea salt and black pepper. Remove from the heat.

To serve, dish out the flounder onto warmed plates, then spoon the sauce over. Place the mussel fritters on a platter in the centre of the table for people to help themselves. A few lemon wedges for squeezing complete the scene.

North Taranaki coastline looking south from Mimi River.

Moving on

West as the seagull flies from Mimi River, the coast is a continuation of black sand fronting low, banded bluffs, rocky outcrops, boulder beaches and estuaries. At all times of day, this landscape is about light — on wet sand, on glistening cliff faces, on the translucent tips of waves, in the fleeting, iridescent colours of the sea, in a blinding strip of sunlight on the horizon. Moment by moment, the scene changes as the waters of the ocean change, surge, roll, sigh.

There is a succession of small coastal settlements. Urenui domain, where a slow river exits to the ocean, is a popular summer destination, famed for its motor camp, golf course and colony of baches. You're not a Taranaki kid unless you've belly-surfed on the mud flats at low tide or shrieked at the heat in the iron-rich sand as you sprint across to the surf. There's another camping ground at Onaero River mouth, where the same processes that carved the sisters at Tongaporutu have formed similar twin pillars — perhaps these are the brothers?

272 *Coasters*

IT'S A GAS

Further west, the cliffs become lower and you are on the northern edge of the Taranaki ringplain. Suddenly, perched on the lip of the coast and a bit incongruous in this farmland setting, you come to a massive complex of gleaming pipes, towers and clouds of steam. This is the Motunui methanol plant.

Now owned by Vancouver-based Methanex Corporation, it was originally one of a suite of 'Think Big' projects initiated in the 1980s by Rob Muldoon's National Government. During a time of high international oil prices, the Syngas plant was going to reduce New Zealand's dependence on imported products. The plan was to convert natural gas from Taranaki's offshore gas fields and from the onshore Kapuni field into methanol and then synthetic petroleum.

Unfortunately, by the time the plant came on-stream in 1987, oil prices had dropped and it was far less economic. Petrol production ceased in 1997 although methanol continued to be generated until 2004 when it was also closed down. It's all swings and roundabouts, however, and in late 2008 methanol production resumed.

Motunui Methanol Plant, one of the original 'Think Big' projects.

Few people standing on the peaceful, grass-cows-and-sheep countryside surrounding the plant nowadays would know that in 1822 the Motunui plain was the site of a fierce and bloody battle between a Waikato war party and Taranaki Maori after the Waikato people travelled down the coastal route from Tongaporutu. Many died on both sides with the invaders ultimately returning home defeated.

Their losses were not forgotten, however, and 10 years later they returned, armed with guns and thirsting for revenge. Te Atiawa fled to Pukerangiora Pa on the Waitara River and were pinned there for three months until, weak and starving, they attempted to leave. Numbers of casualties vary, with some accounts listing as many as 1200 hunted down, tortured, enslaved or killed. Women and children leapt to their deaths off the cliff to avoid being captured.

A SECOND BATTLE OF MOTUNUI

In modern times, the Motunui area has again been the centre of conflict, but this time in the courts of law. In a battle not unlike that over Wellington's Moa Point, this struggle was to prevent the pollution and desecration of coastal waters. In 1981 the people of Te Atiawa made a claim to the Waitangi Tribunal for the cleanup and protection of the reefs and waters of the north Taranaki coast because they were being fouled by urban sewage and by industrial and agricultural wastes.

The coast, its seas and its bounty, has long been connected to Te Atiawa. It is how the people define themselves, an intrinsic part of their culture, songs and mythology. When the waters are defiled, the people suffer.

By the 1980s, there were increasing reports of contaminated shellfish and of people becoming ill after swimming and diving. The finger was pointed at the Waitara borough and Borthwicks Freezing Works, but it was the application from Synfuels to add more waste from its proposed plant that was the last straw.

In 1983, after two years of hearings, the tribunal found in favour of Te Atiawa. It was a decision with far-reaching consequences because not only were steps taken to significantly clean up the waters locally, there was a flow-on effect on other legislation governing the use (and abuse) of the coast around New Zealand.

As an update, although much improved from the 1980s, the situation in 2010 is not resolved, with surfers and people of Waitara still reporting ill-health from the waters of the river at the ocean mouth.

The city of surf

From Waitara, the journey south travels through a different sort of coast, past the suburb of Bell Block and the region's main airport with its runway parallel to the sea. After the isolated splendour of Tongaporutu and White Cliffs, the shoreline is increasingly claimed by subdivisions, golf courses, shopping centres and houses that jockey for the best views. Al's back in town.

And now he's in Fitzroy. The same waves and wild ocean that sculpt the fabulous cliffs of North Taranaki make this coast a wave-riding Mecca, from Fitzroy to the famed breaks of the Surf Highway 45; around the coast south of New Plymouth.

Surfing in New Zealand has an honourable pedigree. Most people think that riding the waves originated in Hawai'i but it is thought to have been popular in pre-European times in other parts of the Pacific, including New Zealand. Pakeha in the nineteenth century wrote about Maori surfing or whakahekeheke, using whatever was to hand — kopapa or flat boards, logs, canoes and

Opposite: Fitzroy Beach, one of New Plymouth's popular surf breaks.

Next page: Daisy Day's photograph captures Fitzroy Beach on a classic day.

even bags of kelp. Christian missionaries frowned upon it — or, more specifically, at the scantily clad attire worn by those involved — and it fell from favour until 1915 when Hawaiian surfer Duke Kahanamoku toured the country, giving demonstrations and firing people up with renewed passion.

Waves are what Daisy Day and her husband Arch Arthur are all about. Al first spots Daisy in her black wetsuit, cutting an elegant silhouette against the jade face of a wave as she slices across it on her purple board. She and Arch are so passionate about the surf, they have made it their life — running a surf shop, teaching surfing and printing the local surf paper. Every Friday Arch does a show on the local radio station to talk surfing, surfing and more surfing.

The couple live near the clubrooms of the New Plymouth Surfriders Club, founded in 1991 when Arch spotted an unused building in the area of the Fitzroy motor camp and persuaded the council to lease it to him.

'Within a week we had 67 members fully paid up and a society formed,' he says proudly from the clubroom's enviable spot on the foreshore; overlooking the beach. 'I think the council have accepted us: we used to be the toe-rags of society but in the last few years we've paid the rates and paid the dues, I guess.'

Over the years Arch has seen a shift in the council's attitude and

Daisy Day, surf photographer, surf instructor and surf fanatic. She and husband Arch are at the heart of the New Plymouth surf scene.

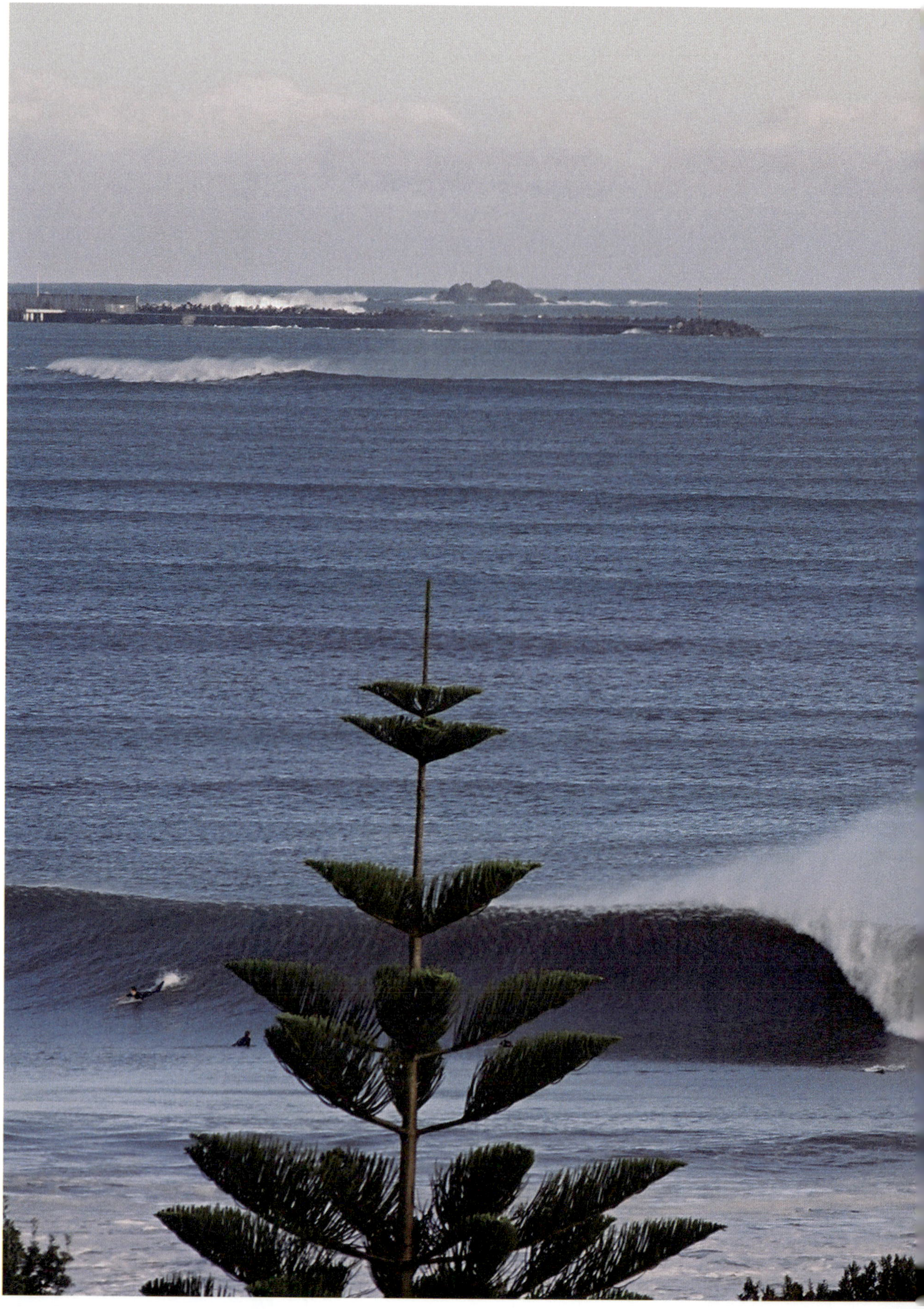

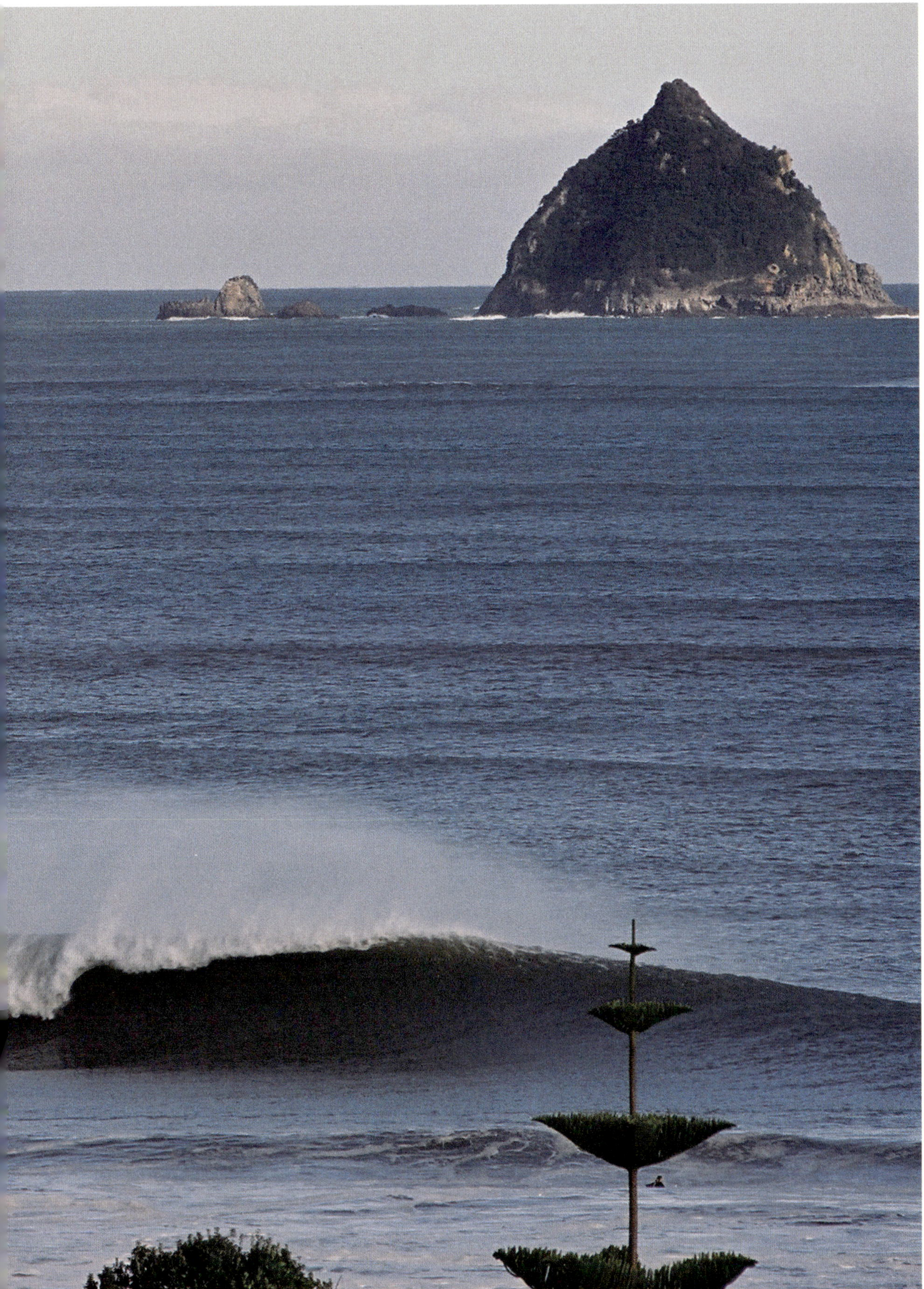

Arch lining up the face of a beautiful Fitzroy wave. With some of the best waves in New Zealand, surfing has become a big part of Taranaki's coastal culture.

approach to New Plymouth's coast and he loves the city's new angle on life. 'New Plymouth has turned itself around in the last few years and now embraces the ocean,' he says. 'It used to have its back to it, looking at the mountain, but now we look at the water.'

SHOOTING THE WAVES

When Daisy moved north from Whanganui, it was in order to be able to combine her love of surfing with her other passion and former career, photography. After training as a cadet on the *Wanganui Chronicle* she worked for many years as chief photographer for the *Taranaki Daily News* and so it was inevitable that when she recently decided to put a book together, the images should be from her collection of surfing photographs — she's been chasing the perfect shot of the perfect wave almost all of her life. Her book, *Thirty Years of Surf Photography*, which contains 150 pages of black and white and colour images of tanned and trim surfin' guys and gals, is a celebration and historical record of the people and places of the Taranaki surfing scene. You can tell by the width of the smiles just how much they love it.

'We're a mixed bunch,' Daisy says. 'All personalities, but we are happy. Some of us have quite intense jobs, but when we're out in the surf it's all chatting about surf — it's not just the young crew, it's our age as well — it's beautiful to be out there. There are so many things — the whole aspect of getting out into that big ocean on a piece of fibreglass, paddling along, smelling all the ocean smells, looking at the wildlife, and catching those waves.'

She even likes to tuck a small camera into her wetsuit. 'Being a photographer, there are different times of day for beautiful light — we have absolutely gorgeous morning light and sunsets. It's the waves, the rocks, the smell . . . it is always different. I just sit out there and forget I'm catching waves . . .'

Al's keen to find out what all the fuss is about and takes Daisy up on the offer of a free surf lesson. He squeezes into a wetsuit, is given a board called the Queen Mary and after some brief beachside instruction is led out into some very average Fitzroy surf. It's not easy but he manages a brief few moments upright before hitting the water. It's enough. 'Even that split second of being up there, I can see what the addiction is all about, I'm just feeling totally elated,' he declares. 'That was extraordinary . . . this could be the start of my surfing career. Take me to the shop, I'm buying a board!'

THE CITY THAT TURNED TO FACE THE SEA

There are walkers on Fitzroy Beach, with children and with dogs; there are joggers and horse-riders; there are kayakers and swimmers and Daisy and Arch's crew, bobbing like seals beyond the breakers. Just above the sand, where great stacks of boulders form a defensive barrier against the sea's nibbling ways, there is a wide, smoothly paved walkway and even more people.

It was not always so.

The port — and its need for railway lines, yards, storage sheds, tanks and associated machinery — claimed the foreshore from early on in New Plymouth's history, just as it had done in many New Zealand centres. The city iself, with its main street several blocks back from the beach, faced inward, with its back to the sea.

But all that has now changed. In 1999 the New Plymouth District Council renovated the foreshore and the most stunning and effective

Al gets the lowdown from Daisy before taking on Fitzroy.

Above: New Plymouth's stunning coastal walkway has helped turn the city to the sea.

Right: Len Lye's Wind Wand.

addition was the city-wide seven-kilometre coastal walkway that was built from the Waiwakaiho River mouth at the eastern end of town to the port in the west. It was designed to fit in with the marine environment, with no edge between the footpath and the sea other than a massive protective rock wall below. There are sections of wooden boardwalk, wooden observation jetties, seats, plantings and grassy lawns on raised mounds. The walkway follows the contours of the shoreline, sinuously hugging the coast, offering different perspectives on the waves, rocks and birdlife below.

In June 2010 the walkway grew another three kilometres east to Bell Block with a stunning new addition, a 68.7-metre span bridge across the Waiwakaiho. The bridge is called Te Rewa Rewa after the nearby Te Rewa Rewa Reserve, once a pa site. The elegant bone-white structure is a major drawcard, its ribs curving across a diagonal like a breaking wave or possibly the skeleton of a whale.

The walkway has won many awards but, best of all, people have taken to it like gulls to the sea. They come at all times of day: on foot, on skates and skateboards, jogging, running, cycling, pushing prams, in tandem, on buggies. It is a huge success.

THE MAGICIAN'S WAND

Al is heading along the walkway towards the heart of New Plymouth, looking forward to meeting his next coaster, engineer John Matthews.

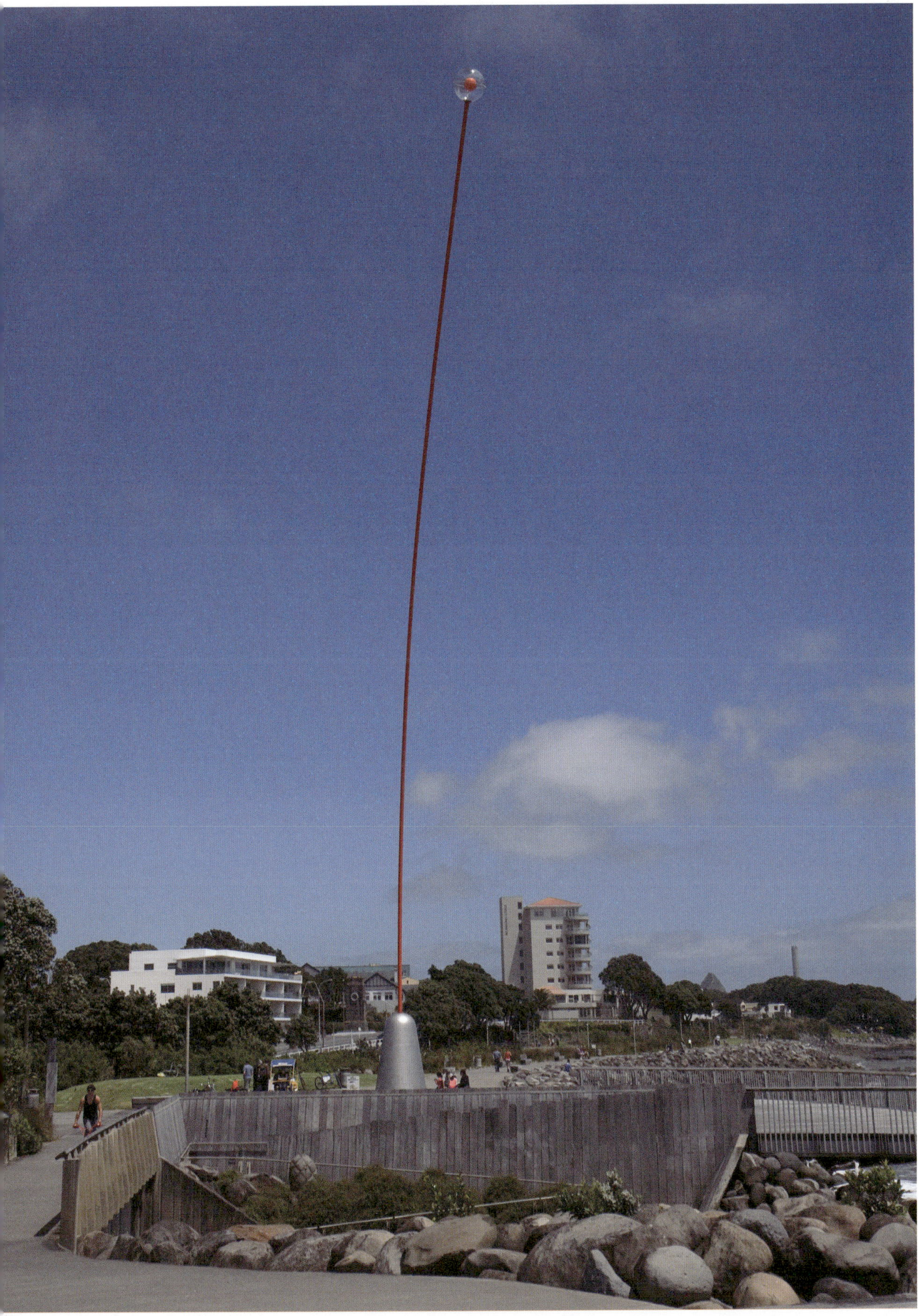

Engineer John Matthews helped bring Lye's work to Taranaki. 'Len used to say that if there's no wind and the wand stands dead straight, if a bumble bee lands on it, it will tilt over!'

John is waiting on the walkway, near to the centre of town. He's dwarfed by a magnificent sculpture, a 45-metre-tall stalk topped by a red sphere encased in a large clear bobble. This is Len Lye's *Wind Wand*: it bows and nods gracefully in the breeze and is a fascinating drawcard of the walkway.

If it were not for John, this would not be here.

Perhaps New Zealand's most internationally acclaimed artist, kinetic sculptor and filmmaker, Christchurch-born Lye was living in New York in 1974 when New Plymouth's fledgling Govett-Brewster Art Gallery approached him, wanting to commission a major exhibition of his work. Lye agreed but he needed the services of a 'genius engineering designer' to lift his ideas off the drawing board and into reality. John Matthews was the man.

He was then a young steel engineer with an interest in art and a connection to the gallery. He put his hand up for the job and flew to New York to meet Lye. They hit it off immediately — they were so in tune that they even had the same *New Yorker* cartoon stuck on their separate walls. It was the beginning of a unique artist–engineer collaboration and ultimately led to New Plymouth becoming the home to all of Lye's works, a major coup for a small provincial city in the southern hemisphere.

It was a partnership forged in heaven. The extraordinary flair of the artist was matched by the equally extraordinary skills of the engineer. 'We had a wonderful time together,' John says. 'He had great enthusiasm for life, was full of ideas — different ideas. He thought outside the paradigm all the time — forced himself to — and was a lovely, lovely person who always had a new way of looking at things.'

Lye's sculptures are always an engineering challenge and the 200-millimetre-diameter *Wind Wand* was no exception. 'That's part of the fun!' says John. Twelve different plastics were used in its construction, allowing it to sway up to at least 20 metres in the wind. It is so finely calibrated that 'Len used to say that if there's no wind and the wand stands dead straight, if a bumble bee lands on it, it'll tilt over!' says John.

The sculpture was installed on the walkway in time for New Year 2000, but the top was damaged by unexpectedly energetic Taranaki winds a month later and needed to be re-engineered using America's Cup yacht mast technology and materials that Lye, who died in 1980, could only have dreamed of. It was reinstalled a year later on 5 July

John Matthews talks about one of his favourite Len Lye pieces, Moon Bead.

2001, the centenary of Lye's birth.

The sculpture also stirred a few winds of its own. In time-honoured fashion there was fierce debate about the work and its price for the city (that is, the ratepayer). As John says, 'there were those who were enraptured by it and those who were enraged'. As if to show that they too could make a statement — and at a fraction of the cost — more than 100 spoof wands sprouted in back yards, gardens and cowsheds across the region, from gumboot-tipped bamboo poles, to miniature front-lawn copies. John even has his own small version at his home overlooking the ocean south-west of the city.

In the end, the wand has triumphed. It's a talking point and a focus for the walkway. Locals are proud of it and take their visitors to see it and have their photographs taken beside it. 'It was very interesting seeing the public psyche change,' John says. 'In the end, a huge number decided that they liked it after all.'

New Plymouth's harbourside wells began producing oil as early as 1865 and, among other things, fuelled the city bus fleet.

From peak to peak

For Al the end of the journey is in sight — Paritutu rock stands in the distance. Ahead lies the business end of the walkway, Port Taranaki with its cranes, chimneys, tanks and rail yards. In between, he passes a rocky stretch of coast below the city's swimming pool with floor-to-ceiling windows that look onto the sea, an inner-city motor camp and, finally, he's at Ngamotu Beach. Protected from ocean surf at both ends by breakwaters, this sheltered bay has long been a family favourite for picnics and at one time was a small version of Wellington's Days Bay, with skating rink, pavilion and donkey rides.

Sited unobtrusively on a corner, there's a small derrick on the shore above the sand. It looks a bit like another sculpture, but unlike the wind wand, it's not moving. It's a small but significant piece of the energy province's history — the original Ngamotu oil well. Until it was closed in 1997, its long arm chugged up and down, as regular as a metronome. The oil from the well was marketed as Peak Petroleum with an appropriate mountain-inspired logo, and among other things, fuelled the New Plymouth bus fleet for many years.

Al has a different peak in mind, however, and is going to need a descent amount of energy to get there. He has his eye on scaling the peak known as Paritutu, his final destination on the Taranaki coast.

THE FINAL CLIMB

Paritutu looms over the port, 153 metres high. It is like an inverted tooth that has had its point knocked off — as in fact, it has. Maori, who sometimes used it as a defensive pa, flattened its top to a platform and, when seen from the sea in 1834, its top bristled with the

Paritutu Rock at Port Taranaki — the end of Al's coastal journey.

stakes of a palisade. Its sides are steep and exposed, with scrubby vegetation. In 1879 and again in the 1920s, its lower slopes were dynamited in the hope that it would yield rock suitable for building the breakwaters. It didn't, and in the end, after it was reduced in size and majesty, it was handed to the New Plymouth City Council to become the centrepiece of Paritutu Centennial Park.

The path to the top is narrow — little more than a goat track with a wire rope to one side — but luckily Al has a sound head for heights. As he nears Paritutu's crest, the view, first of the port and then the shoreline and city to the north, opens spectacularly all the way to the White Cliffs about 55 kilometres away. It's a great place for Al to reflect on this, his final coastal journey.

Along the way he has met coasters whose energy and vitality mirrors the ever-changing environment in which they live — John Cawley, the ocean-loving farmer, John McLean, the artist whose work is steeped with the influence of the coast, Daisy and Arch, whose lives revolve around the waves, and John Matthews, the coaster who made an artist's dreams real.

The richness of these characters is equal to the many others Al has met on his seven coastal journeys. From the mountains of Fiordland to the sandy beaches of the Bay of Islands, it's easy to see why our country's long and varied coastline is an integral, influential and essential part of contemporary New Zealand.

Image credits

All images © Fisheye Films apart from those listed below. Fisheye Films photographers: Peter Young, Nigel Gordon-Crosby, Matt Tuffin, Katherine Bonner and Tracy Roe.

WWW.PHOTONEWZEALAND.CO.NZ

p11 Paul Kennedy 130509; p14 Rob Driessen 250050; p18 Darryl Torckler 254084; p23 Paul Kennedy 17537; p32 Geoff Marshall 201281; p47 Rob Driessen 250034; p52 Forrest Smyth 208846; p72 Tony Brunt 220415; p84 Paul Mercer 218021; p92 Craig Potton 258544; p97 Andy Reisinger/Hedgehog House 131401; p102 Rob Driessen 258192; p120 Richard Parkinson 259991; p137 Craig Potton 280245; p138 Geoff Mason 128616; p141 Nick Millar 252714; p143 Rob Brown 215697; p150 Jason Hosking 280295; p156 Darryl Torckler 118458; p173 Southern Stock 221747; p175 Ian Batchelor 256438; p180 Southern Stock 221746; p190 Gerhard Egger 226239; p194 Jason Hosking 175138; p201 Wayne Tait 258974; p209 Tony Brunt 251347; p212 Colin Monteath/Hedgehog House 300626; p222 photographer unknown 281064; p241 Colin Monteath/Hedgehog House 169092; p243 Steve Dawson/Hedgehog House 253874; p253 Paul Stieller 217814; p254 Harley Betts/Hedgehog House 205829; p260 Craig Potton 301183; p286 Chris McLennan 110545

WWW.NATURESPIC.COM

p21 Rob Suisted

ALEXANDER TURNBULL LIBRARY

p22 Evening Post Collection 35mm-01149-29-F; p27 F-9968-1/4; p28 Sydney Charles Smith, S C Smith Collection, G-46578-1/2; p34 William Mein Smith PUBL-0011-16-3; p37 John Dickie Collection 1/2-034716-G; p40 PAColl-7985-17; p46 A-032-012; p50 F-15698-1/2; p59 Henry Thomas Lock F-15412-1/4; p73 (left) PAColl-5471-021 D Maloney Collection; p73 (right) F-22276-1/2; p89 E M Lovell-Smith Collection F-25246-1/2; p90 F-15696-1/2; p116 Louis John Steele B-077-003; p119 F-8573-1/2; p123 (below) Arthur David McCormick A-004-037; p217 Archives New Zealand/Te Rua Mahara o te Kāwanatanga Wellington Office, F 40047 1/2

PRIVATE COLLECTIONS

p43 Courtesy of Patrick Dellabarca; p60 (above) Courtesy of Jack Devine; p60 (below) Courtesy of Jack Devine; p144 Courtesy of Paul Peychers; p145 Courtesy of Paul Peychers; p159 Shaun Henderson; p160 (below) Shaun Henderson; p161 Shaun Henderson; p162 Shaun Henderson; p177 Courtesy of Gordon Pye; p188 (left) Courtesy of Toby Morcom; p188 (right) Courtesy of Toby Morcom; p245 Courtesy of Garry Brittenden; p272 (below) Daisy Day; p275 (below) Daisy Day; p276 Daisy Day; p278 Daisy Day

CANTERBURY MUSEUM

p214 Bishop Collection, The Weekly Press photograph 1923.53.687

CANTERBURY CITY LIBRARY

p215 The Weekly Press, 9 March 1910, p35, CCL PhotoCD 5, IMG0064

PUKE ARIKI MUSEUM

p259 PHO2002_596; p261 PHO2002_448; p284 (right) PHO2010_0386